Teaching About Family Relationships

Teaching About Family Relationships

Richard H. Klemer
Rebecca M. Smith

University of North Carolina
Greensboro, N.C.

BURGESS PUBLISHING COMPANY • MINNEAPOLIS, MINNESOTA

Printed in the United States of America
Library of Congress Card Number 74-20040
ISBN 0-8087-1991-2

0 9 8 7 6 5 4 3 2

Preface

Teachers are constantly asking for new methods and techniques for teaching family relationships. Although many articles have been written describing techniques and many lists of techniques have been made, no single book has included a full description of methods and techniques for planning and teaching in every area in family relations until now.

Teaching About Family Relationships is written for teachers of family relationships courses. It can be used as a textbook for college methods courses preparing family relationships teachers or for education courses preparing teachers who will teach family relationships as a part of their total job in home economics, health, and social studies.

The introductory chapter explains the choice and sequence for the material in this book and discusses student-teacher relationships. Part One begins with an overall framework for planning and teaching family relationships—the empathetic approach—a unique method to solve the dilemma of teaching both the objective and subjective aspects of family relationships. This section of the book also describes two other overall frameworks that might be used in planning a course and five general teaching methods, using examples from family relationships subject matter.

Part Two presents nine general areas of family relationships. Each area is in a separate chapter which includes a framework of that subject matter and numerous behavioral objectives, each with illustrations of several teaching techniques. There are over 150 objectives and over 400 teaching techniques given throughout the book. This part of the book could be used as the course outline for family relationships.

In Part Three the philosophy of the relationship between objectives, teaching-learning experiences, and evaluation of students' work is presented. Several evaluation items are given in connection with objectives and teaching-learning experiences taken directly from Part Two. A concluding chapter on the future of teaching about family relationships implies that there will be an even greater demand for teaching about family relationships than there is now.

Dr. Richard H. Klemer died before the manuscript of this book was completed, but his contribution is an important and essential part of the whole. His untimely death represented a great loss not only to the School of Home Economics and the Child Development and Family Relations Department of the University of North Carolina at Greensboro but also to the larger public of students and faculties who benefited from his teaching, counseling, and writing.

Recognition is given to Sally Huffman, family relationships teacher, for giving invaluable support and suggestions in the early stages of the manuscript. Gratitude is also expressed to Sharon Welker for editing, to Lisa Josephson for typing, and especially to Elizabeth R. Hunt for editorial assistance and typing the entire manuscript.

October, 1974 Rebecca M. Smith

Contents

Introduction

The study of family relationships is based on substantive theory and can be taught as objectively as any other subject matter. However, both teachers and students may be threatened by some of the topics included in a family-relationships course because personal application could affect their own self-images. If the implication in teaching is that there is a right or wrong way or that a person is normal or abnormal, teachers and students both react to protect their own self-concepts. This possibility that people might be threatened in class is enough to make some teachers very cautious about including certain topics and using certain methods. However, when students are taught concepts, generalizations, and theories as well as the process of decision making, the threat to the self-image is almost alleviated.

Teaching Methods Presented from Two Perspectives

How family relationships is taught is as important as what is taught because students learn best when they are motivated and when there is a logical sequence of teaching-learning experiences used. To give you, the teachers, depth in methods of teaching family relationships, this book presents methods and techniques from two perspectives. One emphasizes the general methods as they are used in family relationships, and the other emphasizes general areas of the subject matter with examples of techniques for teaching.

The first part of this book describes overall teaching approaches and general methods for integrating the broad knowledge necessary for teaching about family relationships. The empathetic approach is a plan for student progression in the ability to empathize with anyone in any area of family relationships. In the literature approach, books, stories, and feature films are the basic ways of showing family situations, and with the research approach, students may research every area in family relationships. This first section also includes five general methods that lend themselves well to family-relationships teaching. These methods are discussion, questioning, role playing, simulation games and exercises, and music and pictures. Descriptions of each of these overall approaches and general methods are combined with examples of their use in studying family relationships to show how students can experience relationships while they learn the subject matter. Through these methods students experience relationships while they learn the subject matter.

The second perspective for presenting teaching techniques is done by dividing family relationships into some general areas and giving examples of how to use various teaching techniques and the general methods appropriate for each area. These general areas are understanding human behavior, communication, intergenerational relationships, interpersonal relationships, human sexual identity, money and work, crises, singles, and differing family forms. These areas were selected because of their pervasiveness and relevancy. Each teaching technique described is listed in connection with an objective so that the teacher knows precisely when to use that technique.

In-depth Teaching for Functional Family Relationships Courses

When any course has a practical-application approach, it is called a functional course. The implication in the past was that, when something was applied, it was taught on a lower intellectual level than when the subject matter was theoretical. However, most scholars in education know that application of generalizations is one of the higher-level intellectual skills (Bloom 1956). This book was written essentially for the application level of intellectual skills, which in turn presupposes the understanding of the underlying concepts. Family relationships courses geared to application could be called functional if the application is also to the students' own personal lives, but these courses must be based on sound theories, principles, and generalizations.

Although application to present and near-future situations is the goal in functional family relationships courses, it is well to remember that nothing can be applied if nothing has been learned. That is, teaching a great deal of basic knowledge about families and about human development and interaction is a prerequisite to application of this knowledge.

However, students do not necessarily apply knowledge just because they have it. The reason for this inconsistency is that learning to apply knowledge is an entirely different form of learning from learning the facts and understanding their use. Therefore, demonstrations and student activities in application are as necessary as good lectures, explanations, and exercises in understanding. For example, students can learn all the concepts of communication and human behavior and yet never use them for promoting better communication or better human interaction if they do not know how they can be used. However, teachers will run the risk of being called the "fun and games" teachers if they use exercises too often or if they use special techniques without the students' seeing the connection with the goals. It is of prime importance always to point out the reasons for the exercises to the students beforehand and afterward.

Establishing Relationships with the Students

Family relationships teachers in particular, and all teachers in general, should be able to relate well to their students. However, to ask all family-relationships teachers to have excellent relationships with all students is to ask for more than may be possible when there are so many factors to be considered.

Teachers must create the initial rapport and continuing warm relationships with their students because family relationships subject matter has the potential of surfacing some repressed attitudes. Should these attitudes manifest themselves in a hostile classroom environment, both the teachers and the students would have a difficult time if there were not sufficient understanding.

To establish this rapport, one must keep in mind the basic needs of human beings, including both the students' and the teachers' needs. Many theorists have listed certain needs that are basic. Some have indicated that these needs are in a hierarchy, whereas others have noted that there is variation in needs by age, and yet others have indicated there are nearly the same needs throughout life. Probably the most widely used is Maslow's (1954) hierarchical list in which he indicated that the highest level of self-actualization—a stage in which a person has reached his potential and has begun to act for the good of others—can only be reached after one has first achieved some self-esteem. Maslow further postulated that even self-esteem could not be gained without prior satisfaction that one was accepted, liked, or loved by family and/or friends. And before any of these three stages in the hierarchy could be reached, a person must feel secure about basic physiological needs—food, shelter, clothing, safety, and maintenance of body functions. Is it any wonder that students who feel friendless are not eager to learn school subjects which would enhance their self-esteems? In the same vein, can teachers reach out to help other people if they have not yet begun to achieve some self-actualization? With thirty or more students interacting with each other and the teacher and with each student operating each day on a different need level, an accepting but challenging atmosphere in the classroom is essential for any progression. Students and teachers who have not yet moved sufficiently into self-actualization cannot easily empathize with others who are still struggling to meet basic physiological needs.

Another theorist, Kagan (1972), would explain needs with other words and possibly some new ways of looking at behavior geared to meeting needs. In fact he called these needs "motives" or "goals" toward which behavior is directed. He explained that these needs vary from time to time, vary in intensity, and vary in rank order. No hierarchy was implied. The four basic needs or motives Kagan proposed are these: the need (1) to resolve uncertainty, (2) to gain mastery, (3) to resolve hostility, and (4) to resolve sexual feelings. Again, these four needs are believed to be in every person of every age to some degree.

The students may be more eager to resolve uncertainty in the beginning of the course, yet they might need to resolve hostility later if mastery were not gained. All of these behaviors may or may not be directed toward the teacher—another reason for the teacher to be aware of the motivating forces of basic needs. When teachers are faced with equally strong personal needs of their own, they cannot perform their duties adequately. Teachers may have uncertainty at home; they may need more mastery; and if both are blocked, the need to resolve hostility may cause misdirected behavior toward the students. However, most of the behavior to meet these needs can be channeled into productive ventures.

Many years ago Thomas (1925) classified needs this way: response, recognition, new experience, and security. Each of the three theorists saw a need for security. Maslow stated that a person must feel secure in one level of the hierarchy before going on to the next, and Kagan stated that security was reached in resolution of the goals. Response, recognition, and new experience are also seen in Kagan's and Maslow's theories. Thomas's new experience or Maslow's reaching for a new height or Kagan's need to gain mastery all tell teachers that students profit from new experiences in their learning. Students will also profit from the teachers' needs for new experiences when teachers provide new teaching techniques to resolve their own needs for resolving uncertainty or gaining mastery.

Recognition and response can easily be met by personal contact, such as calling students by their names and giving recognition to their attempts to answer. Students also gain recognition and response through mastery and through returned papers or projects that have many comments of encouragement, praise, and suggestions for improvement.

Students who complain about teachers' inabilities to explain may really be expressing their own needs to resolve uncertainty and to gain mastery. Teachers who complain that students will not pay attention may be expressing their own needs for response and recognition. As both students and teachers become more aware of their own and others' needs, they will be on their way to meeting higher level needs such as Maslow's self-actualization. Or they may go on to seeking newer unexplored territories to meet the needs of new experience or uncertainty or mastery.

It surprises some teachers when it is pointed out that students who do not respond are not devoid of a recognition need; it may be that students have a greater need for security at that moment. This knowledge alerts teachers to set the stage for acceptance if they want students to respond. Some very good students do not respond, not because of lack of security or lack of need for recognition, but in this case they may have a need for new experience or a need for the uncertainty of challenge. These theories about needs taught early in the course actually cause the students to be more aware of their own, other students', and the teachers' needs as explanations for behavior. The result will probably be better understanding and consequently fewer misperceptions and misguided behaviors.

The Problem of Teaching in Value-Laden Subjects

What students value about families and how they treat other people is so close to them that an objective discussion about these topics sometimes is almost impossible. This near impossibility for objective discussion results because a person's self appears to be questioned when his values are questioned.

An agreement between teachers and students in the beginning of the course to discuss various value-laden topics in an objective non-judgmental way does help. The explanation used in teaching people to gain cognitive empathy helps, too—that is, to study for understanding without condemning or condoning.

Not only do some students object to discussing such value-laden topics as family planning, sexual alternatives to marriage, social mobility, and male-female role changes, but the community may also actively object. Some college campus communities may also object. However, little or no repercussion occurs when teachers teach the generalizations and theories operating rather than advocating any one particular behavior. In fact, teachers may believe in and carry out behavior that is somewhat different from the traditional; however, if this behavior does not harm the sensibilities of most of the students and the community, and if these teachers teach the process of decision making instead of pressing their own non-traditional view, they have fewer problems.

Because of the difficulty in teaching value-laden family relationships objectively enough for the students to learn the subject matter and yet subjectively enough for the students to gain personal growth, the empathetic approach was developed (Klemer 1965 and 1970). In this approach the students progress throughout the course toward a greater empathy for people in every topic of family relationships studied. The empathetic approach has been carried out for five years in the classroom and has been found to satisfy all the criteria for teaching family relationships. The next chapter explains how to use the empathetic approach as an overall framework.

References

Bloom, Benjamin S. *Taxonomy of Educational Objectives, Handbook I: Cognitive Domain.* New York: David McKay Co., 1956.

Kagan, Jerome. *Understanding Children.* New York: Harcourt Brace Jovanovich, 1972.

Klemer, Richard H. "The Empathetic Approach to Teaching Family Relations." *Journal of Home Economics* 57: 619-625, 1965.

———. *Marriage and Family Relationships.* New York: Harper and Row, 1970.

Maslow, Abraham H. *Motivation and Personality.* New York: Harper and Row, 1954.

Thomas, William I. *The Unadjusted Girl.* Boston: Little, Brown & Co., 1925.

Teaching About Family Relationships

Roy
Buchanan
Saturday 8:00 Nov 2nd
Guilford College
Dana Auditorium
Greensboro, N.C.
$2.00 Guilford Students
$4.00 All Others
Flavor

Part One

General Methods For Teaching About Family Relationships

Family relationships is a subject that can be taught on an objective, intellectual level, but it is difficult for the students not to become subjective as they apply this knowledge. In fact, teachers themselves find family relationships to be filled with values, attitudes, and personal meaning. Yet, to be effective, family relationships must be taught through the substantive theory and the intellectual processes of decision making. A unique framework for teaching family relationships, the empathetic approach, was designed to encourage both subjective and objective teaching and learning. This overall approach, described in Chapter 1, introduces our basic philosophy for teaching about family relationships; that is, students who learn to empathize with other people by applying theories and generalizations about human behavior also learn to understand themselves better.

Chapters 2 and 3 present two other overall strategies, the literature approach and the research approach, both of which give a unifying framework for the goals and methods of teaching family relationships. Even when these approaches are used, to be able to empathize with others is suggested as a major goal. The literature approach provides a framework of books, stories, and feature films as the media for applying knowledge about behavior and the family that is learned in class. In fact, the occasional use of literature is excellent for illustrative material in other strategies.

The research approach should be used when the students are sufficiently sophisticated to question the source of knowledge and to understand some simple methodological processes in research. The outcome of this method is that the students appreciate the concept of validity of subject matter. It puts them in the position of synthesizing rather than consuming knowledge.

The remaining five chapters in Part One present general classroom methods rather than overall planning frameworks. While the planning frameworks can be used as classroom methods at times, these five methods–discussion, questions, role playing, simulated games and exercises, and music and pictures–are not intended to double as strategies. These methods are discussed in depth because of their appropriateness for teaching about relationships. Any of the five general methods and three approaches can be used to teach any area of family relationships, and numerous examples of how to implement them in the classroom are given.

Chapter 1

The Empathetic Approach

The empathetic approach to teaching family relationships is one in which the students progress throughout the course toward better cognitive empathy. There are two types of empathy–emotional and cognitive. Emotional empathy occurs when people empathize with others because they have had some of the same or similar experiences. Cognitive empathy is that understanding of others' behaviors because of a knowledge of the generalizations of human behavior. Cognitive empathy is understanding without condemning or condoning. Although progress toward emotional empathy is not one of the goals of the empathetic approach, emotional empathy enhances cognitive empathy.

The empathetic approach can be an overall strategy or framework for the course in family relationships. Plans are made for the progression of the students through personal feelings and beliefs to explanatory principles and generalizations. Throughout the course the various areas of family relationships are taught for the content and behavior generalizations, yet the students study the areas with greater and greater cognitive empathy as each area is taught.

This approach also teaches students to be able to look at the situation from many perspectives. One of the goals is to be able to empathize with each person; therefore students can explain behavior from the point of view of each person in each situation.

The empathetic approach in studying family relationships can be a very exciting experience for students. It may even be a heady experience for those who have never really put themselves in another's place or who have never done much introspection. But when the method is used, the students' personal learning grows so rapidly and is so meaningful to them that they become intrinsically motivated.

Through this method the students gain great understanding about relationships in a breakthrough moment of insight. These insights can take place vicariously through studying the experiences of others. Therefore, a large part of the empathetic approach will involve case presentations that show conflicts and attitudes in present-day human relationships. As the students empathize with the various people in the cases, they will gain insights, draw inferences, and propose alternatives that could lead to solutions of the problems presented. When these insights, inferences, and solutions are in keeping with the students' own value systems and personalities, the results have immediate meaning for their own lives, much more so than when they only hear other peoples' generalizations and interpretations. Because the insights are the students' own solutions, they can constitute important learning.

Such writers as Berne (1961), Cottrell (1969), Glasser (1965), Harris (1967), and Weinstein (1969) have placed emphasis upon the individual's interpersonal-relationships ability as indicative of good emotional health. Experience in empathizing adds one more avenue to better interpersonal relations. Klemer (1962, 1965, and 1970) developed the empathetic approach to teaching for better relationships, and Smith (1970) used and refined it in the classroom.

All too often, when people think they are empathizing, they are really sympathizing. Empathy is such complete identification with another person that for the moment they can think as that other person does. This *total* feeling is rare, and the students must constantly work toward it rather than achieve it all of a sudden. Sympathy is like empathy except that in sympathizing, one feels a detachment, an objectivity, a relief that one is not there, but still a genuine concern for the other person. Probably it is easier to sympathize because one can stay apart. To empathize students will find a wavering, a desire to feel with, a desire to criticize, a desire to explain, but in the end they will have a feeling of "I understand that he had to do what he did under those circumstances." At the same time they will be able to know whether they would or would not have done the same thing because of their own conditioning and circumstances.

A very quick and sensational way to teach students the difference between sympathy and empathy is to tell the following story in a dramatic way.

> Look out the window! That car just ran into the other one! The car in the back has a smashed headlight and a crumpled fender! The car in the front just stopped suddenly. The car in the back had no recourse but to crash right into the other car! There is a young girl driving the car in the front and young boy driving the car in the back.

Ask the students to react to the story. The most general comments will be, "Is anyone hurt?" "I surely would hate to be that boy." "I wonder who owns the car." "Wonder what his father will say?" "It makes me sick to think about it." "What did the front car stop for?" These reactions are mostly sympathy. Tell the students they have just done a good job of sympathizing. They will react mildly, but then tell them you can make them empathize!

Then tell them to get into the back car under the wheel and, "Say what the boy said!" The reaction will at first be a roar of laughter. Encourage them to come out with what the boy said. Some really honest comments will pour forth. Say to the class, "You are beginning to empathize; you are *feeling with* the boy!"

Empathy is more than this reaction, but this exercise will make a great impression that sitting in someone else's seat makes a world of difference from just watching from the sideline. If the students said what they would have said had they really been in the car themselves, then they are using their own value system; if they said what they have learned boys probably say under such stress, then they are using past knowledge to mimic behavior. If, though, they said what boys usually say under stress and at the same time neither approved nor disapproved and knew that this might not be their own reaction, then they are empathizing.

Teacher Reaction to the Use of the Empathetic Approach

Teachers who have a need for classroom control through telling the students what to think and how to solve problems will feel uneasy with the empathetic approach at first. But, as the students learn to apply facts and generalizations in solving relationships problems, they begin to need no outside control for their learning.

In effect, the empathetic approach takes the students out of the role of the passive absorber and makes them leaders–and yet partners–in the learning process. It opens channels of communication among students and between students and teachers.

The empathetic approach is not without its disadvantages, however. First, it takes much more time to arrive at a personally acceptable conclusion than it does to accept a ready-made solution. A great deal of time is used when students make statements which are irrelevant, repetitious, or mistaken. Teachers may want to push on. Many students want to be given the "right" answers. In fact, some students feel that they are entitled to all the knowledge a teacher possesses regardless of whether or not the information can be used to solve personal problems.

There are many human-relationships problems which are unsolvable and many more which have more than one workable solution. In the beginning this uncertainty about the best answer leaves teachers and students feeling a bit as if the study of relationships has no answers at all. But, herein lies the value of the empathetic approach. The teacher who perseveres in the face of students' frustration will, after a very few weeks, have a group of learners who are beginning to see the complexities of relationships. These same students do not want anyone to tell them the "right" answer; they want to work it out for themselves as they listen to other students' insights and attempts to explain.

This does not mean that the students do not want teachers to express feelings and solutions and values at times. They do. And teachers should occasionally tell how they would apply generalizations and how they would empathize using their own values. Needless to say, expressed values must be publicly defensible. Students want to be led to their own decisions through their own reflective insights. They want some definite directions by which they can guide their lives.

Yet after all of this, the empathetic approach is so stimulating and exciting that it is an adventure in understanding, in communication, and in personal and family growth.

The Empathetic Approach as an Overall Strategy

Any relationships course, no matter who the relationship involves (men and women, parents and children, girls and boys, teachers and students, employers and employees), can make use of the empathetic approach. The objective in using such an approach is to enlarge the students' understanding of how another person feels and why he behaves as he does, even when they cannot subscribe to a particular point of view. It is conceivable that such an approach could be used in a history or geography course to understand how people of differing nationalities feel and behave, in a sociology class to understand how people in differing groups feel, or in a foods class to understand why people have differing food tastes and habits.

When planning a course, teachers should weave in the activities which lead a student to empathize. Not every class period will be used to get at the students' feelings and to analyze case materials. Obviously, many class periods will be used in presenting subject matter in various ways and in teaching the students how to apply principles.

Students can be taught to begin to empathize even when teachers do not use the empathetic approach as the overall strategy. It may be used only when the course outline suggests that empathy is necessary for the level of understanding desired. For example, in a family relationships class there may have been an overall strategy of comparative research (See Research Chapter) in which important research studies were replicated with class members or with an outside group and the findings compared with the textbook findings. But, in the comparative research framework use of the empathetic approach could help the students understand how it feels to be "just average" or "highly improbable" or "abnormal."

Within any relationships course there are certain areas which require more understanding than others. These areas could be in-law relationships or some crisis periods or any others which seem to the students to warrant in-depth discussion. In these areas the empathetic approach would be most appropriate.

One of the major problems with occasional use of the empathetic approach is that real empathy is developed over a period of time. This process will be discussed in the next section.

The Process of Learning to Empathize

Skill in empathy takes time. There is also a developmental process involved in gaining this skill. The five stages which seem to be identifiable will be presented in the order in which most students develop them. Empathy evolves throughout the course although all five parts of the process given below may have their beginning after the students have read only one case.

The process of becoming an empathetic person usually begins when students (1) can express their own feelings without needing to explain those feelings. The next stage is (2) to combine feelings and principles learned earlier from any source to interpret behavior.

An abrupt change must occur at this point or growth is stunted. The students must now (3) divorce themselves from feelings and limit their discussion of the situation strictly to the application of generalizations. The students must stay at this stage long enough to feel competent in both subject matter and ability to apply generalizations. Very soon thereafter the students must (4) do some introspection. If introspection is done too soon in the process, they are too emotional to look at their own values and attitudes objectively. But after they have learned to explain behavior by applying generalizations, they can apply this technique to their own behavior. It is the students' own value system through which all learning is finally perceived. The last part of the process is for the students (5) to analyze their own reactions to situations and class discussions. A question which in the end separates empathy from sympathy is, "What would you have done had you been in the same situation, remembering that your conditioning differs from that of the person in this situation?"

The teacher has to plan for this progression. In the very first lesson teachers can give the students an overview of all five stages by reading a case such as the case of Mary and Al reprinted later in this chapter. First help the students learn the difference between empathy and sympathy by using the automobile accident described earlier. Then read the case study, and tell the students that they may not express anything except feelings as it is read. Encourage them to express their feelings by stopping at intervals. Some students will use actual feelings such as, "This burns me up!" or "I feel nauseated." Others who are not accustomed to expressing feelings will instead make attempts at explaining the behavior such as, "Al acted that way because he had had so little money," or "Mary had every right to tell him that." With a mild suggestion, but not a rebuff, ask these students, "But how do you feel?" Teachers may have to express their own feelings once in a while.

About half-way through the case, encourage them to begin to combine feelings and explanations. A little later on, limit these to explanations and finally, after the case is over, go back and take one of the characters in the case and tell the students that they must explain the behavior of that one person with no criticism whatsoever—only with understanding based on generalizations about behavior (some of which they may have learned from former classes and experiences). Many of the students will have difficulty, indicating that they cannot condone the person's behavior, whereupon teachers should gently remind students that condoning and condemning are not a part of the assignment—only explanation is asked for.

THE CASE OF MARY AND AL*

Mary is now twenty and Al is eighteen. She came from a well-to-do banking family in Spokane; he from an ex-coal miner's family in Black Diamond, Washington. He is a freshman and she a junior at the University of Washington. Al and Mary knew each other for only three months when they decided to get married. Mary's family, shocked and disappointed, forbade her to marry. So Al and Mary went to Coeur d'Alene, Idaho, on a weekend and were married anyway.

After they were married Mary's parents seemed to become resigned to the idea. Al wanted to drop out of school and go to work in Black Diamond, but Mary's parents offered to pay all the college expenses for both of them and even to provide money for an apartment in Seattle if they would both continue in school. Al didn't think much of that (the truth was he was failing in several subjects anyway), but, because it seemed to be what Mary wanted, he agreed to it.

Al is very close to his family. Al's mother, a plump and friendly woman, has always done everything for the men in the family, picked up their clothes and keep her little house immaculately clean. She feels this is a woman's role, as do her menfolk. Al's mother goes to church regularly, and she talks a great deal about religion and what's right, although her grammar is poor and some of her ideas are a little vague. Al's father is a quiet, bashful man who works hard and doesn't like to dress up in city clothes, but who believes in being the boss in his house.

For the first few months of the marriage everything seemed to go well. On the weekends when Al's folks didn't come to visit, Al and Mary traveled the 20 miles to Black Diamond to see them. (Mary's parents rarely came because Spokane was 290 miles away.) But Mary began to get a little tired of Al's folks and their talk about hard-shelled religion. Besides, when Al's mother was around, Mary always felt as if she didn't do enough for Al. His mother would scrub the apartment

*From pp. 14-15 in *Marriage and Family Relationships* by Richard H. Klemer. Copyright ©1970 by Richard H. Klemer. Used by permission of Harper & Row, Publishers, Inc.

when she came and bake and sew for Al. Al's people never offered to help pay any of the young people's expenses, even though Mary felt they could provide a token now and then. Whenever Mary mentioned this to Al, he got quite angry and told her he was going to quit school and go to work in Black Diamond.

A month ago, Al reminded Mary that his mother's birthday was coming on the twenty-first of the month and said he had invited his folks over for that weekend. He gave Mary a little money and asked her to buy his mother a fancy nightgown. Mary was fed up by this time and said some ugly things about Al's people coming over all the time. But she got the gown with the money Al had saved, and Al didn't say much more. A week later Mary's people wrote that they would be in Seattle on the twenty-first en route to a resort in Las Vegas. Since the apartment was small, Mary asked Al to uninvite his folks. "After all," she said, "they come all the time." Al refused. Mary got the nightgown and tore it to shreds. Al stamped out.

Three days later, Al came back. He said he had talked with his mother, and she had sent him back to apologize and resume his Christian duty to his wife. He also said that his folks would not be coming to stay overnight. Mary was relieved and immediately invited some of her college friends to meet her parents on the twenty-first.

On Sunday afternoon the twenty-first, just as Mary was serving tea, Al's folks pulled up in their 1959 Plymouth. Al had told them it wouldn't be convenient to stay overnight, but he had not said they shouldn't come at all.

Mary blew her top. She screamed at Al's folks and told them exactly what she thought of them. Al told her to shut up. This made her even more furious and she kicked him. Al didn't say any more; he just took his mother by the arm and walked out.

It is now five days since Al left. Mary is tearful; she really loved Al, she protests. She thinks she should stay on in the apartment, wait for him to come back, and then apologize. But her parents have urged her to go with them to Las Vegas and get a quick divorce. She wants your advice.

Questions to Evoke Insight into Own Behaviors

A part of the empathetic approach is for students to understand their own reactions to situations. These reactions are based on their own conditioning. Understanding this helps them see why they can empathize but not become that other person. Questions such as the following may be asked to help students understand their own behavior.

1. Think back to the beginning of the case and remember how you felt about certain behaviors. Were you able to explain the behaviors with good generalizations?
2. Now, put yourself into one of the roles (Mary, for example) and decide how you would react in each of Mary's situations (from marrying Al to accepting money from her parents to kicking Al, etc.). If you would have behaved differently, determine what in your own background would have

caused this difference. Would Mary have reacted in the same way if she had had your parents and your conditioning?

3. Put yourself in the position of the guests at the tea. How would you have felt, and what would you have done?

Questions to Evoke Predictions

There is a great possibility that there will not be time to ask for predictions if students work on feelings, generalizations, and empathy in one class period. It is, however, possible to ask just the first question below. But, another whole lesson could very well be on how to make predictions. This lesson will need to be taught at intervals throughout the course just as lessons on generalizations, how to empathize, and understanding one's own value system will continue throughout the course.

1. What would you suggest that Mary do now?
2. What effect will the conditioning of all concerned have on the future of Mary and Al?
3. Consider all patterns of past behavior and generalizations about behavior in general, and predict what will probably happen in this case.

Predictions are very difficult for even the astute counselor to make, but lessons in prediction based on past behavior and probabilities in human behavior do make predictions more than crystal-ball reading.

Sometimes students will learn better if several predictions and evaluations of predictions are made. For example, students might be asked to evaluate the four predictions listed below.

Evaluate the Following Four Predictions

1. Mary and Al should stay married. Mary should go to her mother-in-law's home and apologize. She should also begin to learn some of the homemaking techniques Al's mother could teach her. If Al will try, he can graduate from college. With a great deal of love and understanding, Mary and Al will have a happy marriage.
2. If Mary and Al will go back together and talk over the causes of their misunderstandings and learn to communicate with each other, they will have a happier marriage. I predict that Mary will see her error and Al will begin to study harder and and they will see happier days.
3. This was an unfortunate marriage and should end in divorce. Mary and Al have nothing in common. I predict that Mary will ask for and get a divorce.
4. Even though Mary was upset about Al's folks visiting so often, she has learned that she cannot live without Al. I predict that she will study the situation, particularly her parents' and her in-laws' life styles, and take the best of each in planning her own future.

As students continue to learn how to predict, they will need to eliminate the following statements from their predictions and suggestions for the future.

"If they would *just try*, they could get along."

"If they would *learn to communicate*, they would iron out all their troubles."

"They *should* learn to communicate better."

"In the future he *should* plan his time better."

It is very difficult for people to "try" or to do as they "should" or to "communicate" if their needs have changed, or if they have had little previous experience in adequate communication, or if they have no conception of what "should" be done, or if what "should" be done is not possible at the moment.

When students can make statements such as those below, they will have learned that a person's actions usually do have some reason behind them. They will also show that they understand the complexities of human behavior. It is usually late in the course before the students can arrive at this level of prediction, but use the statements now to illustrate application of generalizations.

These statements are indicative of the understanding of and the application of generalizations:

1. Even though Mary and Al come from quite different social levels, their formal educational level will be the same as long as both remain in school. Similarities such as these are in their favor for a more stable future because people with similar values, arrived at through education or family background, reinforce each other's views and in turn build self-esteem.
2. Since young marriages rarely are separate and apart from the families of orientation (in-laws and parents), and since Mary and Al are in need of financial help from Mary's parents, and since the two sets of parents are so different, there is a low probability that the marriage can ever be satisfactory.
3. Although Mary's parents are providing most of the financial support for the family and there seems to be little hardship, they are not supporting the idea of a stable marriage. The fact that Al's mother tells him that it is his Christian duty to be a good husband will carry little weight since his parents are not as influential as Mary's parents. Since young marriages are reinforced by parental acceptance, Mary and Al probably will get a divorce.
4. Although Mary claims she loves Al and wants him back, she is probably feeling more of a sense of loss and a great deal of uncertainty than a love which seeks to satisfy the other person's needs.

(Note: Many relationships generalizations have been substantiated by research and may be found in Goode *et al.* 1971.)

This one lesson is only an overview for the students to see how the empathetic approach works. Teachers will use cases and other materials to help students in each of the five areas (own feelings, combination of feelings and generalizations, application of generalizations only, introspection, and analysis of own feelings) throughout the course. Actually, all five areas may be included each time a case or some situation is discussed, but students will need to dwell on one area on some days in order to gain some skill in that area.

Teaching Students to Recognize, State, and Apply Generalizations About Behavior

A generalization about human behavior is a statement which will explain the responses of people in a large number of situations. Students understand the explanatory value of a generalization better when they learn the *when-then* sentence structure. Here are some examples: *When* the social class level of two persons is greatly varied, *then* the likelihood of their having similar value systems in some areas is diminished. *When* people are under stress, *then* they tend to revert (or regress) to former behavior. *When* an overall cultural value abounds, *then* individual values which differ from this cultural value are difficult to maintain. Obviously there are other ways to state generalizations, but in the early stages, sticking to one way pays great dividends.

The examples given are written on an abstract or general level and would need to be applied to specific cases to have meaning to the students. The students will learn more quickly if they are given a short list of generalizations and class time is used for illustrating how generalizations are applied rather than just memorized. The statement "*When* people are under stress, *then* they tend to revert to former behavior" as applied to the case of Mary and Al explained that when Mary had had all she could take of Al's folks, she did three things which could be called regressive (childlike) behavior: tore up the nightgown, screamed at Al's folks, and kicked Al. Another illustration is that of Eliza in the play "My Fair Lady" who reverted to her poor grammar and pronunciation when she was under stress.

Generalizations appear sterile until some examples or statements are given. Use examples from the case of Mary and Al to bring some generalizations to life. Since many generalizations may be used to help explain the interactions in the case, some of the propositions listed in Goode et al. (1971) might be applied in the form of generalizations.

Application of Generalizations About Behavior

1. *When* two people of differing social classes marry, *then* it is usually a happier arrangement when the man is of the higher social level because (a) men in this society are still considered the head of the house, (b) couples tend to live in the social class of the husband, (c) financial help is more acceptable from the husband's family.
2. *When* couples of differing social classes marry, *then* there is often friction between the in-laws because of differing expectations and behaviors.

3. *When* people of differing backgrounds are on the same college campus, *then* they do not appear as different as when they are off campus because of the insular setting of the campus (protected from outside pressures and peer reinforcements of behavior, making almost all behavior appear more right).
4. *When* people are of a lower social class, *then* they tend to be more rigid in male-female role behavior and in the religious role because the people are more provincial (limited in geographic mobility).
5. Wives feel inadequate *when* mothers-in-law (or mothers) show how well they can manage a home. Mothers-in-law and mothers may feel jealous of the youth and new ideas of a young bride and rationalize this feeling by their showing their expertise.
6. People tend to regress (use childlike tactics) in their behavior *when* pushed beyond their limits.
7. People tend to continue a behavior *when* they are rewarded for that behavior.
8. Children tend to become more like their parents as they get older, especially *when* there has been a good relationship between the parent and child.
9. Gifts are generally more acceptable *when* they are not basic necessities.
10. Exogamous (mixed) marriages can work *when* there is a distinct meeting of needs between the partners and when the people around them approve of the marriage.

Individual Analysis of a Case

A meaningful learning experience for each student occurs when he analyzes a case for himself and puts the analysis on paper. In making this private analysis the student needs some guidelines. No matter whether the case is analyzed on paper or in a large or small group, the process of learning remains the same. It is important for the student to identify with the feelings of all the people in the case. Then by using all the generalizations about human behavior he knows, the student can arrive at, by his own insights, a solution which is adequate and which is acceptable to him.

The following guidelines are provided for the student to use in analyzing cases. There are three major parts: applying generalizations, empathizing, and predicting. The following steps are for applying generalizations about behavior to the understanding of the case.

1. Read the case several times and make a point of using all the feelings and facts in the case.
2. As you read and reread, make a note of all the generalizations of human behavior that are operating.
3. After you have read the case and have written down generalizations,

insights, and feelings, then imaginatively manipulate these without rational restraint; generate a brainstorm.

4. Speculate on what may not be included in the case and on hidden meanings. Try to put yourself in the person's place and "feel out" meanings. Be careful to identify these feelings as assumptions and not facts.
5. Using your notes, write out an interpretation relating the generalizations to concrete events in the case.

The second part in case analysis is to empathize completely with all the people in the case. In the beginning, the student is overwhelmed with writing if he is assigned to empathize on paper with all people in the case. Therefore, asking him to select one person is more realistic. An essential part of the empathetic approach, however, is that each student can eventually empathize with any or all of the people, especially those with whom he does not immediately identify. This is really the test of having arrived at being empathetic. Here are some guides for the student in empathizing with each person in a case, one at a time. It is essential to practice taking the other's point of view.

1. Reread the case with only one person in mind.
2. Using the assumption that behavior is prompted, explain that person's behavior on the basis of generalizations.
3. When explaining the behavior, use only that person's actions; do not explain by condemning others in the case.
4. In explaining or empathizing, accept all the behavior as having a reason, being careful not to judge the behavior.
5. Continue to remind yourself that no one is wholly right or wrong in a situation, but that behavior is what the person saw or felt he had to do at that moment for some reason. That reason is stated by you as the generalization which is operating.

You may need to remember that generalizations are not always learned from others or from books; common sense is one of the important tools in the empathetic approach. Heider (1958) pointed out that common sense is the hunch that starts nearly all scientists out in their search for support of their speculations.

The third part in the case analysis is predicting what will happen. Or some people say it is answering the question, "What can be done now?" This is the most difficult part for anyone, whether he be a seasoned counselor or a beginning student; however, the ability to predict or plan for the future is the mark of a person who uses a rational approach to life's problems. The students will almost invariably start their predictions in a framework of "oughtness" or suggesting what the people in the case "should" do. These prescriptions are based on the students' conditioning that there are certain ideal expectations of people in this society. Once the students can see the connection between what people have been conditioned to do, the pattern of their behavior, the general behavior of people in these situations, and how people tend to behave in particular situations, then they can more realistically predict the outcome.

As stated earlier in this chapter, one of the pitfalls in early predictions is that the students tend to say, "If the person would just *try* to get along, he could." Students have so often been accused themselves of not succeeding because they did not try that it is difficult for them to see that there are more forces operating than just a mere lack of motivation on the part of one individual.

Predictions are based on generalizations about behavior equally as much as explanations of past actions are. For example, if the major problem in a case is conflict between a husband and wife from differing cultures because they are living in a neighborhood which strongly opposes the persons of the outgroup, little help is gained by suggesting they try harder. When one bases the explanation of the problem on the generalization that "people tend to be more comfortable among people who approve or reinforce their behavior," no amount of "trying harder" will help the situation. A better prediction is that the couple will have a more satisfactory relationship if they move to surroundings more accepting of so-called mixed marriages. Part of the problem could be explained by the generalization that "people tend to revert to former behavior when they return to those surroundings in which the behavior is reinforced." If, in fact, one member of the couple changed when he returned to his former surroundings, then it is a sound suggestion that the couple move if relations are to be improved. There are many more explanations of behavior which can help predict the future. A different way to teach students to predict is to read two or three future courses of action and have them substantiate why they would predict one over the other. The main help you can give your students is to continue to show them how behavior is influenced.

The first time students analyze a case on paper, you may ask that only one of the three parts (applying generalizations, empathizing, or predicting) be done, later adding the others. Too much assigned at one time may overwhelm the students. Another suggestion for the first case analysis is to tell the students that no grade will be registered for that analysis. This freedom encourages greater creativity and flow of thought. These three parts to case analysis may be used throughout the course.

Group Analysis of a Case

Teaching a group of students how to analyze cases in class by explaining how to apply generalizations, how to empathize, and how to predict is only the beginning to an entirely different aspect of the empathetic approach. This aspect is the growth of each student as a participant in an open classroom discussion. The ultimate learning in the empathetic approach is not the ability to empathize with all people concerned but the insights each student gains about his own behavior. Not only will the students learn more about how to analyze cases, they will begin to apply this learning to empathizing with their fellow students and understanding their own relationships with others.

There are always some students who speak out immediately in class and some who say nothing. Students who speak out early may or may not know the answers. The *same* can be said of students who remain quiet. The real understanding comes when it is known why each chose his course of action. The reason for bringing this point out is that students may need to be given some assurance that they can say as little as they want to as long as they know why they have chosen to remain quiet. Some of the nonparticipants may not talk in the group because of fear that what they say will be laughed at or be labeled as wrong. One approach to encourage students to speak out in class is to say, "Your remaining quiet may be depriving others of some wisdom or insight." This comment may have to be followed by, "Even if you don't think you have additional knowledge to add to the class, your question for greater clarification either by the teacher or by the other students may cause a discourse which clarifies the issue at hand for numerous other students."

Just making these statements still may not be enough to get some students to express themselves. Some students need assurance that others will not pounce on them with a derogatory remark such as, "That's wrong," or "What makes you so sure of that?" or "I don't believe that." (Students may be able to take these affronts later but not early in the game.) Use the rules of brainstorming to teach students to be more accepting of others' statements. After the problem is presented, the group members immediately express their solutions no matter how wild. The additional rule is that all solutions are accepted and no one can say, "That won't work!" Try a little brainstorming session with your class using some problem relevant to the group such as, "You are a newlywed couple living in a two-room apartment (kitchen and living room-bedroom combination) and his brother wants to live with you one semester while he is in school. It is temporary and very important that he be able to do this. What arrangements do you suggest?" Accept any answer, especially from those who don't talk much. Take *all* suggestions no matter how weird during a five-minute period. Then sift them to pull out the workable ones.

There is an equally great problem with students who monopolize the class. Some of the students feel the need to be the first one with the "right" answer; others feel the need to help the teacher out; others are in need of attention at all costs; and still others are aware that they do have excellent comments which will benefit the discussion. Even so, one or two students must not be allowed to have the floor too much to the detriment of valuable learning by other students who need to clarify their own thoughts by expressing them in public.

After the stage has been set for freedom to speak, discuss a case in class which the students have analyzed individually prior to coming to class. This procedure can be a "test" of how well the students who talk a lot temper their comments, as well as to see whether or not the quiet ones will speak up. Beyond managing the time used in contributions from the students, another aspect of group discussion which will appear is that the students discover, to their dismay, that they are unable to think of all the aspects their fellow students considered. They may find it discouraging to have spent a great deal of time on a particular case and then realize that there were many insights which did not come to them.

This problem is overcome when the students recognize the need for accepting help from others. As each student gains security, he encourages cooperative discussion and analysis. Freeing the students from having to have a "right" answer is one of the most valuable aspects of open class discussion.

The final step toward maturity in class case analysis comes with the recognition that other students and instructors do not necessarily know the "best" answers. Because relationships and behavior are highly individual matters governed by each individual value system, the "best" answer for any particular individual is the best answer for him.

Another factor in class discussion is to encourage students to stand up for some of the things in which they believe—that is, to make their values explicit. One of the dangers in the "no right answer" doctrine is that people begin to believe that there is nothing to stand on. It gives them an uneasy feeling. A belief in something, a value system which is steady, has always characterized people who have accomplished something. Even so, the students still have a social responsibility not to monopolize the class or to try to force their values on others.

By restating values overtly, the students learn much about themselves. Not only do the values themselves become clear; the students begin to understand what compelled them to contradict, to speak up at one point and not answer at another, to feel hostile at a comment by another, or gratified when somebody else made some comment.

Group class analysis has many advantages over individual case analysis, many of which have been given in this section. Learning and development will not come the first time the class attempts to discuss a case. Case-study maturity may take an entire semester or longer.

Various Ways to Present Case Material

If all cases are presented by the teacher's reading them to the class, then it is little wonder that the students tire of case analysis. Alternatives include a tape recording, acting, student reading, telephone conversation with a counselor, and real persons each telling his or her side.

Tape Recording

Have someone tape a case as if he were talking directly to the counselor or to a good listener or to the class itself. Encourage him to put feeling into stories, but not to overact. Teachers may or may not choose to put a counselor's voice on the tape. The words of the counselor should be mere responses or simple questions to keep the conversation going and not anything which could be interpreted as suggestions.

Acting Out a Case

In an impromptu fashion, have students read the parts in a case just as they might if they were recording it on tape. For variation, have one of them add some to his side of the story. An additional exercise is to have a person play the part of the counselor with the participants. This in no way implies that counseling techniques are taught. Continue this presentation after the class has had a chance to discuss what they have heard, as if it were the next meeting with the counselor.

For a very interesting and challenging learning situation, ask a student or two to play the part of friends to whom the person is telling his or her side of the problem. The students playing the part of the friends react by using all they know about the empathetic approach.

Student Reading a Case

Have a student read a case, mainly so that it is not always the teacher reading. Ask the class members to stop the student every time an insight occurs to them or every time they see a generalization operating. Of course this intermittent discussion of the case could be done no matter who is reading it.

Telephone Conversation

While pantomiming the holding of a telephone and covering the mouthpiece, tell the students that a mother has just called to ask you what to do in the case of her daughter (or a husband about his wife; or a boyfriend about his girlfriend; or an employee about an employer) which you quickly relate to the class. At first the class members will probably say nothing, and you insistently nudge them by saying, "She's on the phone now. What shall I tell her?" whereupon the students get very busy with the problem, the explanations, and eventually what to tell the person on the other end of the line.

Sometimes you have to say, "I will call you back in one hour," which relieves the tension but still pushes the students to think the problem over.

Again, the students will be so taken by surprise that they say to you, "What would you say?" Do you tell? Yes, sometimes an impromptu answer from the teachers is one of the best teaching techniques because students learn a great deal by watching teachers proceed through an analysis and come to some decision.

Persons Relating Real Problems

Occasionally people will relate their problems to a class of students. This must be a problem which can be told in a semi-public place but yet one which is serious enough to cause the students to put a great deal of effort into their discussion. One advantage here is that the students can ask the person to fill in more detail, which is impossible in a written case. (However, do not forget that a very real learning experience comes when students have to speculate on what probably happened in written cases for it is then that they put themselves into the case with the added benefit of understanding themselves better.)

All of these methods lend themselves to an added technique referred to as "in the basket" which means that after you have relayed the case in whatever way you choose, you add some afterthoughts or some bits of information which you "forgot" to tell. Such bits could be, "I need to tell you that the woman is three months pregnant now," or "the man is five years younger than the woman," or "the girl is black," or "the boy was reared in a commune," or "the family lost its money last year," or "the parents are atheists."

Methods Other than Case Presentation

Any time people come in contact with any human-interest story, whether it be current news, a new law, past history, or even a change in policy, they usually react subjectively by expressing their views. In these situations, students can be encouraged to look at all sides and to understand both their own attitudes toward the story and the reasons why a certain behavior or decision occurred. Almost every day the newspaper has one or more articles which could be used.

News Article

For example, read the following news article to the class to get reactions. The major purpose is to see if they can understand their own reactions.

> A 9-year-old girl sentenced to 18 months' detention for stabbing a playmate with a breadknife was sent home today on bail while her sentence is appealed. A judge ordered her release from a home for delinquent children. The length of the sentence for such a young child raised a storm of protest by lawyers who pointed out that no child

under 10 could be arraigned. She had stabbed an 11-year-old girl in the chest during a quarrel. The girl suffered a partially collapsed lung.

Current Commercial Film or a Film in the Classroom

At some time during the semester, there will be a commercial film at the local theater which involves human relationships. If it is not possible to assign such a film, some films may be ordered from educational film companies. The same techniques for using a case are applied to the film.

Recent Law or Policy

Suppose there is a new decision such as the January, 1973, Supreme Court decision to allow abortions with limited restrictions. Students react to decisions such as this with some conviction. A class discussion allows them to express their views, think through why they feel as they do, and listen to other students' views with an empathetic ear. News such as this can be used anytime in the course. If used early it will have the advantage of bringing out feelings which the students are not yet aware they have; if used near the end of the course, it will have the advantage of giving the students the opportunity to test their own empathizing ability, their willingness to listen, their willingness to take a stand and substantiate it, and their ability to predict some outcomes based on generalizations.

Short Story

Sometimes a short story can bring out feelings a person is not aware of. The following story can be too threatening to some students, but it can also be used to help students better understand themselves. (See also de Maupassant's "The Piece of String" in the chapter on Literature.)

WHO IS IN THE CAR?

Family:

Man who traveled quite a bit

Woman who did not work and who traveled with him some

Three children—eight-year-old son; ten-year-old daughter; fifteen-year-old daughter

Situation:

The father had gone to the West Coast on a two-week trip. The mother had flown out to be with him the last few days of the trip. They almost never fly together in case of an accident.

On the night the parents were to arrive home, the children heard on the news that a plane from the West Coast had crashed. A business friend was to meet each of the parents who were to arrive about one and one-half hours apart.

The children did not know which of their parents had been on the plane.

The son thought, "I hope it wasn't Dad, for we had planned a camping trip next week. But what if it was Mom—who would cook my food and kiss me goodnight?"

The ten-year-old daughter thought, "It can't be Mom. I didn't get a chance to tell her I was sorry for yelling and refusing to clean my room. But maybe it's Dad."

The fifteen-year-old quickly thought, "My Dad must come home. We can't make it without him. But Mom—suppose it's Mom?"

About that time car tires were crunching on the gravel driveway. It was the car of the man who went to meet the plane.

Questions such as the following might be used to spark discussion:

1. Who do you hope is in the car and why? For this family? For your family?
2. Is the story so personal that you find yourself not thinking?
3. What cultural conditioning causes us to lack objectivity?
4. Should parents prepare children for death? At what age?
5. What age children should hear this story?

Using the Empathetic Approach with Students of Varying Social Levels

Having students of varying social levels in a class has concerned teachers of family relationships for some time because of the knowledge that differing value systems tend to be associated with differing social levels. It is very difficult to see someone become aware of his social level if he has not been aware before, especially if it is lower than he had imagined it to be. It is also difficult to teach normative behavior with proscriptions and prescriptions of the varying social levels when the students are looking for the "right" answer or when the community or society holds to one norm as if it were "right" for everyone.

These very problems give much material for learning to empathize, part of which is the learning of one's own value system, how it developed, and how it will probably continue to develop. In the process of learning about varying value systems and the development of these systems, students gain the knowledge necessary for empathizing with another's behavior.

Some answers to questions of, "Why don't they do better?" or "Why don't they try?" or "Anyone could stay clean," or "Why do they reject materialism?" may be found in knowledge of behavioral expectations of varying social levels.

Since social levels tend to be based on amount of income and education, a concommitant belief is that a person is less than good the farther down on the social scale he goes. Understanding that there are differing value systems within the income-education-determined social levels helps students keep from condemning someone because of his income level.

The book (Roth 1959) and movie (1970) *Goodbye Columbus* is illustrative of a family that moved up about two social levels in one generation. The upward movement, however, was in income of the father and education of the children. The obvious lack of change in behavior or social graces or attitudcs brings home the notion that social levels carry many facets besides money.

The teacher will have to be very discreet and supportive as the discussion centers around ethical behavior associated with social levels. The case of Mary and Al earlier in this chapter lends itself to the discussion of varying social levels and all the implications.

Evaluating Students' Empathizing Abilities

Empathizing ability follows a patterned process in development just as the acquisition of other abilities does. Assure students that their first attempts will not be graded but that written work will be read, with general comments made about where the students appear to be. The final grade should reflect the point at which the students have arrived and not an average of the poor attempts and the superior attempts, condemning many of the students to an unreal "average" assessment of their abilities. The first case analysis may be given a grade purely as base line data so that the student and teacher have a record of the progress made.

The final evaluation is made both on written cases and on group-discussion maturity. When evaluating the case (or film or story) analysis, look for an indication of progress in the students' ability to recognize and state the generalizations operating. Another part of evaluating empathizing ability is to see if the students can in fact be objective about explaining others' behavior without condemning. Also when students can make predictions based on past behavior, current conditions, and probabilities about the future, then they have achieved a high level of empathy.

It is quite difficult to keep a record of class-discussion maturity and self-evaluation, and you may have to call on the students to keep this record. Each day or intermittently, the students can be asked to note insights gained about themselves and to interpret their feelings and expressions in class.

Summary

The empathetic approach to teaching family relationships is one in which teachers plan from the beginning to teach students to look at a person's behavior from his point of view. Every topic from mate selection to money in a family relationships class lends itself to the empathetic approach. The students are led through a progression of (1) knowing their own value systems and how these value systems affect their behaviors, (2) applying generalizations about behavior, and (3) using both of these ideas in empathizing with each person involved without condoning or condemning.

Although the teacher may use the empathetic approach only occasionally or with particular subject matter in the course, it is far more effective when used as the overall strategy. It takes time for students to be able to use a combination of understanding themselves and understanding others and to know how one affects the other. Empathy can be emotional, but a rational approach is emphasized in this book.

Since literature is an excellent way to present life situations in which to learn how to empathize, the next chapter deals with the literature approach. The two approaches are very compatible.

References

Berne, Eric. *Transactional Analysis in Psychotherapy.* New York: Grove Press, 1961.

Cottrell, Leonard S. "Interpersonal Interaction and the Development of Self." In *Handbook of Socialization Theory and Research*, edited by David A. Goslin. Chicago: Rand McNally, 1969.

Glasser, William. *Reality Therapy.* New York: Harper & Row, 1965.

Goode, William J.; Hopkins, Elizabeth; and McClure, Helen. *Social System and Family Patterns: A Propositional Inventory.* Indianapolis: Bobbs-Merrill Co., 1971.

Harris, Thomas A. *I'm O.K.–You're O.K.* New York: Harper & Row, 1967.

Heider, Fritz. *Psychology of Interpersonal Relations.* New York: Wiley, 1958.

Klemer, Richard H. "The Empathetic Approach to Teaching Family Relations." *Journal of Home Economics* 57: 619-625, 1965.

———. *Marriage and Family Relationships.* New York: Harper & Row, 1970.

———. "Student Attitudes Toward Guidance in Sexual Morality." *Marriage and Family Living* 24: 260-263, 1962.

Roth, Philip. *Goodbye Columbus.* New York: Bantam Books, 1959.

Smith, Rebecca M. *Instructors Manual.* For *Marriage and Family Relationships* by Richard H. Klemer. New York: Harper & Row, 1970.

Weinstein, Eugene A. "The Development of Interpersonal Competence." In *Handbook of Socialization Theory and Research*, edited by David A. Goslin. Chicago: Rand McNally, 1969.

Chapter 2
The Literature Approach: Books, Stories, Feature Films, and Plays

Literature, including feature films and plays, is a way of studying family relationships that combines the social and cultural milieu, including interaction of specific people in specific situations, sometimes the background, and inner thoughts and feelings of the characters. Students can identify or empathize more easily with the people in literature than they can with abstract concepts. Varying interpretations expressed by the students help them understand the part that individual perceptions play in every attitude displayed or decision made. The double bind often exhibited in these life situations gives the students an excellent illustration of how a flexible organization of a set of values operates in human interaction. Somerville (1964, 1966, 1971, 1972, 1974) has developed the literature approach in great depth and others have supplemented her work (Bigner 1972; Channels 1971; Clear 1966; Kenkel 1969; Smarden 1966, 1973).

A great variety of family settings can be visited through literature. With the mobility of society and the mixing of various cultural groups in the schools, there is a need for literature which gives examples, case studies, and knowledge about the way different families live. Literature also offers vicarious experiences in painful areas such as illness, bereavement, divorce, and hard luck.

One of the best attributes of literature in the study of human behavior is being able to relate the specific behavior in the story to generalizations about behavior. It shows the students how generalizations must be applied with exceptions.

Even though the students identify strongly with one of the characters in the story, the objectivity allows them to challenge and critique the action of that character.

Using the Literature Approach

Teachers may decide to use the literature approach for an overall strategy for an entire course. In so doing they would have to have a very large collection of short stories, novels, fiction, biographies, poetry, and the like to supplement the text or outline from which to teach the principles of behavior. With each of the areas of relationships, literature would be used for examples or application of generalizations.

It does not matter whether the generalizations are presented before or after the assigned reading. If they are presented beforehand, the students do not get the full import in the beginning but spot the use of them easily while reading; if the generalizations are presented afterward, the students show great moments of insight as they have the illustrations in their head while you lead the class in organizing and outlining the generalizations.

There are many ways to assign and make use of literature. Early in the course the reading assignments should be from short stories readily available to everyone in the class so that the group concept will form. After some basic generalizations have been studied, a variety of stories and books may be assigned so that individuals or small groups may read and compare different stories.

As the students begin to read more individual stories and books, the teacher may ask them to point out how generalizations about relationships operate in explaining the behavior of the characters. They may also write about the personal insights they each have gained in reading or viewing a work and from class discussion. The literature approach is a natural combination with the empathetic approach. In fact, how could the two really be separated?

More often than not, there will be a limited number of any one book or short story. In this case assign one book to a small group of students. Have them discuss the book among themselves or have them do the book review as a panel in front of the class. Individual written reports do not allow for the important classroom interchange, but some are necessary for the student and the teacher to get a more complete picture of each student's development. Stories may be used on examinations by asking the students to relate the story material to generalizations about relationships. Another way of examining is to have the students compare two stories.

The first session is crucial to the outcome of the use of the literature approach. On the very first day have a short, short story either mimeographed for individual reading in class or have one of the students read it to the class. Do not read it to them. Do not tell them what to look for before it is read. By doing so, the spontaneity of reaction and feelings is taken away, and the stage for a teacher-dominated class may be set. The goal is to have the students learn through insights of their own, very much as in the empathetic approach.

Each story requires two readings just as all films need to be seen twice—first to get the feel and second to analyze the behaviors. Preferably there should be some time between readings.

Since the literature approach is inevitably tied in with discussion, the chapters on discussion and questions should be reviewed before using this approach. Several teaching techniques using literature are described throughout the book. A shortened story is presented here with the directions for using it in class.

FOX AND SWAN*
by John L'Heureux

The crazy situation had begun normally enough a year earlier when they were graduate students at Harvard.

Caryl Henderson was a tall plain girl who at twenty-eight decided her chances of marriage were slender and that if she wanted to have any kind of fulfilling life, she had better set about making it herself. And so, once she was accepted at Harvard, she quit her teaching job at Cambridge High and entered the Ph.D. program in English. She had resolved upon intellectual happiness, the doors to other kinds being closed to her.

Francis Madden had long since chosen his vocation when he came to Harvard. He was a Jesuit. After three years studying theology, in the year he was to be ordained, he began to ask himself—as he often had before but this time with peculiar insistence—if this were what he really wanted to do with his life. Too many of his Jesuit friends had been ordained to the priesthood only to leave and get married within a year or two. Not that route for him. And so he postponed his ordination and, after a great deal of ecclesiastical maneuvering, arranged to work for his Ph.D. at Harvard while making up his mind about the priesthood.

. . . Their relations continued in much this way throughout the summer. As Francis' love for her had changed Caryl into an attractive woman, his physical affection for her made her a free one. Her years and years of strict Catholic upbringing fell away in that one night. She was liberated. She had always given away things she owned, but now she was able to give herself and she gave lavishly. Surprisingly, her sense of freedom extended beyond herself and, where she had wished for nothing better than to marry Francis, she now wished his happiness above all else. It was this selflessness, though he would never have guessed it, which made him most uneasy.

Francis, on the other hand, felt daily more constricted, more obliged. The Catholic training, the involuted mental discipline of the Jesuits, which he had happily and with ease cast off in his first love for Caryl, returned to him now and possessed him completely. He was haunted by a sense of sin he had not known in years. He felt he should break off with Caryl, but she was all he had, and he was not sure that perhaps he might love her almost as much as she loved him. Still, he felt obliged to visit her often and to call each day, and this worried him. It seemed to deny his freedom. And when he was with her they would invariably begin kissing and petting and then that would mean another guilty morning and a trip to the confessional. By this time he was rotating priests, but they all told him the same thing: unless he planned marriage, he should end the relationship. Furthermore, she seemed oblivious to his maddening need for something more than just being naked in bed with her. This, he thought, is what they really mean by the frustration of a faculty. He had left the Jesuits for freedom to be himself and he was being something he could not even recognize. He had quit graduate studies to write and he spent most of his time worrying about not writing. Summer passed this way and now much of the winter.

After reading the story, the class could discuss the following points:

1. Does this story seem to express real feelings of people with strong conditioning, or does it lecture to you about the evils of intercourse?
2. What is your conditioning that would cause you to have one of the two impressions above?
3. Why did Francis feel liberated at first but more caught than ever later?
4. How can being loved make a person more beautiful?
5. Speculate on why Caryl does not feel as obligated to succeed in her profession?
6. Why would Caryl's selflessness bother Francis?

A different way to use the literature approach is to have two students read the same article or book and have them discuss the book so that they will become more aware of differing views on the subject. By using pairs instead of having a whole class discussion, each person has an opportunity to express himself. After each pair has read the same literary selection, they may begin a dialogue by following the outline given below. They can skip any section they prefer not to talk about. The major goal is to improve communication skills and to gain a greater insight into their own interpretations. Each one finishes each statement, and when appropriate the listener repeats or interprets what the speaker has said. Channels (1971) called this technique "Dialogue Duo."

DIALOGUE DUO

1. My name is . . .
2. I live . . .
3. I would describe my family as . . .
4. Right now my dating status is . . .
5. The most important thing I learned from this novel was . . .
6. The outstanding lesson for family life was . . .
7. The motivations and values of the characters were . . .
8. The behavior principles operating seemed to be . . .
9. I would have done these things differently: . . .
10. My philosophy in this area of life is . . .
11. Right now I am feeling . . .
12. If I were asked to evaluate this novel I would say . . .

And yet a different way to use the literature approach is to apply relationships principles to the understanding of behavior in a story by comparing the story (book, short story, film, play) with professional materials directly related to the generalizations about behavior which are operating. See the list below for some examples (Channels 1971).

Book, Short Story, Film or Play	**Professional Materials**
Lost Horizon (Hilton 1933) (Feature film, 1973)	"Alternative Models from the Perspective of Sociology" (Cuber 1970)
Paper Moon (Brown 1971) (Feature film, 1973)	"The Single-Parent Family: A Social and Sociological Problem" (Burgess 1970)
	"The Father-Daughter Relationship and the Personality Development of the Female" (Biller and Weiss 1970)
My Fair Lady (Loewe 1956) (Play and film)	*Science and Human Behavior* (Skinner 1953)
Of the Farm (Updike 1967)	"Of Social Values and the Dying: A Defense of Disengagement" (Kalish 1972)
A Letter to My Wife (Koffend 1972)	"The Inexpressive Male: A Tragedy of American Society" (Balswick and Peck 1971)

Some of the classic stories are excellent for use in family relationships classes because they allow the students to see the generalizations about human behavior operating without the students' getting immersed in current jargon and activities. The following selection from de Maupassant's "The Piece of String" is an example of how a false perception is virtually never forgotten no matter how hard the victim tries to change others' perceptions. To make this story more useful in class, read the section on perception in the chapter on Understanding Human Behavior.

THE PIECE OF STRING
by Guy de Maupassant

Master Hauchecorne, of Breauté, coming in to Goderville, was making his way towards the market-place, when he perceived on the ground a short piece of string. Master Hauchecorne, thrifty like every true Norman, thought that anything was worth picking up that could be put to any use; so, stooping painfully, for he suffered from rheumatism, he picked up the bit of thin cord, and was carefully rolling it up when he observed Master Malandain, the saddler, standing in his doorway, looking at him. They had once had a difference about a halter, and owed each other a grudge, for both were by nature inclined to bear malice. Master Hauchecorne was seized with a sort of shame at being thus seen by his enemy, grubbing in the mud for a bit of string.

He abruptly hid his spoil under his blouse, then put it in his trouser's pocket, and pretended to be still looking on the ground for something he could not find; finally he went off towards the market, with his head poked forward, bent nearly double by his rheumatism.

He was swallowed up at once in the slow-moving, noisy crowd, disputing over its interminable bargainings. Peasants were punching the cows, moving hither and thither, in perpetual fear of being taken in, and not daring to make up their minds; scrutinizing the seller's eye, to try and discover the deceit in the man, and the blemish in his beast.

The women, placing their great baskets at their feet, had taken out their fowls, which lay on the ground with legs tied together, eyes wild with fright, and crests all scarlet.

They listened to the offers made, and held out for their prices with wooden, impassive faces; then, suddenly deciding to take the bid, would scream after the customer as he slowly walked away:

"Done with you, Master Anthime. You shall have it."

Then, little by little, the market-place emptied, and, the Angelus ringing midday, those who lived too far away straggled into the inns.

At Jourdain's, the big dining-room was crowded with guests, just as the huge courtyard was crowded with vehicles of every breed, carts, cabriolets, wagonettes, tilburys, covered carts innumerable, yellow with mud, out of trim and patched, some raising their two shafts, like arms, to the sky, some with nose on the ground and tail in the air.

Right up against the diners the immense fireplace, flaming brightly, threw a mighty heat on to the backs of the right-hand row seated at table. Three jacks were turning, garnished with chickens, pigeons, and legs of mutton, and a delectable odour of roast meat, and of gravy streaming over the well-browned crackling, rose from the hearth, bringing joy to the heart, and water to the mouth.

All the aristocracy of the plough dined at M. Jourdain's, innkeeper and horsedealer, a shrewd fellow, and a "warm man."

The dishes were passed, and emptied, together with mugs of golden cider. Every one told the story of his bargains, and asked his neighbour about the crops. The weather was good for green stuff, but a little damp for corn.

Suddenly, from the courtyard in front of the house, came the roll of a drum.

All but a few, too lazy to move, jumped up at once, and flew to the doors and windows, their mouths still full and their napkins in their hands.

Finishing off the roll of his drum, the towncrier shouted in staccato tones, with a scansion of phrase peculiarly out of rhythm:

"This is to inform the inhabitants of Goderville, and all others—present at the market, that there was lost this morning on the Beuzeville road between nine and ten o'clock, a black leather pocket-book, containing five hundred francs and some business papers. It should be returned—to the Town Hall immediately, or to Master Fortuné Houlbrèque at Manneville. A reward of twenty francs is offered."

The man went by, and presently the dull rumble of the drum was heard again, and then the crier's voice, fainter in the distance.

Every one began discussing the event, calculating the chances of Master Houlbrèque's recovering or not recovering his pocketbook.

And so the meal came to an end.

They were finishing their coffee when the brigadier of gendarmes appeared at the door, and asked:

"Is Master Hauchecorne, of Breauté, here?"

Master Hauchecorne, seated at the far end of the table, answered:

"Here!"

"Master Hauchecorne," proceeded the officer, "will you be so good as to come with me to the Town Hall? The mayor would like to speak to you."

Surprised and uneasy, the peasant gulped down his cognac, rose, and stooping even more than in the morning, for the first steps after resting were always particularly painful, got himself started, repeating:

"All right! I'm coming!" and followed the sergeant.

The mayor was awaiting him, seated in an armchair. He was the notary of the district, a stout, serious man, full of pompous phrases.

"Master Hauchecorne," said he, "you were seen this morning to pick up, on the Beuzeville road, the pocket-book lost by Master Houlbrèque, of Manneville."

The peasant, in stupefaction, gazed at the mayor, intimidated at once by this suspicion which lay heavy upon him without his comprehending it.

"Me? me—me pick up that pocket-book?"

"Yes, you."

"On my word of honour, I didn't! Why, I didn't even know about it!"

"You were seen."

"Seen? I? Who saw me?"

"M. Malandain, the saddler."

Then the old man remembered, and understood. Reddening with anger, he said:

"Ah! he saw me, that animal! Well, what he saw me pick up was this string, look here, M. le Maire!"

And rummaging in his pocket, he pulled out the little piece of string.

But the mayor shook his head incredulously.

"You won't make me believe, Master Hauchecorne, that M. Malandain, a trustworthy man, took that piece of string for a pocket-book."

The enraged peasant raised his hand, spat solemnly to show his good faith, and repeated:

"It's God's truth, all the same, the sacred truth, M. le Maire. There, on my soul and honour, I say it again."

The mayor proceeded.

"After having picked up the article in question, you even went on searching in the mud, to make sure a coin or two mightn't have fallen out."

The poor old fellow choked with indignation and fear.

"To say such things! . . . How can any one . . . telling lies like that, to undo an honest man! How can any one?"

Protest as he would, he was not believed.

They confronted him with M. Malandain, who repeated and substantiated his story. The two abused each other for a whole hour. By his own request, Master Hauchecorne was searched. Nothing was found on him.

At last the mayor, thoroughly puzzled, dismissed him, warning him that he was going to give notice to the public prosecutor and take his instructions.

The news had spread. As he went out of the Town Hall the old man was surrounded, and all sorts of serious or mocking questions were put to him, but no one showed the slightest indignation. He began to tell the story of the piece of string. They did not believe him. Everybody laughed.

He went on, stopped by every one, stopping every one he knew, to tell his story over and over again, protesting, showing his pockets turned inside out, to prove that he had nothing on him. The only answer he got was:

"Get along, you sly old dog!"

He began to feel angry, worrying himself into a fever of irritation, miserable at not being believed, at a loss what to do, and continually repeating his story.

Night came on. It was time to go home. He set out with three neighbours, to whom he showed the spot where he had picked up the piece of string; and the whole way home he kept talking of his misadventure.

In the evening he made a round of the village of Breauté, to tell everybody all about it. He came across unbelievers only.

He was ill all night.

The next day, about one o'clock, Marius Paumelle, a labourer at Master Breton's, a farmer at Ymauville, restored the pocketbook and its contents to Master Houlbrèque, of Manneville.

This man declared that he had found the object on the road; but not being able to read, he had taken it home and given it to his master.

The news spread through the neighborhood. Master Hauchecorne was informed of it, and started off at once on a round, to tell his story all over again, with its proper ending. It was a triumph.

"What knocked me over," he said, "was not so much the thing itself, you know, but that charge of lying. There's nothing hurts a man so much as being thought a liar."

The whole day long he talked of his adventure, telling it to people he met on the roads, to people drinking at the inns, and even at the church door on the following Sunday. He stopped perfect strangers to tell them about it. He was easy in his mind now, and yet—there was something that bothered him, though he could not exactly arrive at what it was. People had an amused look while they were listening to him. They did not seem convinced. He felt as if a lot of tattle was going on behind his back.

On the Tuesday of the following week he went off to Goderville market, urged thereto solely by the desire to tell his story. Malandain, standing at his door, began to laugh as he went past. Why?

He began his story to a farmer of Criquetot, who did not let him finish, but, giving him a dig in the pit of the stomach, shouted in his face: "Get along, you old rogue!" and turned his back.

Master Hauchecorne stopped short, confused, and more and more uneasy. Why was he being called an "old rogue"?

When he was seated at table at Jourdain's inn he began again to explain the whole affair.

A horse-dealer from Montvillier called out:

"Come, come, that's an old trick; I know all about your piece of string!"

Hauchecorne stammered:

"But it's been found, that pocket-book!"

But the other went on:

"Oh! shut up, old boy, there's one who finds, and another who brings back. All on the strict Q.T."

The peasant was thunderstruck. He understood at last. It was insinuated that he had caused the pocket-book to be taken back by someone else, an accomplice.

He tried to protest, but the whole table began laughing.

He could not finish his dinner, and went away, with everyone jeering at him.

He returned home, ashamed and indignant, choking with anger and bewilderment, and all the more overwhelmed because, in his artful Norman brain, he knew himself capable of having done what they accused him of, and of even boasting about it afterwards, as though it were a feat. He realized confusedly that it would be impossible to prove his innocence, his tricky nature being known to all. And he felt wounded to the heart by the injustice of this suspicion.

Then he began again to tell his story, making the tale a little longer every day, adding new reasons every time, more energetic protestations, most solemn oaths which he thought out and prepared in his solitary moments, for his mind was solely occupied by the story of the piece of string. They believed him less and less as his defence became more and more elaborate, his arguments more subtle.

"H'm! that's only to cover up his tracks," the hearers would say behind his back.

He was conscious of all this, but went on eating his heart out, exhausting himself in fruitless efforts.

Before the very eyes of people, he wasted away.

Jokers now would make him tell them the "piece of string" to amuse them, as one makes old soldiers tell about their battles. His spirit, undermined, grew feebler and feebler.

Towards the end of December he took to his bed.

He died at the beginning of January, and in his last delirium still protested his innocence, repeating:—

"A little piece of string . . . a little piece of string . . . look, here it is, M. le Maire!"

Using the empathetic approach, empathize with the man who was misperceived. Apply the following generalizations to explain why it is difficult to change others' perceptions.

Generalizations about Behavior

1. That which is learned in a surprising situation tends to be more firmly conditioned than information learned in ordinary situations because of the

strength of the reinforcement (Skinner 1953). Fear of punishment was a strong negative reinforcer in that society, especially among the lower class people.

2. That which is learned first tends to be more firmly conditioned than that which is learned later (Skinner 1953).
3. When a person appears to be overreacting to a situation, sometimes he is perceived as. and may be trying to show the opposite of reality (as in reaction formation in the psychoanalytic theory).
4. When an event is perceived as reality, the consequences are real (Thomas 1917; Rogers 1961).

Films and Plays

To avoid a heavy reading assignment and to account for variations in student interest, include as a part of the literature approach feature films at commercial theaters, on TV, at college union showings, and from a company which rents commercial films (Jones, updated periodically). Also, include written plays. Do not overlook the use of music from the sound tracks of movies or music from plays themselves. Since teachers are not always sure what commercial film will be showing or when it will be shown, a surprise assignment when one happens to be announced at the theater may mean more than one that was planned in advance. Interestingly enough, almost any film or play seen late in the course is applicable because so many generalizations can be found operating. Previewing before assigning is always preferable but, late in the course, a newspaper review will suffice.

One problem, of course, is making sure everyone sees the film. Both money and time may be factors. Teachers usually know the students well enough to know the money problems. One movie a semester is rarely a financial strain, but some of the students may make teachers think it is, just because it has been assigned. However, student-teacher relationships are usually good enough by this time for dissension not to happen. If the film is shown on the college campus, students may be able to go together to see it. There is usually a very good film selection on television at reasonable hours. Since most homes have a set, this would not be an extraordinary assignment. If other family members prefer to see another program, it would be an interesting assignment to see how the students handled this family relationships problem. In cases in which a student is working, or ill, an alternate film will need to be selected for him to see, or he may be assigned a novel to read and report on.

Besides reading and discussing, students may be asked to present a play as another part of the literature approach (no time should be spent memorizing parts). The Family Service Association's *Plays for Living* are designed for classroom and group discussion use. Many films are in play form. Selected parts of the plays may be read. A selected part of *I Never Sang for My Father* (Anderson 1970) is excellent for teaching how adult children and their aging parents relate. This and other plays are available in paperback. Again, have available as many copies as there are parts to play.

Selecting and Collecting Stories, Books, and Plays

There has to be a beginning. A sufficient supply of books, articles, stories, plays, and films is very difficult to obtain. However, do not wait for that ample supply before making some use of literature. Students are one of the most excellent sources teachers have. Introduce the idea of the approach and they will begin to compile a bibliography of books and stories for the class. Information about this literature should include a written summary, a list of concepts covered, behavior principles operating, and how the characters solved their problems. Although donations from the students may be accepted, their keeping their books may be the beginning of their personal library, a goal any teacher would wish for the students.

Some of the literature collected in the beginning will not be as good as teachers would like, but they should keep all of it until they can afford to be selective. The major criterion for selection is its adequacy in revealing insights. A second criterion is to get as many clear stereotypes of subcultures as possible, for the literature approach is the individual approach, the Rashamon approach (one in which individuals tell it as each sees it). From these individuals, generalizations will emerge.

The Short Story Index (Cook and Monro 1965) may be one of the best sources for titles. The annual (since 1941) publication in paperback, the *Best American Short Stories* (Foley 1972), is also an excellent place to find stories. Since the book is a paperback, feel perfectly free to tear the book apart into its individual stories so that several students may read at one time. If the end of one story and the beginning of the next are on one page, photocopy that page so that each story is complete. Staple each story into a file folder and label. File them by story title with a good cross referencing system, and later a particular story may almost always be used in one study area of relationships. Many other sources (Guernsey 1971; *20 Grand Short Stories* 1967; Updike 1966; and popular magazines) are available.

Book reviews from the newspaper, popular magazines, libraries, and publishing houses give you leads for new materials. The teachers of literature may be the best source. Once word gets around that literature is being collected, teachers get many donations.

Summary

Although literature may mean only books to some people, it includes articles, plays, and feature films. The holistic approach of literature keeps the application of generalizations about behavior in its proper perspective. By reading a book or viewing a feature film, students empathize with one or more of the characters and in turn learn more about themselves.

If books are the major medium, getting an adequate supply of books and having time to have read them will mean that the teacher will have to develop the literature approach through the years. There are some compendiums with teaching suggestions available, however. Also, the students may be more than willing to help start a collection, including a list of generalizations operating in each book or short story.

Feature films are a too-often overlooked medium for family-relationships courses. The films shown recently on television are also new enough to be very useful for today's students.

The empathetic approach of the last chapter, the literature approach of this chapter, and the research approach of the next chapter are all suggested as overall frameworks for the entire family relationships course. However, a whole course framework is not the only way each of these approaches may be used. Each of them lends itself to being used as a part of the total course.

References

Anderson, Robert. *I Never Sang for My Father.* New York: New American Library, 1970.

Balswick, Jack D., and Peck, Charles W. "The Inexpressive Male: A Tragedy of American Society." *The Family Coordinator* 20: 363-368, 1971.

Bigner, Jerry. "Parent Education in Popular Literature 1950-1970." *The Family Coordinator* 21: 313-320, 1972.

Biller, Henry B., and Weiss, Stephen D."The Father-Daughter Relationship and the Personality Development of the Female." *Journal of Genetic Psychology* 116: 79-94, 1970.

Brown, Joe Daniel. *Paper Moon.* New York: New American Library, 1971.

Burgess, Jane K. "The Single-Parent Family: A Social and Sociological Problem" *The Family Coordinator* 19:137-144, 1970.

Channels, Vera. "Family Life Education Through the Use of Novels." *The Family Coordinator* 20:225-230, 1971.

Clear, Val. "Marriage Education Through Novels and Biography." *Journal of Marriage and the Family* 28:217-219, 1966.

Cook, Dorothy E., and Monro, Isabel, eds. *Short Story Index 1959-1963.* New York: H. W. Wilson, 1965. (A recent supplement includes 1964-1968.)

Cuber, John "Alternative Models from the Perspective of Sociology." In *The Family in Search of a Future*, edited by Herbert Otto. New York: Appleton-Century-Crofts, 1970.

Family Service Association. *Plays for Living.* New York: Family Service Association of America. (These are continuously being published.)

Foley, Martha, ed. *The Best American Short Stories 1972.* New York: Ballantine Books, 1972. (Published every year)

Guernsey, Otis L., ed. *The Best Plays-Indexes.* New York: Dodd-Mead, 1971.

Hilton, James. *Lost Horizon.* New York: Pocket Books, 1933 and 1960.

Jones, G. Williams. Consultant. *Dialogue with the World.* New York: Films, Inc. (Updated periodically.)

Kalish, Richard A. "Of Social Values and the Dying: A Defense of Disengagement." *The Family Coordinator* 21:81-94, 1972.

Kenkel, William. "Marriage and the Family in Modern Science Fiction." *Journal of Marriage and the Family* 31: 6-14, 1969.

Koffend, John B. *A Letter to My Wife.* New York: Dell Pub. Co., 1972.

L'Heureux, John. "Fox and Swan." In *The Best American Short Stories, 1972.* New York: Ballantine Books, 1972.

Loewe, Frederick. *My Fair Lady.* New York: Coward-McCann, 1956.

Maupassant, Guy de. "The Piece of String." *Yvette–A Novelette and Ten Other Stories.* Freeport, New York: Books for Libraries, Reprinted, 1971.

Rogers, Carl R. *On Becoming a Person.* Boston: Houghton Mifflin Co., 1961.

Smarden, Laurence E. "Marriage in Magazines." *The Family Coordinator* 22: 177-182, 1973.

———. "The Use of Drama in Teaching Family Relationships." *Journal of Marriage and the Family* 28: 210-223, 1966.

Skinner, B. F. *Science and Human Behavior.* New York: Free Press, 1953.

Somerville, Rose. *Family Insights Through the Short Story.* New York: Teachers College Press, Columbia University, 1964.

———. (a) "Creative Literature for Study of the Family;" (b) "The Literature Approach to Teaching Family Courses;" (c) "The Short Story and Family Insights in Secondary Schools." *Journal of Marriage and the Family* 28: 213,214,223, 1966.

———. "Death Education as Part of Family Life Education: Using Imaginative Literature for Insights into Family Crises." *The Family Coordinator* 20: 209-224, 1971.

———. "The Future of Family Relations in the Middle and Older Years: Clues in Fiction." *The Family Coordinator* 21: 487-498, 1972

Somerville, Rose, ed. *Intimate Relationships: Marriage, Family, and Lifestyles Through Literature.* Englewood Cliffs. N.J.: Prentice-Hall, 1974.

Thomas, William I. "The Persistence of Primary-Group Norms in Present Day Society." In *Suggestions of Modern Science Concerning Education,* by H. S. Jennings, *et al.* New York: Macmillan, 1917, pp. 159-197.

20 Grand Short Stories. New York: Scholastic Books Services, 1967.

Updike, John. *Of the Farm.* New York: Alfred A. Knopf, 1967.

———. *The Music School.* New York: Alfred A. Knopf, 1966.

Chapter 3

The Research Approach

Students often are unaware that all knowledge comes from some type of research, whether it be personal observations or highly structured, controlled research. Some of the questions raised in any course are "How do they know?" "Where did they get this?" "Who said so?" and "What is the real truth?" These questions can be answered in part by having the students conduct some research on their own. The major benefit from this approach is not so much in adding new knowledge to the family relations content but in teaching the students where knowledge comes from, how to judge the conclusions from research, how to replicate research in order to verify the findings, to compare findings over time, and to gain new knowledge for themselves.

Conducting Research in the Classroom

By using the research approach, the teacher could require that students do some research in every area of family relationships, or the class could be divided into smaller groups and each group be given an area to research. They would compare their findings with those presented in the textbook. If the class is small, the whole class could participate in all of the research projects. The advantage of the large class is that it allows for more different areas to be researched at one time. On the other hand, in the small class each student has the advantage of being a part of several research projects rather than being in on only a few projects.

Students are angered when old research data are presented as evidence (or support) for an author's conclusions about a relationships area, for example the area of dating. A quick survey of the class members provides a ready bit of present-day data which shows similarities and differences between the old data in the text and the new data. If the class is large and varied, the data are more reliable. If the responses can be made anonymously, the data are more reliable.

For even greater impact, give the students a short questionnaire about dating which is similar to the research presented in most textbooks. Do not allow them to put their names on the questionnaires. They will assume that you will tally the responses and report to the class later. Instead, take up the questionnaires, shuffle them and return them to the class members so that no one is likely to get his own paper back. Then, tally the data right in front of them by asking for a show of hands for each question. The students will not be at all reluctant to share the responses on the papers because they are not their own.

The immediate knowledge of the outcome of the questionnaire and the immediate comparison with the data in the book has a lasting effect on the students. Many times the new and the old data are almost exactly the same, reinforcing the fact that some things do not change "with the wind." Kerckhoff and Boytala (1969) also found that students have another learning experience from this technique; they will be either more suspicious of research data or more accepting of research data according to how honest they themselves were in answering the questions.

Framework for the Research Approach

The purpose of the research approach is to teach the students (1) the basic tenets of research methodology, (2) how to interpret conclusions, (3) how to use research findings, and (4) that replication of research is necessary for reliability of the findings.

Introduce the research approach as the overall framework for the course in the beginning or immediately after a topic has been undertaken for study. When the subject matter has been taken from various research reports, question the research findings, if the students do not do it first! Upon questioning the findings, the teacher can question the methodology, and questioning the methodology can lead to teaching what is acceptable.

After several episodes of questioning research findings because of methodology, students may begin to doubt that the findings of some study apply to them or to the particular day and year; at that point the idea of replicating some of the research either in or out of the classroom will be appropriate. Have them go outside to collect data–from other students, children, parents, or whatever group is similar to that originally researched.

Even though teachers will be tempted to teach a whole unit on research methodology in the beginning, the students will benefit more if they are taught certain aspects of research all through the course. The various methods of data collection need not be taught at one time–only that method being critiqued in the research topic of the moment. Only recently has there been much experimental research in the study of total family interaction and most of this research was through simulated games on the one hand and organized different life styles on the other. Some experiments which have not been well controlled have occurred from suggestions from behavioral therapists.

Research as an overall framework can be high key or low key. If it is too high key, it will alienate the majority of students who have probably taken the family relationships course for personal application. Teachers may use the research approach only as their own guide for conducting the class. To do this, teachers would merely teach the cautions of research as they would teach any other topic. Teachers could also have students participate in research as an occasional project while learning the principles and methodology of research rather than basing the entire learning experience on actually doing research. Straus (1969) designed a book for teachers to use in doing simple, partial replications of research in class. Instruments and worksheets for analysis are included.

Cautions in Using Research Conclusions

Sophistication in research and statistical techniques is not necessary for the use of the research approach; however, some appreciation and knowledge of research is necessary. Much of the research is purely a description of certain aspects of people or of a relationship. That is, a percentage of people is determined (1) who marry at a certain age; (2) who say they are happy in marriage; (3) who have in-law trouble; (4) who are child abusers; (5) who have sexual problems; etc. Along with giving the percentages of people who are in any one category, a description of certain attributes is sometimes given such as: most of those who marry very young are unhappy at home, immature, and erratic; most of those who say they are happy in marriage are conventional, goal seeking, and have good self-concepts. Too much research stops with these percentages. But even more important than this, the findings are then stated as conclusions or facts and are very often imputed to everyone.

The major fallacy in using statistics in research findings about human relations is that they are usually not generalizable. A second fallacy is the inappropriate use of actuarial-type predictions from percentages. That is, when it is found that a certain percentage, say 65 percent, of people have certain characteristics, the prediction is falsely interpreted to mean that everyone has a 65 percent chance of having these characteristics.

A third problem in using statistics to help make decisions is the confusion of prevalence with excellence. If it is found that most of the people act a certain way, one cannot automatically assume that that behavior is best. Because "everyone is doing it" is no more a justification for doing it than when a child uses just this plea when begging for permission to wear a certain garment. In some cases what "everybody" is doing may be the best for those who are doing that particular thing but not best for another specific person.

A fourth problem in research is finding that even the experts disagree in their conclusions about some topic they have researched. This leaves the students in the turmoil of making decisions for themselves after having been conditioned to accept the word of the experts, the word of their elders, and the results of research. An equal dilemma may occur if teachers do not know how to judge conclusions from research (Klemer 1970).

Some basic guides to judging conclusions from human-relationships research are summarized below (Kerlinger 1973):

1. The conclusions may be applied no further than to the people who were measured or to the group of people for which the measured sample was representative. For example, characteristics of college students on one campus do not apply to the general public or to all college students.
2. The conclusions may be acceptable only if the data were collected with valid and reliable instruments. For example, a questionnaire must ask questions which really obtain information about the concepts being measured and the questions must be interpreted the same by all. For reliability, the questionnaire must be testing the same concept throughout and must test the same concept time after time.
3. The conclusions may be acceptable only if they predict behavior of others in an accurate statistical manner. For example, that mixed marriages will be more likely to be fraught with problems than are marriages between similar people is an inaccurate prediction even if the sample were representative of all marriages. The accurate conclusion is that there are more problems in mixed marriages, but the prediction must be drawn from the explanations of why and when there are more problems in mixed marriages. Then it would be accurate to predict that in mixed marriages (a) couples who are young, (b) who live in a traditional neighborhood, (c) who are rigid in their beliefs, and (d) whose parents are unacquainted are *more likely* to have problems. The opposite prediction is that couples in a mixed marriage who are (a) older, (b) better educated, (c) on a higher social level, (d) flexible in their beliefs, and (e) whose parents are not involved are *less likely* to have problems. But to predict that people in mixed marriages are more likely to have problems than people in marriages of similar people is too simple.

Making Use of Research Conclusions

Generalizations are made all the time. Some are from long observation; some are from vague feelings; some are from hard research data. The most important outcome of statistical research is to further validate or refute theoretical propositions (Burr, Mead, and Rollins 1973). In the end no matter how much research data or how many generalizations are available, a judgment or decision has to be made if problems are to be solved.

Even when it is found by research that a majority do tend to behave a certain way under certain conditions, there is still the realization that there is a minority who do not. Therefore in making judgments or speculating on behavior, it must always be remembered that, "Some do, some don't." If this idea is kept in mind, the person who does not fit the generalization or majority is at least looked at as an individual with some understanding that behavior may be caused, but not by the same thing in different people.

Research conclusions do have an important place even if they are limited. Every bit of information which explains a little better why people behave as they do helps teachers as they are at times called upon to counsel with people, give advice, make judgments, and set up situations whereby people respond.

Knowing what people generally do in certain situations is a quick way to make a judgment when speed is necessary. It is a way to set a framework for reacting to people. It is a way of predicting before all the facts are in. And generalizations are a safety factor so that teachers will not be caught completely unaware. For example, to generalize that men are aggressive helps to understand, expect, and predict their behavior.

But alongside the generalizations must be an open mind and a whole set of facts which are not generally applicable, but which may impinge so strongly on the specific situation that they become the important factors and not the generalizations. For example, as the generalization is made that men are aggressive (that is, that on the average men are more aggressive than women), the other factors must be remembered: that men have varying aggressiveness according to the situation, that some men are more aggressive than other men, that some women are more aggressive than some men, and that aggression can be both overt and covert. To be specific, in working with a particular man, people at first expect a certain aggressiveness and then find the man is not as aggressive as expected, whereupon it is remembered that normal and average are not the same and that he is within the normal range. After this it is found that his lack of aggressiveness was situation-specific and that his aggression varied. So what can be done with all this information? This leads then to a possible value judgment—it is best for this man to act the way he does.

No generalization or research finding substitutes for a person's own value judgment. Value judgments come from what people believe to be good or right, and this judgment comes from cultural expectations, observations of outcomes, and what fits their needs. Obviously some value judgments must fit the cultural norm more than individual needs. At any rate, research findings do help with some final decisions according to one's own values, whether these values are (1) to believe research findings without question, (2) to use only those findings which support individual values, or (3) to weigh research findings against past beliefs and reconcile the differences.

Teaching Techniques

1. *To understand that the **generalizability of research findings** can go only as far as the representativeness of the sample goes.*
   a. In a research study involving 410 students (160 men and 250 women) at one college in 1958 (Bell and Blumberg 1970, p. 167), 65 percent of the women and 44 percent of the men felt they would be going too far by having sexual intercourse during casual dating.
   Which of the following statements are true so far as to which group and which period of time? What is wrong with the false statements?
   (F) (1) In 1974, 65 percent of college women and 44 percent of college men felt they would have gone too far by having sexual intercourse during casual dating.
   (F) (2) In the late 1950s, 65 percent of college women and 44 percent of college men felt they would have gone too far by having sexual intercourse during casual dating.
   (F) (3) In the late 1950s, 65 percent of women and 44 percent of men felt they would have gone too far by having sexual intercourse during casual dating.
   (T) (4) In 1958, 65 percent of the 160 men and 44 percent of the 250 women questioned at one college said they felt they would have gone too far by having sexual intercourse during casual dating.
2. *To be able to reconcile that **conflicting conclusions** from different researchers are a result of dissimilar subjects, eras, concepts, and methods of gathering information.*
   Three sets of two conflicting conclusions are listed below:
   a. People tend to marry people like themselves rather than opposites. People tend to marry people with complementary needs.
   b. The economic factor is not significant in divorce or marriage adjustment. Money ranks in the top three factors which cause disagreements in marriage.
   c. American families are becoming democratic companionships. American families are still traditional in most of the important role definitions.

   If, in fact, these six conclusions are valid from data given, how can one use the conclusions in solving a particular problem at hand?
   a. One way is to apply the conclusions only to groups similar to the ones from which the data were taken.
   b. Another way is to realize that both conclusions should be used in considering a problem.
3. *To be able to use research **findings about the minority** as well as the majority in making decisions.*

a. Consider the following descriptions of the majority and the descriptions of the minority, remembering that the minority is still a part of the group with whom you will have contact; and, therefore, the minority characteristics must be remembered so that absolute stereotyping does not occur.

Descriptions of unwed mothers who keep their children

Majority: Desperately need someone to love.

Minority: Want the child because it is an expression of love and because they realize their capacity to rear children.

Descriptions of girls who marry under eighteen years of age

Majority: Need to get away from home, have a strong need to have adult status, or have poor self-images.

Minority: Are ready to marry and are capable of realistically managing an adult relationship.

b. Discuss the following statement: Waller (1970) said that statistics may be used imaginatively and case studies unimaginatively. No generalization can be so clearly buttressed by facts as one which is definitely supported by one or two well understood cases; generalization from statistics is ever more tenuous and inconclusive than generalization from persons.

4. *To understand how **to predict from percentages.** Actuarial interpretations are not relevant to human behavior.*

a. Consider the following findings from research:

(1) Seventy-five percent of married couples have trouble with in-laws. Twenty-five percent of married couples do not have trouble with in-laws. Which of the following statements is more likely to be true about the research findings?

(F) 1. Every couple has a 75 percent chance of having trouble with in-laws.

(T) 2. Seventy-five percent (or three-fourths) of all couples have a 100 percent chance of having trouble with in-laws and 25 percent (or one-fourth) of all couples have a 100 percent chance of *not* having trouble with in-laws.

The likelihood is determined by the situation involved. Under certain circumstances such as parental approval of the marriage, maturity of the couple, financial capacity of the couple, and maturity of the in-laws, there is every likelihood of *no* in-law problems or nearly 100 percent chance of *no* in-law problems.

(2) Fifty percent of all teen-age brides are pregnant at the time of marriage.

Which of the following statements is more likely to be true?

(F) 1. Every teen-age bride has a 50 percent change of being pregnant at the time of marriage.

(T) 2. Fifty percent of the teen-age brides have 100 percent chance of being pregnant at marriage and 50 percent of the teen-age brides have a 100 percent chance of *not* being pregnant at the time of marriage.

The likelihood is determined by the situation involved. Under certain circumstances such as the girl's early dating experiences, lack of parental supervision, immature judgment about the consequences of sexual intercourse, need for close relationships, and the older age of the mate, there is every likelihood of a 100 percent chance of pregnancy at marriage.

(3) One-fourth of all marriages end in divorce.
Interpret this finding with respect to predicting what will happen to any one marriage.

(4) One-fifth of all houses in one town are substandard.
Interpret this finding with respect to predicting the quality of housing in the next five years in that town.
Even in the year of the research, clearly there is no way that one could say that every house in that town has a 20 percent chance of being substandard in the future. When comparing these data about nonpersonal matters with personal matters such as in-law trouble, the reasoning that every couple has a 75 percent chance of having trouble with in-laws is unjustified.

5. *To be able* ***to apply correlation coefficients*** *to explaining behavior. If two variables, for example, the amount of income of one of the spouses and power in that family, have a correlation coefficient of +.70, the first impression is that there is a strong relationship between the variables and that power can be predicted when the income is known (see Kerlinger 1973 for a complete discussion on correlation).*

Three misinterpretations are inherent:

a. To find the true amount of variance explained by the +.70 correlation coefficient, multiply .70 by .70 to get .49 or 49 percent. This notes that only 49 percent or less than half of the variance (or relationship) is explained by the +.70 coefficient. If less than half of the relationship is explained by this high a correlation coefficient, then keep in mind that the income level is not as potent a predictor of power in the family as one might expect.

b. The second misinterpretation is that no cause and effect relationship may be claimed from a correlation coefficient. That the amount of money caused the power is not proven by subjecting findings to a correlation statistic. Only one other means may be used to determine a greater cause and effect relationship. There has to have been an experimental design in which spouses were given varying amounts of income to see if higher amounts would increase power in the family. A good *ex post facto* design could ascertain this information. An *ex post facto* design is one in which it is assumed that the experiment took place in real life and the researcher merely used excellent methodology to get the information from the people so that no contamination or confounding of the data occurred.

c. A third misinterpretation is that a specific amount of increase in income will be related to a predictable increase in power. This interpretation may not be made unless the data were subjected to a regression analysis, a statistical operation which indicates prediction power.

Even so, the correlation coefficient does give a better understanding of what factors may be related.

When teachers are analyzing a case or counseling with students or teaching generalizations about relationships, knowing how factors are related does help.

6. ***To understand whether there are any real (significant) differences in the characteristics between two groups of people.***

a. Explain the difference between these two statements (see discussion below):

(1) The personality trait of dominance is *significantly* related to power. Those people with a personality trait of dominance usually have the power.

(2) A personality trait of dominance is likely to account for some power in a marriage no matter who makes the most money.

In (1) the term "significantly" implies that the data gathered has been subjected to a statistical test which compares the mean (average) measure of dominance of those who have the power to be enough larger than the mean (average) of those spouses who do not have the power to say that these two groups are different from each other.

In (2) the statement merely says that the level of dominance is probably higher for those spouses who have the power, but there is not enough difference between the groups to claim dominance as a trait that goes with power. It also implies that some of those who do not have the power may have a personality characteristic of dominance.

b. When two groups are compared statistically, the results are usually presented in the following form:

There will be a significantly greater ($p>.05$) number of divorces from marriages when the couple is under 18 years of age than when the couple is over 18 years of age.

Three ways to interpret this finding are listed below:

(1) This means that the finding that "three divorces for every four

marriages of couples who marry under 18 years of age" is enough larger than the finding that "one divorce for every three or four marriages of couples who marry after 18 years of age" to say that the two groups of couples are different.

(2) It also means that this difference will occur between every two such groups of couples drawn from the same population (assuming the sample is representative) ninety-five times out of a hundred. (The symbol $p>.05$ means that the probability is equal to or greater than 95 percent that the difference will occur.)

(3) It also means that this difference will not occur between every two such groups only five times out of a hundred (probability is equal to or greater than .05 that the finding of real difference is an error).

7. *To compare and contrast research techniques about knowledge and attitudes toward some area of family life and be able to make viable use of the combination of techniques.*

The following is an example of how comparing research techniques could be used in one area of family life. The area chosen is arbitrary.

Area: Knowledge and attitudes about venereal disease (other areas can be mixed marriage; homosexuality; arguing; equality between the sexes; personality development; premarital sexual relations).

Three different research methods: Inventory, survey, and experiment.

a. Survey

Interview or survey the entire class about their attitudes toward venereal disease using the following short schedule.

(1) Have you ever known anyone who had VD?
(2) How well did you know this person?
(3) Were you disappointed when you found out? Why?
(4) Did you attempt to stay away from this person after you found out? Why?
(5) Did you suggest any method of alleviating the VD? Why or why not?

b. Inventory

Give the entire class the VD Knowledge Inventory (McHugh 1966).

c. Experiment

Before experimenting with the class (experimental condition or treatment will be three different films) divide the class into thirds and give each person in the class the same short situation (below) to respond to. Then show each third a different film on VD, each of which approaches it differently: one which uses a scare tactic such as *Dance Little Children*; one which uses a moralizing tactic such as *The Innocent Party*; and one which uses a straightforward health care and prevention tactic such as *VD: Name Your Contacts* (order these films from your State Department of Public Health).

Give the students this situation prior to the film:

> Your 14-year-old daughter is very open about her discussion of boy friends and beach parties and being more mature than you were in your day. Lately she has been spending much more time in front of the mirror and noticeably more time with cosmetic or medicinal preparations from the drugstore.

Question: What would you suggest to her?

This is the situation presented after the film:

> Your 14-year-old sister appears to be much more mature than girls were when you were 14. She tells of her encounters and how she handles them, using very cosmopolitan attitudinal comments. Lately she has been spending more money on cosmetic and medicinal preparations from the drug store.

Question: What would you suggest to her?

Discussion following the use of each of the three research techniques:

a. Compare the findings from the three research techniques: Inventory, Interview, Experiment.
b. Compare the three techniques for validity of the technique for gathering data.
c. Consider the value in the use of a combination of techniques.
d. Assess the errors involved in the techniques such as prior knowledge of the subject matter, differences in attitudes prior to the research, and the limited effect one short film or other experimental variable could have.

Applying the Theory Rather Than the Specific Findings

Theories are developed after observing that certain relationships between factors are predictable. Empirical research is carried out to test these theories. However, teaching from the theory, rather than from the supportive empirical findings, is the important thing (Burr, Mead and Rollins 1973).

For example, that a person with high self-esteem is easier to work with is a postulate consistently substantiated by empirical research. Would it not be better to discuss relationships problems in the context of the self theory (Rogers 1961) which states that energies are used to maintain self-esteem? This would be an explanation of the problem rather than a memorization of the statistical findings.

Research findings show that most people have in-law problems. To stop here explains nothing. The theory is applied by saying, "When an in-law's self-esteem is lowered, he uses his energies to protect or raise his self-esteem rather than to promote good relationships." The question is, "What might be the reasons for loss of self-esteem in a daughter-in-law and mother-in-law relationship?" Some suggestions are that the daughter-in-law feels inadequate for her new wife role when the mother-in-law may have a loss of self-esteem if the daughter-in-law constantly brings to her wife role new ways which seem to be more efficient. On the other hand, a person does not feel threatened or suffer a loss of self-esteem if the other person does not make an obvious point of being better. It is probably the loss of self-esteem rather than the fact that they are in-laws that causes the problems. The point being made here is that the theory is the applicable portion of research results, not the specific finding.

Support for the postulate that people who have good self-images and who are not burdened with problems will get along better in any situation is found in "Step-Kin Relations" (Duberman 1973). The specific finding that step-kin get along about as well as blood-kin is important enough in itself, but the discussion of this finding implies that the real mechanism for a good relationship is the abilities for relating that the people bring to the group.

In the research on "Extended Kin Relationships in Black and White Families" (Hays and Mindel 1973), it was shown that the following assumptions are made without justification: (1) If a particular family structure does not approximate the dominant American model, then that family form is considered abnormal; and (2) because the nuclear family fits the needs of an industrial society, then it fits the needs of all people living in an industrial society. However, this study was conducted within the proposition that: individuals from different subcultures operate in a different social situation; therefore their family structures must be different. Upon studying black families, it was found that blacks visit more, include a larger number in the kin network, live together more, get more help, etc. To stop here explains nothing. The conclusion and discussion of these findings was that an extended kin network is a more salient structure for black than white families because of a need for more aid and comfort in a hostile environment which is a different social situation from the white norm in America. Without discussion and a propositional framework within which to explain the findings, they would have little real use. This is another example in which the theoretical framework more than the findings is the most important part of research.

Summary

The research approach in teaching family relationships shows students how to evaluate research findings through participation in research. As the students participate, they become aware of where family-relationships subject matter is gained, the cautions in interpreting and applying research findings, and how good research is planned and carried out.

The three overall strategies for the entire course in family relationships—

empathetic approach, literature approach, and research approach—may be combined, used only in some courses, or used only occasionally throughout the course. No matter what the overall strategy, discussion is a major classroom technique used in clarifying and teaching subject matter. Discussion is the topic of the following chapter.

References

Bell, Robert, and Blumberg, Leonard. "Courtship Stages and Intimacy Attitudes." In *Marriage and Family Relationships* by Richard H. Klemer. New York: Harper & Row, 1970.

Burr, Wesley; Mead, D. Eugene; and Rollins, Boyd C. "A Model for the Application of Research Findings by the Educator and Counselor: Research Theory to Practice." *The Family Coordinator* 22: 285-290, 1973.

Duberman, Lucille. "Step-Kin Relations." *Journal of Marriage and the Family* 35: 283-292, 1973.

Hays, William C., and Mindel, Charles H. "Extended Kinship Relations in Black and White Families." *Journal of Marriage and the Family* 35: 51-57.

Kerckhoff, Richard K., and Boytala, Sandra P. "Classroom Research as a Teaching Method in Family Life Education." *The Family Coordinator* 18: 14-21, 1969.

Kerlinger, Fred N. *Foundations of Behavioral Research*, 2nd ed. New York: Holt, Rinehart and Winston, 1973.

Klemer, Richard H. *Marriage and Family Relationships.* New York: Harper & Row, 1970.

McHugh, Gelola. "A Venereal Disease Knowledge Inventory." Saluda, North Carolina: Family Life Publications, 1966.

Rogers, Carl R. *On Becoming a Person.* Boston: Houghton Mifflin, 1961.

Straus, Murray A. *Family Analysis: Reading and Replication of Selected Studies.* Skokie, Ill.: Rand McNally Co., 1969.

Waller, Willard. "The Old Love and the New." In *Families in Crisis*, edited by Paul Glasser and Lois Glasser. New York: Harper & Row, 1970.

Suggested Films

Dance Little Children (1963, 25 min.). Kansas State Board of Health, State Office Building, Topeka, KS 66612.

The Innocent Party (1959, 17 min.). Kansas State Board of Health.

VD: Every 30 Seconds (1971, 17 min.). Alfred Higgins Productions, 9100 Sunset Boulevard, Hollywood, CA 90069.

Chapter 4

Discussion

Why is the discussion so important? When a student hears himself explain something aloud and sees others react, he can clarify his thinking. By hearing another person do the same thing, he can further clarify his thinking. By observing his own reactions to others, he gains even further insights about his way of thinking. Reflecting on issues may be one of the best things that happens in a discussion because the student takes this one skill with him to use later as he makes decisions. From reflecting and discussing, the student who arrives at a position or stand with substantiation has begun to see the great value in going through the process, for he has a product in the recognizable form of a position.

Discussion is one of the best methods for clarifying thinking, but the topic for discussion should be made clear. The topic may have been suggested spontaneously, or it may have been planned by the teacher as a part of the course. The topic may have been introduced through reading, or the teacher may have asked a question or made a controversial statement.

The students must also be made aware as to whether the purpose is for (1) a value judgment or (2) an explanation of fact (Hyman 1970). If the purpose of the discussion is to make a value judgment, then opinions are more acceptable as the discussion ensues even though they will eventually have to be substantiated; in an explanation, the students' statements should be nonpersonal and based on accurate information. In both types, the students will have to support their statements, but in the end the conclusion from explanation is based on fact.

The inputs of the teacher and sometimes the students are a part of keeping the discussion moving toward the goal—to get an answer to the original question. This may be done by summarizing a few statements that have been made and then asking another question to keep the students searching. Teachers can clarify statements by restating them and by giving some examples. Ask for a tentative conclusion or application of the conclusion to help the students see how close they are to the goal.

Sometimes the most pertinent thing to do is to redirect the students from discussion to activity. The students may find they do not have enough information to continue the discussion and will be more ready to do various things to get more information, for instance reading, small group discussion, or viewing some visual aids.

Knowing when and how to help the students draw some conclusions is an ability that is sometimes more difficult than keeping the "talking" going on. When teachers are clear about the question under discussion, then they are more likely to know when enough information has been brought out. Letting a discussion drag on is a misery. Teachers, therefore, may be tempted to push too fast or not give students the time they need for reflective thought because they are confusing "dragging on" with "time to think."

As soon as the students are ready, ask for some conclusions or tentative hypotheses. If the students are not yet able to draw conclusions or make generalizations, then do it for them and show them how to arrive at the decision that enough information has been gathered.

The length of the class period, the intellectual ability of the students, the maturity of the students, the excitement of the topic, and the seriousness of the topic will all affect the time to begin to draw the discussion to a close.

Discussion Involving Values

Little real discussion can begin until students get beyond personal preferences. It is all right for them to express preferences, but these ideas need to be taken further. Definitions of terms, supporting evidence for their preferences, valid generalizations, and criteria for judging these preferences will have to be presented before the class can see the difference between socially accepted values and personal preference. If the students do not have sufficient evidence or facts, then the discussion should be brought to a close until the information is gained.

The outcome of issues being discussed will need to be evaluated. Teachers are able to manage the flow of the discussion better if they help the students understand that there are several ways to evaluate a point (or opinion or position). Three ways to evaluate are: (1) in terms of preferences (Which life style do you like best?); (2) against a set of criteria (If the function of the family is to socialize all members of the family and to act as executor for family activities, which life styles perform these functions?); and (3) in terms of the consequences of the action (If you choose to stay single yet adopt a child, what effect does this have on you and on the child's life, and can a single person provide as adequate care as a married couple who adopt a child?).

The major difference in leading a discussion about values and one in which you are trying to get the students to use logic in examining and understanding more about a problem is that in valuative discovery the students are not pushed by the teacher to stay with a certain line of thinking; they are allowed to express feelings and thoughts at large (Grainger 1970).

The following is an example of a discussion from which a value judgment is to be made.

Question: Should monogamous marriage (one person at a time) be the ideal?

Points you should have in mind before going too far in this discussion:

1. Monogamy is the only lawful marriage in the United States.
2. Group marriages even though they are purported to exist are not yet lawful.
3. Monogamy has been by far the most likely type of marriage in most societies.
4. People do not change easily.
5. The variations in living arrangements within monogamous marriages have occurred more covertly than overtly because of fear of reprisal.

The following is an example of how such a discussion might proceed:

Cathy: One man and one woman is the way marriage is intended.

John: By whom?

Cathy: By nature, by God, by people, that's who!

Alice: But many societies didn't believe that.

Teacher: Shall we assume from the beginning that monogamous marriage is a man-made law and discuss it from that view?

John: Now we know who intended the one man and one woman marriage—we human beings did.

Teacher: But why? How does one begin to value this behavior?

And the discussion goes on until the students are aware that values tend to come from that which has been useful over time.

Discussion for Explanation

When teachers ask the students to explain something, they should be careful that they are asking for an explanation and not just a definition ("Explain what a nuclear family is.") and not just a description ("Explain how to become a better communicator."). An explanation is both the information and the generalization necessary in answering "why" questions ("Explain the fact that the nuclear family is almost universal in the United States," or "Explain why ability to communicate differs from person to person or from situation to situation.").

Part of the problem in good explanations is that either not enough information is given or no generalization or conclusion is drawn. When asking the question teachers may have to reask it to be sure the students know how complete an answer is wanted.

The following is an example of a discussion in which the goal is an explanation.

Question: Why has monogamous marriage been the most prevalent type throughout the centuries?

Points you should have in mind before leading the discussion:

1. Even in countries where polygamy (one person married to two or more people) was practiced, monogamy was also practiced.
2. To have polygamous marriages the central figure must have enough wealth and land holdings to maintain the large family.
3. Monogamy, on the other hand, is a way for less wealthy–even poor–people to have a married relationship.
4. Monogamy is more practical in a mobile society.

The following interchange shows how the discussion might proceed:

Cathy: Monogamy is the most prevalent because it is the right way.

John: Right for whom?

Cathy: For everyone.

Alice: What makes it right?

Teacher: Let's compare monogamous and polygamous marriages as to the relationships, intricacies, the wealth necessary, and the types of societies which encouraged each.

Levels of Conclusions

The students will need to be shown that conclusions come in differing levels and that the highest level is difficult to reach early in a discussion, or early in the students' experiences in discussion. The highest level occurs when students begin to ask why and when they have already arrived at cause-effect relationship judgment. Both of these levels are deeper thought processes than the more simple "ought" type statements based on the reasoning that "this is the way it is because it's right" without any substantiation.

If students were discussing the topic of endogamous marriages (between persons of similar race, nationality, class, etc.), especially within a socioeconomics class, an early judgment–possibly the one which incites the discussion–could be that "people ought to marry their own kind." After some views and also some substantiation for the judgment are stated, a higher-level judgment would emerge in the form of, "When people of similar socioeconomic classes marry, their values are similar, and they are more likely to have a satisfactory marriage." Most discussions stop here. There is an even further questioning which asks why this is so, and the judgment might well evolve as, "People of similar values tend to reinforce each others' behavior, resulting in a feeling of well-being, an atmosphere which is non-threatening and good toward promoting basic human needs."

Issues to Discuss

The most difficult issues for discussion are those without an absolute answer, such as values or moral truths, yet these values are the very ones that need to be subjected to discussion, using every means available to challenge, to compare, to explain, to apply, and to gain insight even though an absolute answer for all times is not achieved. (Socrates knew that ethical matters and personal relations are far more difficult to discuss than factual relations are.) Since a good discussion takes much preparation, is very exhausting, and is very time-consuming, only very important issues should be discussed. The fact that the issue is important to the students is sufficient reason for discussion, however.

Since the discussion method which delves into inquiry encourages students to question the issue as well as themselves, it is an excellent method to use in the empathetic approach. Students not only discuss the problems presented in the cases, but they discuss the moral and ethical issues these cases bring up. In so doing, they are clarifying their own values, which is the essence of the empathetic approach.

Discussion is best used when there is an issue that needs to be thought through by a number of people. Discussion is an excellent method to use when studying valuative matters (such as social values), morals, or evaluations (best for what? better than, etc.) The goal of discussion is to find a solution to a problem through synthesizing the contributions (Bloom 1956).

The realization that issues such as values and morality are far different from factual matters is essential in deciding when to use the discussion method. Teachers and the students who realize that there is no one correct answer when they start the discussion will be more willing to branch out into speculation and possibilities, to try out various approaches, and to look at the problem from differing perspectives. As the discussion progresses from the perplexing issue to consideration of counter ideas to trying out tentative solutions, teachers and the students may have to engage in some fact-finding or explanation through small lectures or discourse or through students' checking up on something.

Discussion as a Means of Discovery

Too many teachers think their job is to "keep the discussion going" with only the simplest notion of the methods of inquiry, levels of learning, types of questions, and the intricacies of human behavior.

When teachers challenge the students by posing questions and situations and then lead them to understanding or generalizing, it is sometimes called insight or discovery. This type of teaching helps students become independent or able to gain knowledge on their own. They gain both knowledge and the method to acquire more knowledge and insight. Students must believe they can discover before they will allow themselves to go through the process. (A reading of Socrates' dialogue of Meno and the boy will encourage students to discuss as well as teach the method of leading students to discover.)

Doubt and uncertainty are the motivating forces for discovery. Testing findings against other conflicting findings and comparing with similar findings help the students know whether or not their findings are acceptable. The problem in challenging students' beliefs, findings, or present knowledge is that it is very disconcerting for them to find they are wrong. In order to maintain trust between the students and the teacher, students need to be reminded that this is a method of inquiry and is not intended to embarrass anyone. Teachers may also have to remind students that the creative person is the one who takes time to answer and who is willing to give lots of answers, many of which will be off base but many of which may lead to an acceptable solution of the problem. Teachers may also have to say that an off-base answer or a partial answer may be just the impetus another student needs to clarify his own thinking. In other words, several attempts by several students may actually add to the ideas of other students, and the person who reaches the answer first is not necessarily the only one responsible for reaching it.

Comic relief also reduces tension when you have countered a student's defense too strongly. Reassurance from a laugh helps the students know teachers are working on an issue and not seeking to undermine them. Another way to ease up on the students is to move to explaining how issues become perplexing and by showing how generalizations apply to the issue. To keep the students from being left feeling exposed or devastated, help them see how far the inquiry has helped them move in developing their self-concepts and that they are now a step further along toward the goal of critical thinking or problem solving than they were before.

Discussion as Motivation

Most teachers think of discussion as the technique which settles a question or finds solutions to problems and, in many cases, this is true. However, discussion can be a very potent motivator when used to get students' opinions about a subject or to lead the students to see and feel a need for more information. This motivating feature of discussion many times is serendipitous —it is an unexpected but very welcome outcome.

When discussion is purposely used as a motivator, teachers would do the same preplanning as they would if it were to be a problem solver. In this case, challenge the students and set up situations counter to their thinking, yet encouraging their own views. In the end, summarize by asking further questions. These questions will be the guide to converging their findings from reading or other fact-finding avenues.

Reasons Why Discussion May Not Work

Some topics are not good discussion material because they require too much explanation or demonstration. An explanation of some of the theories about family interaction or a brief history of the Women's Liberation Movement is better done by lecture. However, both of these make excellent discussion topics when the issue is valuative. Some topics are not important enough to take the time that discussion requires.

If the class is too homogeneous in its views, topics good for discussion will need to be presented from a viewpoint different from that of the entire class, such as one author's viewpoint, rather than expecting the dissension to come among the students.

Teachers Must Be Prepared as Discussion Leaders

No matter what the topic under discussion is, teachers need to have some counter issues prepared as well as some lead questions that will cause perplexity, that will cause insight, or that will cause evaluation of the conclusions. Without preparation the discussion turns into a disorganized opinion-giving session or even a gripe session. A good discussion exhausts both the teacher and the students and therefore cannot be used for too long a period or too often.

Throughout the discussion, teachers will need to clarify points by rephrasing a statement, to encourage further participation, to introduce new ideas, to call for support of statements, and to contribute their own ideas. When teachers do give their own ideas, they are as obligated as the students to give supporting evidence. This exchange in itself will be an excellent demonstration for the students of how to support statements made in a discussion.

Student Preparation for Discussion

Not only must the teacher be prepared, but the students also should be ready for discussion. Student readiness does not necessarily imply having studied prior to the discussion; it can also mean the students' having the cognitive maturity to discuss the topic, the experiences necessary, and emotional strength to take "counterattacks" or to speak out.

One way students can prepare is for them all to read one or more articles of differing views (authors differing or a view that may be different from the usual student view).

Another preparation students must have is the mechanics of a good discussion. They must all know that in a discussion, one student cannot monopolize, a student-teacher dialogue is not discussion, and comments and questions from student to student are expected. The following game is a good way to show how a discussion should be conducted. The ball may be any moderately soft nonbreakable object. The eight or ten students respond after one student reads the successive parts of "Action." Another student reads the part of "Reader" after each action has taken place.

Ball Game—Way to Show a Group Working Together in Discussion

Directions: Eight or ten students form a circle. Two students stand apart from the circle to read the parts of "Action" and "Reader."

Action: The leader has the ball and plays with one other student. The two of them toss the ball back and forth. (Indicate that two students should begin and then continue until another directive is given.)

Reader: This is a discussion group. The chairman or leader has an idea and is sharing it with one member of the group. The others look on.

Action: The rest of the group looks bored, sighs, is distracted.

Reader: This isn't very interesting to them because they have no part; just watching the others is not fun.

Action: Leader tosses ball to a different student who tosses it back; then the leader tosses the ball to another student who tosses it back.

Reader: This is called a discussion, but it isn't; it is only a question and answer period between the leader and individuals in the group.

Action: One other student is included, and the three play triangular catch.

Reader: Now a third person begins to take part. The activity is more interesting right away because there are more ideas and more people to help share in the responsibility.

Action: Now the ball is passed all around the circle. Students smile and act as though they are having fun. The ball is passed to another quickly.

Reader: At this point everyone is included. Now things are really humming. This is a sharing of ideas and responsibilities on the part of everyone in the group. Everyone cares what goes on because everyone is taking a share. In other words, those who share care, and those who care share.

Action: One student fumbles; everyone stops; the fumbler looks embarrassed, and the others look provoked and disgusted.

Reader: What happened here? Well, one student fumbled. The student had an idea that the rest did not like. It is holding up the action of the group.

Action: The ball goes back and forth across the circle; then the fumbler is given another turn.

Reader: Now watch closely. They are giving the student another chance. You see we aren't always right; none of us are, but we should have another chance when we miss, when we get ideas that aren't very good.

Action: Now two students play alone. The others act bored and distracted again.

Reader: The two students playing alone show how a discussion can get sidetracked. Here are two students who are way off the subject and not sharing their ideas with the rest. Notice how this holds up group action. All that the rest of the group can do is watch, and that isn't fun for long. Two people playing alone can surely hold up a meeting.

Action: Now one plays alone tossing the ball up and catching it himself. The ball goes higher and higher.

Reader: Here we see a student trying to get all the attention. See, the ball goes higher and higher–just as he thinks his own ideas get better and better.

Action: Now all the group is working and taking part in tossing the ball.

Reader: Now the whole group is working together again–each one taking a share of the work and responsibility, each one getting ideas before the group and having credit for them. This kind of group activity is productive. It shows that sharing pays because then you can get things done.

Room Arrangement and Management

The maximum number of students for a discussion for even a skilled teacher is around thirty. When there are more than thirty, the so-called discussion is really a lecture with some student-teacher dialogue. The optimum number is from about twelve to twenty. Fewer than twelve results in too little variety in backgrounds.

The horseshoe, or circle, is probably the best arrangement since there is greater chance of trust among students, and there does not have to be any straining to hear and see.

Keep the discussion short, maybe ten to fifteen minutes, especially if the topic is disconcerting and rapidly presented. Obviously all the students cannot participate all of the time; therefore, in a large group there will be several onlookers at any one time. To sustain interest, some students may be asked to observe for later criticism of the discussion. Some students may be allowed to break away from the larger group to discuss on their own or to look up material to bring back to the group.

Students Who Appear Not to Participate

There is a lot to be said for the students who do not speak at all or who speak very seldom in a discussion. There must be diversity for a discussion to get the heat it must have, but if all of the students wished to speak even if they did not attempt to speak, there would be more restlessness than could be handled. Moreover, those speaking would have no audience because the others would be so busy formulating their own speeches they wouldn't or couldn't listen.

The listeners are vital because they cause the speakers to keep on the track or to be more cautious or to perform better. The student who does not speak out may be as active, if not more so, than the speaker in reflecting, in going through the process of change, and in taking a position. The speakers who speak through a compulsion to keep the discussion going are not adding as much to the discussion or gaining as much personally as does the person who really desires to say something. Teachers may need to help the students see the various roles.

It is rare to find an entire group of students in one class having the same informational background, intellect, motivation, emotional security, or verbal fluency to participate totally in a discussion. More than likely, some students will have difficulty following the flow of the discussion whereupon you will need to summarize throughout the discussion. Some students will have the intellect and verbal fluency but need the emotional security teachers can give by allowing time to build up courage, by praising efforts, and by implying, if not telling, the class that all views are important.

Evaluating Student Participation

Since discussion is a group process with individual students showing growth both covertly and/or overtly, the teacher is at a disadvantage in knowing who has grown in which way. Obviously a subjective evaluation or overt participation is one way. A more objective way is to watch for participation which shows growth in ability to look at the problem with some perspective, in finding supporting evidence for problems and statements, and in level of judgments from the "ought" to the causal to the reason for being. (See illustration under "Discussion as a Means of Discovery.")

Variations of the Discussion Method

1. Rap-session or sound-off session: Occasionally allow students to talk about any subject without feeling it is wrong. This freedom gives them a chance to ventilate their feelings in a protected environment.
2. Role-taking in a group: Some or all of the students take on a specific role–possibly someone they dislike or are afraid of or someone in authority or of the opposite sex–and discuss a topic. These people will have to wear labels to remind the others that their comments are not their own but are what they think the person whose roles they are playing would say. Many of the students can take similar roles; in fact, do not have too many different roles represented. This method is excellent for topics which usually get opposing views such as "adoption of children by a single person" or "living together without marriage."

Summary

Although some people have the notion that a family-relationships class is one big discussion about opinions, this idea is far from the truth. The subject matter does lend itself to discussions of all types, and discussion is a very good method in an area so value-oriented. Discussion, however, must have a purpose. Two purposes of discussion are value clarification and explanation. In either case, the conclusions may be on various levels from a simple answer to an opening of new areas to question and discuss.

The various suggestions for leading a discussion will be even better managed when you are also an expert in asking questions—the topic of the next chapter.

References

Bloom, Benjamin, ed. *Taxonomy of Educational Objectives, Handbook I: Cognitive Domain.* New York: David McKay Co., Inc., 1956.

Grainger, A. J. *The Bullring.* New York: Pergamon Press, 1970.

Hyman, Ronald. *Ways of Teaching.* Philadelphia: J. B. Lippincott Co., 1970.

Additional Readings

Bormann, Ernest G. and Bormann, Nancy C. *Effective Small Group Communication.* Minneapolis, Minn.: Burgess Publishing Co., 1972.

Epstein, Charlotte. *Affective Subjects in the Classroom: Exploring Race, Sex, and Drugs.* San Francisco: Intext Educational Publishers, 1972.

Flynn, Elizabeth W. and LaFaso, John F. *Group Discussion As a Learning Process: A Sourcebook.* New York: Paulist Press, 1972.

Gulley, Halbert E. *Discussion, Conference, and Group Process.* 2nd ed. New York: Holt, Rinehart, and Winston, Inc., 1968.

Potter, David and Andersen, Martin P. *Discussion: A Guide to Effective Practice.* 2nd ed. Belmont, California: Wadsworth Publishing Company, Inc., 1970.

Sattler, William M. and Miller, N. Edd. *Discussion and Conference.* 2nd ed. Englewood Cliffs, N.J.: Prentice-Hall, Inc., 1968.

Chapter 5

Questions

No response or behavior is as motivated or as much a person's own as that which is touched off by a question. When a directive is given, students may react like a robot but, when a question is asked, a whole series of thought processes and activities occur. Questions are so vital to the teaching-learning process that practically no learning would occur without one. They start the whole process; they guide intellectual processes; and they even affect the emotional climate of the class. These are the reasons questions are so vital to teaching.

Using Questions

Rarely is one question or one type of question at a time all that a teacher uses in any lesson or class period. Different types of questions are generally used in combination with each other to achieve the goal. One of the major purposes of asking questions is to lead students through a series of mental processes which will culminate in their understanding of a problem and their gaining enough insight to generalize their learnings to a new situation. Almost any number, type, and sequence of question can be combined to achieve this goal. There are three blocks of questions, however, which are part of every exercise in teaching students to think through a problem: (1) the motivating questions, (2) the comprehensive questions, and (3) the application questions. Almost every question mentioned in this book, from the ones which encourage students to feel comfortable to the ones which cause them to gain insights, fits into one of these categories.

In attempting to motivate with questions, the teacher's queries to make the students sit up and take notice may range from those that diverge slightly from the topic to those which chide the students just a bit. In this block there will be those questions that help build rapport and those that ask what would happen if.... After the students' eagerness to know has been developed, questions that help them comprehend can be used to guide learning.

As teachers lead the students through comprehension and knowledge building, they should include questions for getting facts from the very simple "What is . . .?" to those requiring empirical evidence for verification of the answer. Lead the students to compare, to explain, and to apply principles. When students seem to be getting sufficient skill and knowledge, begin asking them some questions to see if they can summarize and draw inferences. Too many teachers stop too quickly here.

The final block of questions will be almost entirely made up of those divergent questions which encourage students to speculate, to evaluate future prospects, to predict, and to create new ideas.

The list of questions below is given to show how one combination of questions could be used in teaching students to understand why rules or traditions get started. From these questions, the students see value in the rules, see whether or not they need changing, and speculate on future actions which may themselves eventually become traditions or customs. The motivating questions or situation could come from a lesson on changing roles of men and women such as, "Why do parents expect their sons or daughters to marry endogamously?" or an assignment to see "Fiddler on the Roof" (a movie about changing traditions).

Motivating Block of Questions

Is a tradition always a tradition? (Current traditions were once new behavior!)

Is a rule always a rule? (A rule yesterday may be unnecessary tomorrow.)

Is a custom always a custom? (What is customary now may be outmoded soon.)

Knowledge and Comprehension Block

What are some traditions or rules?

When did they begin?

Where did they begin?

What were the circumstances which made the rule seem necessary?

How did the rules affect the society (or situation)?

If the circumstances had been different, would the rules have been different? For example, suppose the circumstances had been that everyone had an equal income, would any rules have been different?

What are some rules which fit past circumstances that do not seem to fit now?

Do they not fit now because they no longer have a positive effect?

Work backward and take a recent rule and apply it to an earlier era or society (such as 55 mph speed limit in 1865 or even 1910). Where are the absurdities?

How would you change the rules which don't seem to apply?

How do traditions or rules change anyway? For example, we no longer arrange marriages, we no longer treat wives as property, and we no longer leave property to the eldest son only. Some things that are not so definitely out but are nearly so are the following:

–We rarely see a "hope chest" (holdover from the dowry).
–We rarely see ten or twelve children in a family.
–We rarely see an extended family.

Some things that are debated now are:

–whether the boy or the girl should ask for the date
–whether abortion is an acceptable birth control measure
–whether women should be granted equal opportunity for employment, credit risk, etc., as men

Some things which are still not yet acceptable to most people are homosexual marriages, adoption of children by single persons, etc.

Application Block

Which way do you think the above activities will turn?
What will have to happen in this culture to make changes possible?
What would make the changes imperative?
What would outlaw certain regulations or never allow them to be written?
Why do some rules tend to last and others tend to be temporal (long or short)?

In this illustration of how questions of many types are used in leading students to learn, teachers have to have some skill in asking the right type question to keep the students interested, working, and learning. As long as teachers teach, they will think of questions they wish they had asked, but there is also the possibility that what they asked was quite sufficient. It takes practice. The more teachers ask and the more response they get, the more motivated and skilled they will become in developing questions right on the spot which are invaluable to insightful learning.

Inexperienced teachers and experienced teachers alike need some key questions written down to guide them through the lesson or unit. The thing to keep in mind is that most units in teaching include all three blocks of questions–the motivator block, the knowledge and comprehension block, and the application block.

Questions and the Emotional Climate

Teachers encourage students to respond–and to learn–by accepting their answers. This encouragement can be done in two ways: (1) by praising the answer when it is satisfactory or shows some progress toward a satisfactory answer, and (2) by praising the effort even when it does not add to the search for the answer–possibly by saying, "That is an interesting view."

Many students learn early not to respond to teachers' questions because of frequent and harsh reprimands for their inadequate answers. Students will come to teachers with some of this conditioning against answering in class. One of the teacher's important jobs early in the course is to set the stage for willingness, even eagerness, to respond. Needless to say, mere response is not entirely satisfactory unless a student is in great need of overcoming a fear of speaking in a group. Since it is difficult to know what the students can do, teachers will have to take a chance on some methods. It is a truism that students prefer teacher-acceptance to teacher-rejection. It is also safe to say that students intrinsically want to be able to perform adequately. Basing actions on these assumptions, teachers will actively look for honest attempts from students, and it will become easier to praise and encourage them.

Some responses from students will be very humorous and teachers will do well to show their amusement so long as the answer was intended to be humorous and was neither a *faux pas* nor an attempt to be ridiculous. Teachers may not know why the answer turned out to be funny, but the assumption that students do not want to be rejected will help to keep the student's personal feelings in mind.

Some students need personal teacher acceptance less than others. These students gain their feeling of worth from a feeling of achievement. These students gain a camaraderie with the teacher on a different plane—that of commonality of intellectual achievement rather than commonality of kind words to each other. These students have a hunger for challenging discourse, and they thrive on being able to match wits with the teacher. Rapport is developed in many ways, but acceptance of the student and a mutual knowledge of this is the secret.

Responding to Questions from Students

Students need to see teachers work through answers to their questions without always having the answer on the tips of their tongues. They need to see the process. Typical questions students ask are found in Harris (1968a, b) and Schulz and Williams (1969).

Not only do they want to see teachers look for the answer, but also most students want to know the answer itself. Some questions that appear to be to get the teachers to do the work may really be questions teachers should answer so that the students can get on with the more important problem at hand.

If teachers think students are trying to see if they know the answer, settle it by answering. If teachers don't know, they should say they don't know, but too many "I don't knows" in the teacher's own subject matter field may indicate a lack of preparedness. Be willing to look it up. Do it on the spot.

Be willing and able to say to a student that a particular question he asks may be better at another time—then remember to answer it later. Answer questions so that the student will want to ask again.

What to Do When an Unusual Question Arises

First of all, students aren't really out "to get" teachers, especially in the beginning of a course and particularly when the teacher has not irritated the students. Therefore, teachers must keep visibly calm while they judge the situation. If teachers can consider each question to be an earnest and legitimate question, then answering becomes easier and is much more straightforward. Sometimes teachers tend to put a value on a question that was never intended by the student. For example, when a teacher has read about half a case study that is full of drama with the intention of getting feelings from a class in the empathetic approach and a student says, "Don't you think this is rather melodramatic?" what should a teacher say? Say, "Yes, it is; but so is life itself. Nothing is so emotional and dramatic as some of the situations you students found yourselves in just last week. What were some of them?" At this point the true experiences will be even more overwhelming than any case presentation.

Teachers also have to know why a question shakes them. Are they afraid of making a mistake? Do they feel uncomfortable when students challenge them? Are they afraid of some of the students? It is difficult to make such assessments on the spot; therefore, the safest way is to assume the question is legitimate and deserves an answer.

Why Are Some Teachers So Good at Asking Questions?

There are at least four reasons why any one person is good at asking questions: (1) a knowledge of various types of questions; (2) a knowledge of the subject matter; (3) a desire to get people to respond, and (4) a knowledge of the students who are responding. A good knowledge of questions which elicit certain responses includes an awareness of the types of responses these questions engender. This also implies that teachers know when to use which questions for specific goals.

When teachers know the subject matter well, then they have a storehouse of questions. They are aware of the various similarities or differences about the topic. Having a knowledge of types of questions and the subject matter does not override having a feeling for working with people to bring out the best in them.

Good classroom management is a part of bringing out the best responses. Bringing out the best responses may in fact be the cause of good classroom management. Knowing the types of questions which cause the most excitement, skill in waiting for students to answer, skill in rephrasing a question, and skill in making a series of questions (or developing follow-up questions) that lead the student on to further thinking have a great deal to do with bringing out the best. For example, if a teacher can ask a question that allows a student to tell his knowledge without bragging, the questioner has made the person feel good and in turn has built a good relationship. Teachers who want to bring out the best in students accept attempts at answering, whether they be fledgling attempts or retorts. These teachers are also willing and able to see that some answers from the students may be better than the ones they themselves had in mind. It takes quite a bit of courage for some teachers to say, "That's an excellent answer. I hadn't thought about that."

Teach Students How to Ask Questions

Students are taught to answer questions they did not ask but are rarely taught to ask questions. To question for the sake of understanding, of establishing the real problem, and for the sake of guiding the work toward finding the answers is probably the best thing any student can learn (Hyman 1970). Real life is not set up in a schedule of well-stated questions just waiting for programmed students to give computerized answers. Life just goes on happening until it hits a snag, but it does not ask questions!

As teachers ask students questions and bring out problems, they should encourage their students to question. They will not only learn from teachers' examples, they will also learn better if teachers will explain how they have asked their questions and teach them to develop questions of varying kinds.

Knowing how to ask the question represents a person's hold on what the problem is. How much better educated is the student who has been taught to observe the world and formulate the question which outlines the situation than the student who is programmed only to respond to the question! The tendency of being busy just to look important is an example of producing answers for which no question has been asked.

What question was really asked when the answer given was, "Marriages should last a lifetime." Was the question, "Are happiness and stability synonymous?" or was it, "What happens in a society when marriages end quickly and easily?" or was it "Are children better socialized in a marriage of long duration?" Maybe it was, "How long *should* marriages last?" with never a why at all. How did society arrive at some of these time-honored expectations? Have the questions now changed so that the former answers no longer fit?

People are faced with more answers (responses) or situations than they are with questions although it is believed that life is a series of questions. A situation or problem cries for the right questions to guide the actions. In almost any day students find themselves in such situations as an encounter with a classmate who last week was friendly and outgoing and this week is quiet and distant. Too often no question at all is asked. Did they ask "why?" Usually mere responses such as "I don't like him anymore," or "He's silly" are made instead. If a question is asked at all, the usual first question is "What is bugging him?" Sometimes it is, "What have I done?" But it rarely is as far-reaching as, "Since people don't change that fast, what has occurred? What conditioned his reaction? Am I merely putting my own feelings in this? Do people usually do this in situations such as this? How are others seeing him? Is time all he needs? Does he need approaching or left alone? What are the probable outcomes if I take a specific action?"

Students will not learn to ask questions by being told to ask them. They must have experience. Give them some situations and ask them to state some questions which not only would get at the influences on the behaviors but also would lead to finding some probable solutions.

Another exercise for learning how to question and at the same time to increase communication is to role play a situation in which a student will not talk about a project or experience for some personal reason, such as being a stranger or being normally quiet or feeling uncomfortable or being conditioned not to brag. The project or experience is described to the one playing the "quiet student" in advance of the role playing. A second student is instructed to question the person in such a way that there is both rapport and interesting conversation about the topic. The first time this activity is done may be in a role playing or skit type of exercise with the two students in front of class members. Assume the experience is working at the hardware store during the summer. Questions which tend to elicit better responses in terms of rapport as well as information are these:

"Did you have to learn how to use all that equipment?"

"What did you do to help a person when he didn't know what he wanted?"

"What's the way you used to make a satisfied customer?"

"If you could rearrange the store in some way, how would you do it?" Questions which might hinder rapport are like these:

"Hardware isn't very exciting, is it?"

"Did you know the difference between a hammer and a screw driver?"

"Did you have any customers besides handymen?"

These questions say, "You're pretty dumb if that's all you did."

The TV show, "What's My Line?" used the technique of questioning to elicit information very successfully. In fact, teachers could use that technique in class to give students exercises in questioning. To use the technique to meet the goals of better communication and relationships, teachers would need to change the rules of the TV show somewhat. The person being questioned by the panel would be instructed to play the part of the inhibited but to speak out in conversation when the panel made him want to do so. (In the TV show, "What's My Line?" the person being questioned could give *yes* and *no* answers.)

The students need to know that there are different kinds of questions which elicit specific responses. Students need to observe teachers take a problem and formulate the questions which when answered will solve the problem much as is done in research. Teach them that questions need to be asked to get at causal relationships, to look at situations with a different perspective, to organize the action for answering, and to have some way of determining the value or validity of the answer. Give students exercises or experience in asking questions for various reasons such as:

Communication

To bring another person out

To make small talk

To find out what's troubling someone

To learn how to ease up on questioning when a person feels threatened

Seeking Answers

To help others clarify thinking

To find causal relationships

To get at the root of a problem

The charge to teach students how to question is also a means of teaching them the scope of the subject matter of relationships and the questions which need to be asked in order to learn more about relationships and the whys and hows of living in a social setting.

Levels of Questions

Even though it is believed that learning levels can be classified in a hierarchy—that is, that one level has to be mastered before the next level can be gained—questions do not have to come in a particular order. Six broad levels of cognition have been defined (Bloom 1956). Beginning at the lowest level they are knowledge, comprehension, application, analysis, synthesis, and evaluation. Sanders (1966) took Bloom's levels of learning and developed classroom questions for teachers for each level. Neither of the books implies that teaching itself must begin at the lowest level, that is, gaining facts and knowledge.

In fact, if teachers would ask some questions on the highest level, evaluation, such as, "If the voting public were allowed to choose the limit of children per person and they were given the following options—1, 2, 3, or 4—on what criteria would you base your selection?" students would immediately give an opinion with little basis. After serious discussion about all the ramifications, the students themselves might wish to study more about effects of size of family on child development and family relationships, the reasoning behind encouraging families to rear fewer children, the effects of overpopulation, etc. As the students study to find the answers, they tend to weave all the levels into the solving of the original problem.

Occasionally, teachers approach areas in which the concepts and words are so new and difficult that definitions or some other first-level learning must take place before the students can progress. Sometimes the steps toward the goal of productive thinking and making sound judgments are in the exact hierarchy as Bloom described. For example, in a unit on the development of the self in which common words (e.g., self-system, identity, needs, self-concept, self-esteem, motive), are used in a different but very specific way, the operational definitions are almost a must before any progress can be made. Many times the students and the teacher ask questions beyond the knowledge and ability level of the students, and they have to retract enough to gain that knowledge or ability necessary to answer those higher-level questions. The point is that when teachers know that there are hierarchical levels, know what types of questions fit each level, and know that motivation for learning comes by tantalizing the students with questions to which they do not yet know the answer, then with well-placed connecting, directing, and encouraging questions, the students will work out the answers to the higher-level questions.

It is likely that if teachers would classify questions they would find that they tend to ask too many questions which get at lower-level learning, such as "What are the names of three theories of mate selection?" or "What factors are most conducive to happy marriages?" Each of these questions at the end of a unit could be nothing but statements or names or lists. Begin to insert some questions all along such as, "If after studying three theories of mate selection you were asked to develop one of your own, how would you do it and what would it be?" or "When are the factors most conducive to happy marriages in fact conducive to the unhappiness of marriage?" These last two questions require prior knowledge and prior skills in applying knowledge to new situations as well as some creative ability. They imply that teachers have taught students enough knowledge and skills so that they could answer the questions. Do not overlook the use of these questions as motivators, as a teaching tool for application and creative abilities, as well as a final testing device.

The following categories of learning, summarized from Sanders (1966), include sample questions:

1. Memory category—to recognize or recall information such as facts, definitions, generalizations, and value statements. "What are the expected behaviors when a person is in a new situation?"
2. Translation category—to change ideas into parallel forms; that is, to give the same meaning in other words or in charts or in pictures, etc. "What is meant by 'Unto thyself be true'?"
3. Interpretation category—to discover or use a simple relationship between

two or more ideas such as comparing, cause and effect, generalization, and examples. "How does marriage differ from family?"

4. Application category—to give practice in transfer or training, that is to give real-life situations and ask the student to apply his knowledge and skills in solving the problem. "How would you explain the fact that you recoil when one person speaks and not when another speaks?"
5. Analysis category—to use the parts and processes of reasoning such as that used in inductive thinking, deductive thinking, in challenging fallacies, and in semantics. For example, in a case study the student does a great deal of interpretation and application, but to analyze, he must attach the reasoning of the participants in the case. "What was the process through which the person arrived at this action?"
6. Synthesis category—to do imaginative or original thinking; that is, to discover knowledge that is *new to them*. Much freedom is allowed in a classroom where original thinking is done. Synthesis requires divergent thinking in which the student starts with a problem and offers many possibilities for solutions. Prediction in case studies is an example of synthesis or creative or divergent thinking. Brainstorming is a method used to encourage divergent thinking. "If a person is constantly losing certain friends, excelling in his work, and growing in many abilities, what do you predict his future to be?"
7. Evaluation category—to judge how closely an object, idea, or action meets certain criteria. The student is required both to set up the criteria and to make the judgment, not merely to state whether something is good or bad, or worthy or unworthy. The criteria are a set of standards based on someone's decision about what should be. "Based on enduring criteria for socialization, what are the advantages of communal settings for rearing children?"

Questions encouraging recall of information are almost always a prelude to or a part of moving further into the use of intellectual skills. As an end in themselves, questions of recall are only part of the job of teaching. Some teachers have taught a parroting response and have expected the student to teach himself the application and judgment skills—skills involved in higher mental processes.

Teachers need to know what they want students to do or say—that is, what change is desired in the students—before they can plan the question. If all teachers want is that students show a retrieval system for bringing back facts, then asking a question such as, "What is the name of the basic family unit?" will surely produce a short answer—"the nuclear family." Many types of student responses may be desirable at any particular time. The responses can range from feelings to opinions to recall of information to use of a myriad of intellectual skills.

Questions to Encourage Feelings Responses and Opinions

Feelings responses are encouraged when the objective is to understand that nearly all decisions and thoughts are accompanied by feelings, that feelings differ from time to time and from person to person, that feelings temper judgment, and that any individual feelings response is always right if that is what is asked for. To get a feelings response, use a question as simple as "How do you feel or believe or think?" or as involved as "How does your reaction today differ from your reaction last year to news stories about drug overdoses?" Experienced teachers will immediately remember that students are not all that eager to express their feelings about a topic unless they have had a backlog of reassurances that their feelings responses will not be condemned, for a person's feelings are his very self. Follow-up questions after the simple, "How do you feel?" might be to ask:

"What are the differences and similarities in feeling among the students?"
"How did you get these feelings?"
"Do feelings just come or are they taught?"
"Do feelings sometimes keep a person from looking at the facts?"
"Why are feelings about topics such as drug overdose so intense with some people?"

Other questions which get at feelings but do not use the term within the question are these:

"What would you have said to yourself as you read the news article?"
"What might you say to your mother if she read the article to you and why?"
"What would you think if you heard a group of adults discussing the article?"
"What would be your first thought or action if the news article mentioned your kid brother's name?"
"Do you think the article was fairly reported?"

All these questions would be woven into the discussion in a relatively orderly fashion, although not in a stilted way. Part of the problem hindering good questioning is the fact that teachers are not clear about the objectives of the discussion. There are, of course, some discussions in which getting at some feelings is a happy coincidence rather than a planned sequence of events.

Opinions are very much akin to feelings but they differ in one very important respect. Opinion responses usually carry a personal judgment combined with a feeling and sometimes with sound knowledge. Again, an opinion response will come from as simple a question as "In your opinion, do you think the legal age for marriage should be lowered?" to the complex question of, "Without more research, how much reliability is there in trial marriages being a basis for determining the compatibility of a couple in long-term marriage?"

The objective in asking for opinions may be to find out how much the students know, to help them find out the extent of their own knowledge, to help them distinguish feeling from opinion and both of these from fact, and to interest the students in further study on the subject. Again the studied sequence in leading a group of students to want to research a topic is planned by teachers and is at times used with regular progress, and at other times it may move so spasmodically that teachers may think they are too far off the subject now to ever get the students back. However, a question again comes to the rescue when teachers ask one such as this, "With what probability can you make these statements?" What teachers may have to say instead is, "How sure can you be in making these predictions you have made?" Student responses are the actions which bring the discussion back into focus because they have changed their thinking and action. Questions were only tools to get the responses.

Questions That Encourage Productive Thinking

The higher intellectual skills are the ones students *must* gain in order to be productive and to make decisions about living. Granted they must know the difference among decisions based on feeling, opinion, and limited information, but they must also know the techniques of arriving at responses which represent understanding, use of principles, analysis of situations, and adequate judgment. If we accept the premise that a storehouse of information is essential to making sound decisions, we must also accept the premise that learning the uses of knowledge is distinct from learning the knowledge itself. To learn that the probability of a satisfactory marriage is higher for a couple with similar values in life is far different from *using* that same information when counseling with a couple about their probability of success when certain of their values are similar but others are not. But what are the questions? What is the technique? What is the sequence? Does the knowledge have to come before the question asking for a decision? What responses do you want?

What are the questions which challenge students to use varying intellectual skills? One such question would be, "What values tend to be common among families in your community and how have they affected the behavior of both the parents and the children?" This question forces the students first to recall the values if they know them or to isolate them if they do not know them. They will find that such a question will be too difficult without showing them the process of defining terms, narrowing various rules and expectations to their value base, and then associating and applying these values to the long-lasting behavior seen in the community. Before finishing, students will move on and even force teachers to place a judgment on the good of the values and the behaviors, a thought process which when done properly is considered the highest level. However, teachers will be cautioned to make it clear that judgments made too early may be merely opinions. Students do not automatically move into the higher intellectual skills merely because they have a storehouse of knowledge. They must be taught every single skill even though transfer of ability is possible, and even probable, as students gain more experience.

The answers or responses, then, are important, for these are the objectives; questions are the vehicles on which the students ride in reaching these objectives. Better questions result from awareness of questioning technique and use of questions for various purposes.

Productive thinking requires that a person reason in order to reach a conclusion. Productive thinking occurs from two major types of questions: (1) convergent and (2) divergent (Hyman 1970). Both types are necessary for the students because people are faced with problems that require both types.

Convergent questions are those which cause the students to converge all the facts and generalizations they have on the solution of the problem. When students are asked to analyze a case, they are asked to do convergent thinking because they apply generalizations, they compare what the people in the case have done in relation to what others have done, and they explain why some action has taken place. A specific example of convergent thinking is, "If you could choose (or adopt) parents, what would affect your choice?" Another example is, "How do crises differ from one family or person to another?"

Divergent questions are those in which students are given several pieces of information for which they must create a new idea. They differ from convergent questions in that the students are more free to develop their own conclusions, to generate new ideas, to predict outcomes, and to be creative. In case analysis, such questions are asked when the students are making predictions although the prior data does somewhat limit them. Creativity and flexibility are encouraged when questions are stated contrary to the facts, such as, "If the girl in the case had been five years older than the boy instead of five years younger, would this have changed the sequence of events?"

Questions That Require Verification

Responses may be different from what is expected because the question actually asked for the response given while the teacher thought the question required a different response. For instance, questions may elicit only opinion unless teachers clearly require justification or verification and not just opinion. Three kinds of questions which require verification of response are analytic, valuative, and empirical (Hyman 1970). Teachers, who know the differences in these three ways of asking questions will not confuse the students and, in turn, the discussions will not fail because of the students' apparent lack of informative responses. The three kinds of questions will be discussed below.

Analytic questions are those which ask mainly for definitions which may rarely be doubted—they are accepted. For example, the question, "What is a family?" is actually asking for some acceptable definition within some culture. If students answer that the family is "any group of people living together," they are really giving their opinion since their answer is not the culturally accepted definition. The definition could be made in such sociological terms as "nuclear" (mother, father, children), or it could be the census definition of household, but the difference must be made clear so that the students will know that opinion and specific definitions are different. Confusion may also arise if the teacher is not careful to use exact terminology in asking a question. For example, the teacher may be a bit taken aback when the response to "What is the normal age for marriage?" is, "Thirty." This answer is entirely adequate. The problem arises because "normal" can mean almost any age within the norms of this society when the teacher really meant to ask, "What is the average age for marriage?"—a specific question.

Valuative questions are greater culprits for eliciting opinion than analytic questions, since students tend to base their answers on their own biases. The teacher must make it clear to the students that a valuative question asks for a value judgment based on criteria. A valuative question which asks, "Is a sexual relationship based on love better than one based on physical attractiveness?" immediately asks for some criteria, some set of points on which the relationship is to be judged. If no criteria are set, don't be surprised to get such answers as "I think all sexual relationships should be love-oriented" or "I think love is overrated." Both of these answers could be the beginning of sound valuative answers if the teacher is astute enough to ask further questions to help the students set up criteria for judging a relationship. Such questions as, "How did love and sex become associated?" and "Under what conditions have love and sex nearly always been separate?" and "How did love, sex, and marriage become associated?" and "What are some of the societal and personal outcomes of sexual relationships without love?" Many other questions would bring out that in this society love and sex as a combination were reinforced for security reasons and that love is manifested in caring for another—a component in non-exploitative behavior, a value highly regarded in this society.

Empirical questions, the most asked of all questions, will urge the student to defend his answers by indicating personal observations or observations recorded by others (the more valid and reliable the better). These questions differ from the analytic in that in analytic questions the answers are generally accepted definitions that do not have to be supported by empirical data other than that most people say so. Empirical questions differ from valuative questions in that a judgment is made when answering a valuative question. Empirical questions call for a counting of occurrences rather than evaluation. Such questions as "When babies are born to girls under sixteen years of age, what is the probability of their being normal babies?" Actual statistics without any biases indicate that there is a much greater probability of abnormal, underweight, and stillborn babies of mothers under sixteen than of mothers over sixteen years of age.

Less likely to be recognized as empirical is the question, "Will communes be the form of family living within the next fifty years?" The answer comes from counting those communes in the past and making a prediction on the basis of what has happened.

Confusion or lack of focus in a discussion sometimes can be traced to the questions that inadvertently encourage an answer other than that which the teacher intended. No few students have been chastised for giving the "wrong" type of answer when that was exactly what the teacher unknowingly asked for. Needless to say, students do give inadequate answers to very adequate questions, but the astute teacher realizes this inadequacy and restates the questions, thus building on the responses already given. Valuative questions very readily follow empirical questions since answers from observations give us criteria on which to make our judgments. When students respond with a type of answer that is different from the one expected, the answer can be used to diagnose (1) the teacher's questioning (2) of the teacher's lack of teaching the students that there are different ways to answer questions, and (3) of the students' knowledge and/or ability to answer in differing ways.

Myths in Questioning

There are many myths about questioning: (1) that only certain questions are thought-provoking, (2) that questions with *yes/no* answers do not require thought and lend themselves to guessing, (3) that a "why" or "how" question always draws on higher mental processes, (4) that questions should be used only to make a person think, and (5) that there is a dichotomy of "memory" questions versus "thought" questions. A thought question yesterday from which the students learned the answer becomes a memory question today (Hyman 1970). Myths are dispelled when the question, the context, and the student's mental processes are all considered.

Summary

Questions are the very essence of the teaching-learning process. They can motivate, they can aid in comprehension, and they can show how to generalize and apply knowledge.

When the teacher assures the students questions and/or answers may come from either students or teacher, the climate of the classroom is rich for learning. Questions may motivate or inhibit by the very attitude of the questioner.

Questions can indicate the level of learning expected and can move a student from one level of learning to the next. They can guide productive thinking, but only if the teacher has indicated whether the responses are to be supported with evidence or merely to express opinions. When the response elicits another question that leads to further search for understanding, then the exercise is extremely fruitful.

The next chapter describes role playing as a teaching technique for understanding viewpoints and feelings. The use of questions after the role playing pulls out important points for discussion and integrates them with the feelings. The questions also put the feelings into a framework of understanding generalizations about human behavior.

References

Bloom, Benjamin, ed. *Taxonomy of Educational Objectives, Handbook I: Cognitive Domain.* New York: David McKay Co., Inc., 1956.

Harris, Alan. *Questions About Living.* New York: Hutchinson Educational, 1968a.

———. *Questions About Sex.* New York: Hutchinson Educational, 1968b.

Hyman, Ronald. *Ways of Teaching.* Philadelphia: J. B. Lippincott Co., 1970.

Sanders, Norris M. *Classroom Questions: What Kinds?* New York: Harper & Row, 1966.

Schulz, Esther, and Williams, Sally. *Family Life and Sex Education.* New York: Harcourt, Brace and World, 1969.

Chapter 6

Role Playing

Role playing is reality in practice, for we play a role every waking moment. Role playing makes relationships concrete. It is said that social relationships are abstract and therefore hard to teach, but role playing makes the abstract concrete.

The great advantage of role playing in the classroom is that it increases involvement and makes interaction more real. It increases spontaneity and reduces resistance. Role playing increases self-understanding as no other technique can. Understanding others' feelings takes place almost immediately when one is playing his role. Role playing permits people to act out their true feelings in a permissive atmosphere. It gives students the practice they need in handling situations and tests their resources for facing unanticipated situations. All this interaction takes place in a sheltered environment where the student is privileged to make mistakes as he learns. The teacher is not in the authoritarian role during the role playing scene (Chesler 1966; Hyman 1970; Shaftel 1967).

Management of Role Playing

Role playing is a technique to use when teachers want students to see how people would act in a given situation. They learn generalizations about behavior and they begin to understand feelings. It includes both prepared and spontaneous behavior. The discussion in this chapter will be limited to spontaneous role playing because in family relationships classes we hesitate to use drama to practice "right" ways of behaving. We much prefer to use role playing as a means of allowing students to react in a situation spontaneously and then to use the results to study the reasons for the behavior or the feelings or the insights.

The classic manner of role playing is to present a situation to the students, have the role players finish playing the scene, and then discuss the implications of the scene. Seven guidelines for all role playing, whether it be classic or some variation of the classic type, follow:

1. There must be a reason for using role playing other than entertaining the class (although even a change of pace is commendable teaching). The reasons should involve teaching a principle of behavior and/or helping the students (role players and other class members) gain insight into their own beliefs. For example, role playing might be used to illustrate the behavior generalization that, if two people have differing beliefs, there will be great conflict when one insists on his way.
2. The situation must be emotional; that is, it should build up to an open end of what a person would do or say next. Note that the description of the following situation ends just when you want to know what happened next. A wife who has always worked and made an equal salary to her husband's for a similar job is just told by her mother-in-law that she (the wife) should care for the house because her husband works. Obviously this situation would be explosive in a group of very "liberated" women, but it will still have emotional appeal in any group.
3. Use role players (through selecting or volunteering) who will not feel threatened by playing the role. Since role playing got its start as psychodrama (Moreno 1945) in which emotionally disturbed role players were cast in their own roles so that they could relive and work out their conflicts in a protected environment, people are tempted to cast students in roles similar to their own in order to let them work through their feelings. The teacher must remember that this is a teaching situation, not a therapy group. However, some students in a normal classroom may be mildly disturbed people. The students and the teacher may or may not be aware of this mild disturbance. At any rate, do not cast a student who may not be able to cope with the situation in a particular role. The student who volunteers is saying by virtue of his volunteering that he can handle himself.
4. Give the role players a little time to get into the role. They will need to think about the age, the personality, the pressures of the moment on that role, and the reaction that the person might make. There are times when one player does play himself while the others take on roles.
5. Part of good management of role playing is the selection of the stopping place. The point of role playing is to dramatize some behaviors and not to fill up time. When the players have shown several reactions in an attempt to solve the problems stated, stop the role playing before it drags. In fact, if the role playing is used more to stimulate discussion than for the players to work their own feelings, stop the role playing at a high point even if the students appear to want to go on. This disruption will make the discussion start much more quickly and emotionally than when the playing is "finished."

6. The next step is the one which is usually the least well handled, and that is the discussion which follows the role playing. A suggested set of guides which would fit any role playing scene is the following:
   a. Ask each role player how he felt as he played his role and heard what the other person had to say.
   b. Ask the class members to react to the chosen behavior of each role player.
   c. Give the role players a chance to say how they wished they had acted.
   d. Ask the class members how they would have acted had they been the role players.
   e. To bring out the teaching points, ask what tended to cause or be a reason for the actions chosen.
   f. Sum up by asking for (or in some cases you should tell) generalizations about behavior which seem to be operating in the interaction.
7. If the roles played were very emotional and out-of-character for the players, they must be "de-roled." That is, either call each one by name or ask each of them to say to themselves, "I am (my name)." This process may sound unusual, but a peculiar feeling remains with some people if they are not brought back into their own roles. It also allows them to disown any behavior in the scene by cognitive awareness that there were two separate persons—the role and the self.

An example of a role playing situation which fits the criteria just spelled out is one in which the teacher wants to teach the following: When a person changes his usual role behavior, it is difficult to know how to react to him. The teaching point sounds simple and unemotional, but the role playing must not be. In fact, in real life, situations in which the mother suddenly happens not to be ever-available, as in the instance described, are almost traumatic. Assume the mother has been invited to go out to dinner with someone on the spur of the moment and decides to go knowing there is plenty to eat in the refrigerator for the family. Her teenage daughter also gets such an invitation, which is not unusual for her. The daughter rushes in the house to tell where she is going just as the mother walks out of her bedroom dressed to go. The problem is that there is an aging grandmother-in-law living with them who will need to be cared for. Which of the two will concede? The surprise comes by not allowing either of the role players to know the other's plans. The fact that one of the role players has to give up something makes the situation meaningful, emotional, and intense.

The teacher must be expert in knowing when to stop the role playing scene. This scene is ended just after some important points have been made and just before the scene drags or turns into hilarity. First of all, the scene will have taught just as much by its resulting in a rather high-spirited word-flinging spree as it will by resulting in a resigned mother or daughter encouraging the other one to go. Both scenes would teach that people you depend on need to be consulted before expecting them to do something for you. Both scenes would teach that people react differently in the face of challenge. Some students who were observing would react differently. Ask them how.

The teacher's skill is exhibited in the questions used to bring out the above-mentioned points. Questions such as these may be used: "How did you feel when your daughter raced in to say she was going out again?" "How did you feel when your dependable, ever-present mother was about to leave?" "What did you feel about a dependent grandmother-in-law when you get a once-in-a-great-while invitation to go out to dinner?" "Why do some people choose to yell when they are distressed?" "Why do some people choose to give in ever so quickly?" "If the grandmother-in-law heard the discussion, how do you think she felt?" "Would you have tried to have kept the grandmother from hearing?" "What could have alleviated the surprise of it all?" "Was the mother justified in wanting to go out?" "How did the father fit into this scene?" In addition students themselves are quite capable of bringing out generalizations about behavior the teacher has not yet thought of. When students begin to ask questions and point out generalizations about behavior, the teacher should feel even more pleased that the techniques worked.

Variations in Role Playing

Since the usefulness of role playing is so great, the skillful teacher can use one variation to teach something that another style of role playing may not be able to do. Variations of the classic role-playing technique may be used for a change of pace or to make a different impact or to teach a different point. The variations to be described here are the classic, alternate roles, soliloquy, cut-in role playing, replaying, group role playing, drop in the basket, observer plus role player, reenactment of a past action, and overheard conversation. These variations in role playing will suggest many uses to the teacher. In our discussion, the teaching point is given first; the role playing situation which follows each type exemplifies that variation; and suggested questions follow each situation.

Classic Role Playing

As an example the teaching point may be to become sensitive to the influence of financial goals and values in marriage because, when a person's strongly held values are challenged, he reacts equally as strongly. Also, strongly conditioned beliefs become emotional needs which increase the strength of the behavior.

Select two students to play a young husband and wife. Give each a card describing his (her) part. Do not allow the other or the audience to know what is on each card. Give them time to feel their parts and then tell them to start.

Husband's card: You have been brought up to pay all your bills on the *first day* of each month (not the *second* and never the *third*) because as your father told you this promptness is the mark of an honest, dependable man. You are also on time for all appointments including meals at home. It is the major mark of character. You are settling down to read the afternoon paper on Saturday, July 2, when you notice your wife studiously working at something. You ask her lovingly what she is doing.

Wife's card: You pride yourself on being a very good cook and friendly person. You enjoy working at projects that can be picked up or put down as the notion strikes you, such as knitting or painting. Your employment as a part-time florist encourages your spontaneous creativity, and you profit from it. On July 2 you settle down to write some checks for household bills and are about finished, but you quit since the Fourth, Monday, will be observed as a holiday in business, and no checks would get there until Tuesday anyway. You close the checkbook and are about to suggest to your husband that the two of you do something different tonight when he asks you what you are doing.

Continue to play the scene.

Questions to bring out the importance of financial values (after the classic questions of how each role player felt as he played his role).

1. How many of you think bills should be paid immediately?
2. What are the general rules in businesses about late payments?
3. If businesses give a period of grace, why should the man in this scene be so emotional?
4. What are the personality characteristics associated with immediate payment? Later payment?
5. How does a person with a personality characteristic of compulsion get that way?
6. What other beliefs or values in life affect the way a person spends his money?

Alternate Roles

The alternate-roles type of role playing occurs when the actors exchange roles to get a different view. The actors may need a little time to get started again after they have already played the role once. The teaching point is to understand that the way another person perceives a situation affects his behavior.

Select for the following three positions three students who really have a feeling for these positions: (1) People should have the right not to have any children; no one should have over two children; and you're planning to adopt one child. (2) People should have the right to have as many children as they wish; you've had two and are pregnant with the third. (3) People should limit their children to two; you've had one and would rather not have any more. If you couldn't have any children, you wouldn't adopt one.

Tell the class members the position of each. Send the role players out of the room. Tell the class, but not the role players, that the role players will alternate roles after they have first played their original roles. The class members will be more alert to the strength of the arguments if they have been told that they will alternate roles. After the players have established their positions rather firmly, have them alternate roles and take as firm a stand for that position as possible.

Questions to bring out understanding others' views about bearing children:

1. To the class: What were the major arguments in each case during the first debate?
2. To the players: How did you feel when you first had to think through another role?
3. To the players: How were you able to play the role of another?
4. To the class: How can you see many sides of an argument and still maintain one view of your own?
5. To all: How does behavior change when perception changes?

Soliloquy

A soliloquy is a performance in which one player talks to himself out loud. This soliloquy is, of course, unrehearsed as are all role playing scenes. The player may talk about himself by using stage whispers to the audience. The teaching point is to clarify one's personal philosophy or set of values about accumulating material goods and money.

Ask a student who is verbal enough but who admittedly is not absolutely positive of his philosophy about the topic. The role player will sweep away the cobwebs which have been clouding his set of values (his process of arriving at a publicly stated philosophy), but the class members will benefit from hearing another person hassel with some of the uncertainty which accompanies a philosophy in-the-making.

Questions to help the class members see the process of arriving at a set of values or at a value:

1. To the player: How were you able to argue both sides and yet arrive at your own decision?
2. To the player: Do you suppose that this decision will be altered a little as life continues? Why?
3. To the class: What were the different things he did before he arrived at a decision? Did he go back and forth? How sure was he in the end?

You may even have the class members do their own searching as an exercise.

Cut-in Role Playing

This type of role playing literally allows the audience to get into the act. After the original players have had a chance to get into the act, anyone from the audience may come up to either one of the role players, tap him on the shoulder, and take over the role. The teacher will have to stop the role playing before it gets out of hand. The teaching point is that people act the roles that culture assigns to them.

Wife: You have been married nearly two years. You have been employed the entire time as a science teacher in a junior high school. You were in graduate school for twelve weeks both summers.

In the first few months of your married life, your husband was very generous with his praise about your homemaking abilities and you were pleased.

For more than six months it has been obvious that your husband has begun to expect you to cater to his wishes. Not only that, he has made it clear that housework is woman's work.

Husband: You are employed by a large insurance company as an actuarial assistant. You have worked hard to get this position and are very pleased with your accomplishments. You are also pleased to have a wife who could help you move ahead by making home as pleasant as possible.

The Scene: Wife comes home at 5:00 with a textbook under her arm. She puts in a load of clothes and starts dinner. Husband came home at 6:00 with a newspaper under his arm, goes immediately to the TV, and begins to watch the local news.

He calls: "Hey, Honey, what are we having for dinner? Bring me a cup of coffee and come watch TV with me!"

Continue to play the scene.

After several cut-ins on both sides, stop the role playing and ask questions to bring out feelings and the following points:

1. Distinct work roles of husbands and wives continue to be a part of this culture–variation occurs by own family models, social levels, peer groups, etc.
2. Women tend to reinforce homemaker role early in marriage to please husbands.
3. Women may reinforce homemaker role unconsciously because of a desire to control the management of the home.
4. The chores of housework are obvious whereas chores of management of family business are sometimes without show objects.
5. Most men are conditioned to succeed and to stay permanently employed whereas women are allowed the freedom to work or not work, succeed or be mediocre, change jobs, etc.

Replaying

Replaying is a technique which is effective when the players have learned that their approach could have been different or when the players have gained insight and need to start over. Replaying is also excellent to use after the class members have had a chance to suggest new approaches.

One teaching point is that, when a person experiences something far different from what he expected, he is more likely to react in a confused or regressive manner. Select a girl and a boy to play the part of a couple who have been going steady for four months. They have returned to her home late in the evening. Tell her, but not him, that she is hoping that this relationship will turn into an engagement, maybe even tonight. Tell him, but not her, that he has decided that he must tell her they shouldn't go steady any more, but that he does want to keep on dating her. He starts out by saying "I have something to talk over with you." Play the scene first with players unaware of the other's desires. Then have them replay the scene with players aware of what the other one is probably thinking. Use questions to bring out the difficulty in expressing true feelings when no harm is meant and the difficulty in asking someone to do something when he wants something very different. These questions are appropriate for either the first or the second playing.

1. To the boy: What feelings did you have in protecting the girl's feelings?
2. To the boy: Did you feel as if you wished you hadn't even brought up the subject?
3. To the boy: Did you find the right words difficult to find?
4. To the boy: When did you realize that she expected almost the opposite?
5. To the girl: When did you realize that he was suggesting something very different from what you had in mind?
6. To the girl: What did you want to do when he suggested that you not go steady any more?
7. Why does an opposite expectation aggravate regressive behavior?

Group Role Playing

Several students can role play at one time. Usually it is easier if several are playing the same roles or at least have a common objective while other individuals have specific roles.

One teaching point is that a person reacts to praise on the basis of his own self-concept, his interpretation of the intentions of the praiser, and/or in light of the total situation.

Select three people who will each be given a written description of his role: (1) one is a person who is to act himself, (2) another is told that one person in the group is out to get him, and (3) the third person in the group is told that everyone is plotting against him. Send those three people outside the room. Tell them to keep their instructions to themselves.

Select six other students and give them the instructions that they are to begin a conversation with each of the three other role players, in turn, which will bring out the best characteristics in the role player.

Stop the scene as soon as each role player has established a set of behaviors. Ask the first one to return to the audience. Bring in the second role player and do the same. There is no particular order in which any of these three players should be brought in.

After all three have had a chance to talk with the group of six, begin the class discussion by the usual questions of how each felt and speculate on why each of these three acted as they did. Ask the class to note any differences in the three.

Divulge the content of the cards given to each of the three role players and the instructions given to the group, and then begin to draw out the generalizations of why people react to praise differently. The generalizations involved in the development of the self-esteem will also come out in the discussion if encouraged.

Observer Plus Role Players

Sometimes specific students should be assigned the observer role with the charge to watch for nonverbal communication. They are also told to look for such things as skill in interpersonal relationships, attitudes of the players about preserving their self-concepts, and cultural influences.

The teaching point is that nonverbal communication may be more meaningful than verbal communication.

Role players are not told they are being observed for nonverbal communication. Any of the role playing scenes already described could be used for this exercise.

Reenactment of a Past Action

The teaching point is that conditioning in childhood remains strong because of the immature perception of the situation, the reinforcements used, and the strength of the need to be reinforced.

Tell a story about your own childhood which was meaningful to you. Then, role play the incident in your own childhood using some class member for the other person. Reverse the roles and allow the other person to play *your* role.

One person could play each part alternately as in a soliloquy. This procedure would be very meaningful in understanding how the other person felt and in understanding why the student himself did what he did.

Overheard Conversation

One teaching point is that a person's covert decisions may or may not become overt behavior according to the situation.

Tape record some derogatory comments about a role (principal, boss, teacher, parent, child, teenager, neighbor, etc.) Have a person playing that role listen to the tape. The actor then soliloquizes his feelings after he hears the tape. He decides what he can do to change his image.

A person who plays the part of the one whose voice was on the tape enters the scene, and there is a face-to-face encounter. The first person must carry out the decisions he made after listening to the tape or decide what the alternative is.

Class Members as Part of the Role Playing

Using the class members for more than observers is another way to vary the effectiveness of role playing. You may try giving a small group (or the entire class) of students a list of the generalizations which the role playing is intended to bring out. They will be more alert to the interactions and to the generalizations in action.

Another way to put the students into action is to divide the class into as many sections as there are roles to play. Have them play the assigned roles in their heads as the real role players are acting out their roles. What happens is that the class members will feel the emotions of the role players and may even be tempted to tell what to do or not do. Or you could just ask them to observe their assigned role player's nonverbal behavior as a learning experience in nonverbal communication.

Spontaneous Role Playing

Spontaneous role playing in the middle of a class discussion is an outstanding way to get students to see and feel a point of view. Stop the discussion and say, "Suppose you were the father, and your son had just said he thought you stunk. What would you say?"

Another spontaneous (or planned) role playing is when an issue comes up which divides the class. Make the division physical by putting those who are on one side of the issue on one side of the room and those on the other side of the issue on the other side of the room. Then ask students from one side to ask questions of the students on the other side. Stop this exercise within a short time if the sheer numbers of supporters cause one or more students to aggravate the other side more than discretion should allow. Several issues which have divided classes are these: parents paying for a married child's education; abortion; women not working; and easy divorce laws.

Other Variations

There are many other techniques for getting students to assume a role. Each technique in the following list is briefly described.

1. The telephone call–Number the students. Dial a number and start the conversation.
2. The pairs–Pair the students. Give each a specific role and situation.
3. The alter-ego–Each participant in the role playing scene has a person

standing behind him who plays the part of both the id (devil) and the super ego (angel). As the scene progresses, the other self (alter-ego) says in stage whispers what was really going on in the speaker's mind.

4. The audience knows but the participants do not–Tell the audience what the whole scene is all about, but do not tell the participants all. The anticipation increases audience interest.
5. The unexpected question–Get volunteers for four or five roles in authority. Get volunteers for four or five roles of children. Give the children specific questions to ask those in authority. (More interest is stirred when audience knows the questions in advance.)
6. The last half of a film (or case)–At a point in the film when a decision is to be made, stop the film. Have students play the rest of the film.
7. The musical chairs (or role reversal)–When two or more people are playing roles, have them reverse (if two) the roles or move to various roles as in musical chairs, possibly even dropping one of the roles out each time to see how the situation changes.
8. The unfinished cartoon–This can be done in pairs at their seats rather than in front of the group.
9. The teacher role plays student-made situations–The teacher asks for the situations in advance and then, taking one of the parts, structures the scenes.

Topics for Role Playing

The topics for role playing are an inherent part of each lesson you teach, but there are times when you are not aware of the situations in which role playing would be an excellent method. The following list of situations and people will give you a start on which ones are suited for role playing. (Use these in Chapter 10 on Understanding Human Behavior.)

The Person Who

1. Will not listen

   A self-righteous mother will not listen to her fourteen-year-old daughter explain why she was late.

   A father will not listen to his ten-year-old son's description of his science project.

   A wife will not listen to her husband talk about the problems of his business.

   A teacher will not listen to an eight-year-old girl's explanation of why she could not finish her homework.

   A husband will not listen to his wife on any subject.

   Points about People Who Will Not Listen

   a. Some people who will not listen have been conditioned to believe that they are right.

b. Some people do not understand that to listen does not mean acceptance or approval.
c. People who will not listen may be distraught because of their own anxieties.
d. Some people will not listen either because they do not want to be bothered or because they have heard the same story too often.
e. Some people will not listen if they are afraid they are wrong.

2. Talks incessantly

   A fourteen-year-old girl talks incessantly about herself around her girl friends.

   A young wife (who is home all day) talks incessantly around her husband.

   An eight-year-old boy talks incessantly around his father.

3. Listens empathetically

   A sixteen-year-old boyfriend listens as his sixteen-year-old girl friend tells about her first test failure.

   A mother listens as her fifteen-year-old daughter tells about her boyfriend who has a new girlfriend.

   A husband listens as his wife tells about her insecurities at work.

4. Thinks someone is out to get him when they are not

   A young man in his first job is sure that one of the four fellow employees who is complimenting him is really out to get him.

   An older woman reads malice into every word said by the three women to whom she is talking.

   A fourteen-year-old boy is urged by his math teacher to study harder.

5. Thinks he is mistreated

   A wife (who works full-time in a job comparable to her husband's) is approaching her husband about sharing the housework.

   A sixteen-year-old son is talking to his father about getting a new car.

   A young woman with three children who wants no more is talking with her husband who does not believe in birth control.

6. Over-eagerly wants to make a good impression

   A young man is talking to his prospective father-in-law.

   A new teacher begins in a newly racially integrated classroom.

   A fifteen-year-old girl talks to a senior boy at a football game.

7. Is in a dilemma he loses no matter what the decision

   A seventeen-year-old girl who has agreed to drive the others to a ballgame finds her mother (who does not get to go out much because someone has to stay with an invalid grandmother) has also planned to go out that very night.

   A husband who can get promoted if he moves approaches his wife who can get promoted only if she stays.

8. Knows he is right, but no one will believe him

   A young mother who is employed provides a variety of foods in the refrigerator for breakfast for her growing family and her husband tells her mother-in-law.

Cautions in Role Playing

There are times when teachers will wish they had not suggested role playing because it either falls flat or they get no volunteers or it turns into a hilarious scene. What could be done if no one, absolutely no one, volunteers? Obviously the whole thing could be dropped. Most teachers understand that the reason for the lack of volunteers is probably a fear of failure. In this case, allow the players to sit in their own seats as they play the roles. Or let them play their roles in the rear of the room while the rest of the students face the front (Shipman 1964).

If the role players turn out to lack sparkle and enthusiasm, call a halt and discuss the issue from there. However, the situation can be changed by turning the role playing into a cut-in type, a role reversal type, or even a soliloquy.

Another quite innocent thing can happen when teachers tell the players to act naturally. Some players do just that and some things are said which are not normally said in the classroom. If this happens and if it bothers the students, the explanation can always be that they were just playing a part. Literary license and dramatic license have abounded for centuries!

A problem which is not so easily handled will result when the students lack the ability to think through the problem and get completely off the track. However, if these students do perform, even when they diverge from the problem at hand, the feelings and the thoughts which were generated can be discussed.

Audience reaction during the role playing scene is occasionally disruptive, but that can be handled by noting that the students who have sounded off are really a part of the act. Capitalize on this by switching to cut-in-role playing or by bringing out in the discussion how different people do react differently in the same situation.

Role playing should not be overdone. It should be used when it is the very best way to get students to see a point or feel how someone else feels or to see how someone else would approach a situation. Never should it be used just to entertain, but it may be used for motivation. It seems that the more rigid, highly achievement-motivated student does not learn as well by role playing and may tire of role playing more quickly than those students who are somewhat introspective.

The teacher may take a role occasionally, but usually it is better later in the semester when the students are aware that the teacher's performance is not there to be copied. The role the teacher takes should not be one of authority.

Role playing in the classroom should be used to teach something, not as an underhanded device to change someone's personality. It is, however, a highly successful technique for gaining insights, especially for the role players themselves.

Summary

Role playing is used for bringing the abstractions of relationships into concrete behaviors and in turn teaching generalizations about behavior as almost no other method can. Students who watch the role playing benefit as much as the players do when they are instructed to be part of the scene in reality or vicariously.

What makes role playing most effective is the fact that the teacher knows the generalizations that would or could operate in a certain situation and has designed the situation and the questions for the discussion to bring out these generalizations. Numerous variations in life scenes from the contrived (reversing roles) to the usual (playing typical well-known roles) to the unusual (reacting to an unexpected behavior) show how the generalizations continue to operate.

When the students know they are playing a role and believe their actions will be accepted as coming from that role, they are more comfortable and gain far more than when they are fearful of being seen as themselves. Yet, the very acting of the other role gives them additional insight into their own and others' behaviors.

Simulation games and exercises, the topic of the next chapter, are another way to allow the students to participate without the fear of reprisal so often felt when they are reacting as themselves. Although simulation games and exercises are more structured than role playing, they, too, teach much about behavior. The teacher, again, must guide the learning with careful preparation and leading of the discussion to bring out the generalizations involved.

References

Chesler, Mark, and Fox, Robert. *Role-playing Methods in the Classroom.* Chicago: Science Research Associates, 1966.

Hyman, Ronald. *Ways of Teaching*. Philadelphia: J. B. Lippincott, Co., 1970.

Moreno, Jacob L. *Psychodrama and the Psychopathology of Interpersonal Relationships*. New York: Beacon House, 1945.

Shaftel, Fannie R. *Role-playing for Social Values*. Englewood Cliffs, N.J.: Prentice-Hall, 1967.

Shipman, Gordon. "Role Playing in the Classroom." *Improving College and University Teaching*. Winter: 21-23, 1964.

Chapter 7

Simulation Games and Exercises

People use strategies every day to handle decision making in either a strong or mild conflict situation. Real-life situations may be simulated in the classroom so that the students may experience all facets of decision making.

Simulation games differ from role playing in that role playing is noncompetitive and semistructured, whereas simulation games usually involve competition, structure, strategies, and a payoff. The word "game" itself is a blessing and a curse all at once. Therefore, when using games, always refer to them as "simulated games for learning." In the classroom a game is used to allow the student to play without the penalties of reality.

Simulation Games*

When students actually take part in a simulation game, they get all the experience of having taken the "bull by the tail" without the panic and probable bodily danger involved. They learn to plan strategies and make decisions in the face of other players who may be helping or hindering them. The game situation allows them to learn how to apply strategies which they might not have time to learn in a quick real-life situation, yet, should a similar situation be confronted later, their experiences in the games may be automatically put into use in real life. If the students make an error, they have the satisfaction of knowing that it is a game, not a life or death situation (Osmond 1970).

Since there is no game without rules, or without following the rules, the students learn why rules are necessary and that the teacher is not the sole enforcer of the rules. The players themselves enforce the rules; each player at times and of his own accord actively does this.

*Many of the ideas in this chapter were given by Edith Murphy and Phyllis Rollinson, students at the University of North Carolina at Greensboro.

In certain games students play as if they were in a life situation with all the decisions and possibilities; in other games they begin to understand what happened in their past to make them react this way now. Students who have difficulty bridging the gap between regular classroom teaching and future goals can play games and may close the gap within the hour.

Use of Simulation Games in the Classroom

Any time students reorganize themselves into groups for active participation, there will be extra noise and excitement but, if this hyperactivity is expected and if kept to a livable amount, teachers and students can continue. It also takes time to play the game. Many teachers would prefer merely to list the sociological and psychological principles and eliminate the experiential part, but to continue only lecturing may turn the students off for days on end. This time would be more valuable in experiential exercises, would it not?

The larger the class, the more activity and noise, but so long as there are enough games for each group, large classes are little problem. There will probably not be enough of one game for a large class, but many different games may be played at once and then rotated. Another method for large classes is to have an equal number of observers as players for each game. Observers could vicariously learn and could watch expressions of the players.

Summarizing Learning from Simulation Games

Even if no summary is made at the end of a game, the students will have learned. However, some games are played to teach something not always caught by the students.

When students play the "Man and Woman" game (Tavris and Wexo 1971), rules, strategies, chance, and planned-in pitfalls are rich learning experiences in themselves, but the discussion afterward is stirring. As a part of all simulation games there must be a session afterward in which the teacher and the students critically examine the concepts and processes simulated. During a game the students are so emotionally keyed up that they may miss the subtle processes—a situation not unlike our own loss of clear thinking when we are upset (a point to teach in itself).

Prior to the use of the simulation game, teachers would have had a reason for the students using the game—to apply generalizations, to see a total picture of a theory at work, to see others in action. At the end use leading questions such as; "Why did you choose this strategy over another one?" "Why are the consequences different for different strategies?" "What is the expected outcome for certain strategies?" "What do you understand better now about this theory than you did before?" "What do you understand better now about people than you did before?"

Games may be a way to measure a kind of problem-solving intelligence that escapes conventional measurement (Abt 1970). Simulation games are not just another teaching technique, but they become a living part of educational and psycho-sociological theory. Students learn the relationship between variables and the outcome of good and bad decisions, and they learn a great deal about themselves and others in the process. In evaluating the learning experience, students are able to put into words many generalizations in the "If . . . then . . ." type of statement which shows they have learned the basic theories. Moreover, student behavior actually changes in the course of the game. The students change strategies and make decisions. This change goes even beyond the usual expectation of attitude change.

Simulation Games and the Unsuccessful Student

Unsuccessful students many times do better in simulation games than in the usual classroom methods. Simulation games are so different a way of teaching that underachievers do not have the negative stimulus which prompts them to use their conditioned failure response. In fact, both unsuccessful and successful students achieve in simulation games. It has been found that some students who are not able to perform in a regular classroom situation, especially on a test, have been able to arrive inductively at abstract rules while playing a simulation game. The major difference between these underachieving students and other students is that the underachievers cannot verbalize the rules even though they can use them with shrewdness (Boocock and Schild 1968).

The fact that many students can understand a rule and use it without verbalizing it makes it even more important to link games with other learning activities. The insights and generalizations may be verbalized by the teacher, if necessary, when the students cannot verbalize them.

Not only do these formerly unsuccessful students gain greater knowledge through simulation games, but success in playing also increases their belief in their own ability to affect destiny. The lack of this ability is believed to affect the lack of occupational success in lower socioeconomic groups (Chilman 1968).

Even though critical thinking is necessary in a simulation game, students of all ability levels can play the same game at the same time. The slower students sometimes learn better from the brighter students than from the teacher. They observe the brighter students' moves and strategies and can copy without fear of being watched by the teacher. Chance in a game allows everyone an opportunity to make good plays occasionally, whereas little chance is possible in teacher-controlled lessons.

Simulation games are motivating for both the slower or disinterested students and the brighter students but for different reasons. The slower students need action and immediate results. The brighter students get an opportunity to develop and try different strategies.

Simulation Exercises

Simulation exercises are more like role playing than simulation games in that there are no strategies or props. There is, however, a semi-structure and a purpose. Students are put into the act of physically feeling an abstract concept such as how it feels to have too many demands at once. They are put into the act of really paying full attention to someone for the first time in their lives. They gain insights in ways that lecture and discussion never have given them before.

In fact, role playing, simulation games, and simulation exercises are the laboratory of a relationships course. The reasons for simulation exercises are the same as for role playing and simulated games–motivation, different ways of learning for people with different learning styles, a change of pace for others, gaining of insight, and greater transfer outside the classroom. The suggestions for management are the same and questions and discussion are equally as necessary. Cautions about the participation in and discussion of simulation exercises–and role playing and simulation games as well–are not to make a person play against his will or probe too deeply in the question period about why any one student did what he did. This is not a therapy session.

Simulation Exercises for the Classroom

1. *To understand more fully that there is a* ***universal desire to be accepted****, either through being touched or being listened to.*
   a. Slap Rap* (Lewis and Streitfeld 1972). "Converse" with your partner by slapping him or her on the arms or shoulders. Your partner answers the same way. This continues as in ordinary conversation. Express any or all emotions you feel.
   b. Hand Conversation* (Lewis and Streitfeld 1972). With knees touching and eyes closed, "converse" with your partner by touching and feeling only each other's hands. Express any or all emotions you feel.
   c. Out in the Cold* (Lewis and Streitfeld 1972). Form groups of about six to eight students each. One student at a time voluntarily leaves the group and walks away for a few minutes and then returns but does not talk to anyone. The intact group should whisper. Each student in the group does this activity voluntarily. (Vary this procedure by the group's telling someone to leave or not allowing someone

*Used by permission of Harcourt Brace Jovanovich, Inc., New York, from *Growth Games* by Howard R. Lewis and Harold S. Streitfeld. Copyright © 1970 by Howard R. Lewis and Harold S. Streitfeld.

to leave. Be sure the students are stable enough to handle this. Remind them it is a game.)

Questions for discussion after any one of these exercises

(1) When did it change from being a class exercise to gaining insight or realizing a feeling?
(2) Did you feel foolish? Why? Did this change later?
(3) Did you object to touching? Why?
(4) What is the difference in being touched or accepted as part of a group (person) and in being apart from that group (person)?
(5) What has taught you these feelings?

Major points

(1) There is a universal desire to be accepted.
(2) There are different ways of being accepted.
(3) Acceptance implies you "measure up."
(4) Touching someone whom they do not know is unacceptable, but not rejected, by some people.
(5) Touching someone whom you do not know may engender revulsion or fear in the other.

2. *To gain insight into beliefs about male-female dominance.*

a. Master-Slave* (Lewis and Streitfeld 1972). One male and one female student (or same sex acting the parts) are needed. First one of them stands on a chair and the other kneels in front of the chair. The one in the chair puts his (her) foot on the other's back. The one on the floor begins to crawl away. The one on the chair presses hard to keep the person from crawling away. Then reverse positions.

b. On a Pedestal* (Lewis and Streitfeld 1972). One person stands on a chair. The other sits on the floor or in a chair. Then they carry on a conversation. Later reverse positions.

Questions for discussion after either of these exercises

(1) Did you feel comfortable in one position more than the other?
(2) Did old memories of one's controlling you return?
(3) Did you feel uncomfortable in one position because of the gender of the other person?
(4) What insights did you gain as you were in one position or the other?

Major points

(1) Some women may feel more comfortable in the subordinate position but feel ambivalent because of societal expectation of equality.

(2) Some men feel uncomfortable in the dominant position but feel ambivalent because of societal expectation of the strong man. Even though this is changing, there is still a cultural lag (Ogburn 1922).

(3) Some women may feel more comfortable in the dominant position and admit it and are surprised at the resentment of the group.

(4) People sometimes deny their feelings even to themselves when it is against either cultural expectations or childhood conditioning.

(5) There may be a time and place for both positions.

3. ***To understand that people react to situations in self-preserving ways especially when their self-esteem is attacked (Rogers 1951).***

Satir (1972) has delineated five patterns of reacting: (a) placating (agreeing, smoothing, feeling worthless, and acting demure); (b) blaming (accusing, disagreeing, feeling unsuccessful, and pointing accusing finger); (c) computing (being ultra-reasonable, correct, feeling vulnerable, and sitting stiffly composed); (d) distracting (using words that are irrelevant and make no sense, feeling this is no place for them, with body in constant motion); and (e) integrated (using words and actions that are relevant and rational). Get three or four volunteers to argue some point. They may or may not be told about the five patterns to begin with. The other students would be informed, however, so that they could analyze the words and actions.

It is also possible to have the four volunteers actually take the first four patterns to role play. At first, students should assume the body postures described and face each other for one whole minute. Then start the argument.

Topics for arguing

People over thirty are squares.

Black people are foolish to date white people.

People born in the United States of parents born in other countries are not Americans.

Divorce is usually a result of selfishness.

Children kill marital happiness.

Sexual relationships between consenting adults is their business and no one else's.

Questions for discussion

(1) Did you feel comfortable in the position you chose?

(2) Can people change types during the course of the conversation?

(3) Did you notice a stronger stance the harder your self-concept was being hit?

Major points

(1) There is an inherent need to preserve the self; even when we admit

error, we are saying, "See, I am good enough to admit when I'm wrong," thus preserving the concept of honest self.

(2) Strategies or ways of preserving self are learned over the years by modeling or reinforcement.

(3) Ways of preserving self can be tempered or changed as one learns different ways that are more satisfying.

Other simulated exercises are described and referred to throughout Satir's book (1972) and the four volumes of Pfeiffer and Jones (1971).

4. *To bring about an awareness of the various facets of **nonverbal behavior** that are exhibited when an emotion is felt.*

Have the students demonstrate in some nonverbal fashion an emotion selected from several possibilities.

Make several sets of cards with one of six emotions written on each card. Some emotions to select are love, anger, hate, apathy, loneliness, joy, fear, excitement, admiration, shyness, shock, anxiety, etc. Select three positive and three negative emotions. For each emotion, make four cards but on each of these four cards put one of four nonverbal ways of expressing each emotion: facial expression only, arm movements only, body and leg movements only, or a combination of any of these ways. This makes twenty-four cards per set. For example: hate–facial expression only; hate–arm movements only, etc. (This can be mimeographed on heavy paper and cut into cards.)

Divide the class into groups of four to six with one observer-recordkeeper. Give each group two sets of cards (forty-eight cards). The dealer shuffles the cards and deals them one at a time until all the cards are dealt. Beginning with the player on the left of the dealer, each player selects a card to demonstrate that emotion in the manner designated. The other players guess the emotion being demonstrated. Each one who is correct may demonstrate that manner and/or emotion in his turn. Those who guess incorrectly must remove from their hands all cards with that manner of expression connected with any emotion. The player who gets all incorrect guesses must also remove all cards from his hand with that manner of expression on them. The object in the end is to have the greatest number of cards after each round. The penalty of having to remove cards from a hand not only lowers the number one has, but also lowers the choices of different types of emotions and manners of expression. The observer-recordkeeper is given a chart on which to mark the emotion selected by each player.

Discussion

Stop after one round of play so that there will be time for discussion. Draw a chart on the board to tally which emotion was selected by each player in each group. Use this tally for discussion. (More negative emotions will probably be used at first.)

Emotion chosen by position

Emotion:	Player 1	2	3	4	5	6
Anger						
Hate						
Loneliness						
Shyness						
Joy						
Love						

Major points

(1) It is easier to show anger and hate because of the action involved.

(2) There are fewer active behavioral manifestations for love, shyness, and loneliness than for anger and hate.

(3) There has probably been more reinforcement and modeling in public for negative emotion (for instance, reinforcement in the form of attention as parents have reprimanded children for anger).

(4) Actions of anger and hate are generally associated with strength.

(5) Actions of love, loneliness, and shyness are generally associated with weakness.

(6) All emotions, negative or positive, have a point of "overcomeness" (Zetterberg 1966).

5. ***To analyze strategies people use in problem solving.***

Play the "WHO DUNIT?" game (Daly and Reeves 1972).*

Select six people for each group to play the game or solve the mystery. Select six (or fewer if there are not enough students) other people to observe. Each observer is assigned (or selects) one player to observe without the knowledge of the player. Each observer is to keep notes on strategies his player uses and also to observe total group effort.

Each player is given one of the six information slips and is told to find out "who dunit?" After ten minutes, whether the mystery is solved or not, stop the procedure and ask the observer to report to his group.

Observers guide questions

Observers (Group Interaction): As you observe groups discussing, keep these questions in mind and any specific people to whom they apply.

How well did the group stick to its job?

How well did the group get information from its members?

*"Who Dunit?" a game demonstrated and distributed at the National Council on Family Relations in Portland, Oregon, November 1972. Used by permission of Ronald Daly.

Who talked the most? To whom?
Who talked very little and why?
What was helpful in discussion and not helpful?
Who influenced the direction of the discussion?
How did they exert influence?
How did the group test for agreement?
Were people able to say what they felt? Why and why not?

Observers (one person observed): Compare the person you observed with the others.

Did that person take the lead? When?
What other position did that person take? How?
Ask that person if this is typical of his usual behavior in a group.

Information Slip #1

WHO DUNIT?

Although you may tell your group what is on this slip of paper, you may *not* pass it around for others to read.

Your group members have all the information needed to find the answer to the following question. Only one answer is correct. You can prove it.

Who Killed Bianchi?

Some of the information your group has may be irrelevant and may not help solve the problem.

Information Slip #2

WHO DUNIT?

Although you may tell your group what is on this slip of paper, you may not pass it around for others to read.

Information

Bill Bianchi was shot to death at close range on a lonely country road late one night. It was raining at the time. The police soon established that the murder was commited by one of four men—Al, Jack, Joe, or Tom—and the gun that was used belonged to one of the four.

Information Slip #3

WHO DUNIT?

Although you may tell your group what is on this slip of paper, you may not pass it around for others to read.

Information

Al was questioned and made the statements listed below. Two, and only two, of the statements are true.

1. I didn't do it.
2. Tom did it.
3. Sure I own a gun.
4. Joe and I were playing poker when Bill was shot.

Information Slip #4

WHO DUNIT?

Although you may tell your group what is on this slip of paper, you may not pass it around for others to read.

Information

Jack was questioned and made the statements listed below. Two, and only two, of the statements are true.

1. I didn't do it.
2. Al did it.
3. Joe and I were at the movies when Bill was shot.
4. Bill was shot with Joe's gun.

Information Slip #5

WHO DUNIT?

Although you may tell your group what is on this slip of paper, you may not pass it around for others to read.

Information

Joe was questioned and made the statements listed below. Two, and only two, of the statements are true.

1. I was asleep when Bill was shot.
2. Al lied when he said Tom killed Bill.
3. Jack is the only one of us who owns a gun.
4. Tom and Bill were pals.

Information Slip #6

WHO DUNIT?

Although you may tell your group what is on this slip of paper, you may not pass it around for others to read.

Information

Tom was questioned and made the statements listed below. Two, and only two, of the statements are true.

1. I never fired a gun in my life.
2. I don't know who did it.
3. Joe doesn't own a gun.
4. I never saw Bill until they showed me the body.

(Incidentally, Joe did it, but don't tell.)

Bring the class together to discuss strategies and feelings and whether simulation games do allow a person to bring out some of his true nature.

Major points

(1) The leadership strategy of a person, whether it be to take over immediately, to sit back and do nothing, to look the situation over and then organize the group, or to logistically put every step down and analyze, will come out in ten minutes of serious playing.
(2) As the seriousness of the game (or seriousness of the teacher that the problem must be solved) is realized, the more anxiety is evoked and the more energy students use.
(3) Anxiety gives some people energy but takes it away from others.

Summary

Simulation games and exercises differ enough from role playing to have been presented in two separate chapters. Even though all three are structured, they differ in degree–games being highly structured, exercises somewhat structured, and role playing structured only to describe the situation and type of player. The three also differ in the behavior involved. Games have rules and a goal; exercises include much nonverbal behavior; and role playing is verbal and open-ended.

All of these methods are simulations and are the laboratory of a relationships course. They give concrete examples to support the theories of behavior. The teacher, however, must plan to use them in the appropriate context and must organize the discussion to bring out the generalizations.

All students do not learn equally well in every teaching situation whether it is lecture, discussion, active participation in research, role playing, or simulation games and exercises. On occasion, other media may serve the purpose of learning the subject matter of family relationships. Music and pictures may be used in some instances to fit the learning style of some students or the mood of the concept being taught. No matter which method a teacher uses, the foremost goal must be for teaching the students to understand and use generalizations about human behavior. The next chapter describes how to use music and pictures.

References

Abt, Clark C. *Serious Games*. New York: The Viking Press, 1970.

Boocock, Sarone, and Schild, E. O., eds. *Simulation Games in Learning*. Beverly Hills, California: Sage, 1968.

Chilman, Catherine S. "Child-Rearing and Family Relationship Patterns of the Very Poor." In *Sourcebook in Marriage and the Family*, 3rd edition, edited by Marvin B. Sussman. New York: Houghton Mifflin, 1968.

Daly, Ronald, and Reeves, Joan P. "The Use of Human Interaction Laboratories in Family Life Courses." Paper presented at the National Council on Family Relations, 1 November 1972, at Portland, Oregon. Mimeographed.

Lewis, Howard R., and Streitfeld, Harold S. *Growth Games*. New York: Bantam Books, 1972.

Ogburn, William F. *Social Change*. New York: Viking Press, 1922.

Osmond, Marie. "The Method of Simulation Games in Family Life Education." Paper presented at the National Council on Family Relations, 10 October 1970, at Chicago. Mimeographed.

Pfeiffer, J. William, and Jones, John. *A Handbook of Structured Experiences for Human Relations Training*. Vols. 1, 2, 3, and 4. Iowa City, Iowa: University Associates Press, 1971.

Rogers, Carl R. *Client-centered Therapy: Its Current Practice, Implications, and Theory*. Boston: Houghton Mifflin, 1951.

Satir, Virginia. *Peoplemaking*. Palo Alto, California: Science and Behavior Books, Inc., 1972.

Tavris, Carol, and Wexo, John B. "Woman and Man—A Game." *Psychology Today* 5: 44-56, 1971.

Zetterberg, Hans L. "The Secret Ranking." *Journal of Marriage and Family* 28: 134-142, 1966.

List of Games and Companies

Games Research, Inc., 48 Wareham St., Boston, Mass. 02118
"Insight" (Perception of personality)

The Hyphen Consultants Ltd., 12007-40 Avenue, Edmonton, Alberta, Canada
"Two-to-One" (To improve communication)

MACSCO, Box 382, Locust Valley, New York 11560
"The Games People Play" (Recognizing social actions and their consequences)

Psychology Today Games, Del Mar, Calif. 92014
"Body Talk" (Communication of emotions without words)
"Woman and Man" (Bias of traditional man-woman relationships)
"Blacks and Whites" (Nature of the black-white relationship)
Simile II, 1150 Silverado, LaJolla, Calif. 92037
"Star Power" (Insight into a three-tiered society)
Unitarian Universalist Association, Division of Education and Social Concern, 25 Beacon St., Boston, Mass. 02108.
"Hang Up" (Empathy and tolerance about racism)
Western Publishing Co., Inc., 850 Third Ave., New York, N.Y. 10023
"Generation Gap" (Structure of power and interdependence of the family)
"Ghetto" (Experience of life in deprived areas of the city)
"Life Career" (Planning for the future)
"Consumer" (Decisions about buying)

Chapter 8

Music and Pictures

Every student has his own learning style just as every teacher has a unique teaching style. When the two are in tune, both the student and the teacher benefit. Since neither person may be completely aware of these styles, several different methods must be incorporated in teaching concepts of family relationships. The use of music and pictures may be more effective for teaching certain concepts to certain people, and their use may also complement other methods in teaching certain concepts. That is, a concept that was not really clear with the use of one method or another may come into focus with the use of both methods, for instance, music and role playing; pictures and discussion; simulated exercises and music; pictures and the empathetic approach; literature and music.

It is very difficult to get students–and some fellow faculty members, for that matter–to realize that music is not a stereotyped method of entertainment. Also the use of pictures to teach attitudes and relationships as well as the history of the family is seen by some as "cutting out pictures." When teachers become comfortable and skilled in the use of music and pictures and when teachers have definite concepts and generalizations to be learned, they will be able to select appropriately for both content and student needs.

Music*

Probably no method encourages students to give more attention to the subject at hand than music does. Sometimes it is the words; sometimes it is the rhythm; sometimes it is the change of pace; but always music tells its story to attentive ears.

Music may be used in every topic about relationships from communication

*Many of the ideas in this section were given by Sarah Shoffner (faculty member), Roby Kerr (student), and Adair Rountree (student), Child Development and Family Relations Department, University of North Carolina, Greensboro, N.C.

to philosophy of life to role relationships. Certainly love and crises are amply represented in music. Even in the general techniques of teaching, such as discussions,* questions, role playing, and the empathetic approach, music is aptly used.

Current music will catch the immediate attention of the students, and it should be used more than older songs for teaching certain concepts. A variety of songs which are both current at this writing and classics that students will continue to recognize are listed to show how much may be used in teaching about relationships.

Many of the recent songs are thought provoking in that they describe a person's feelings as he goes into depression or they chide the parents or the adult generation for their lack of concern. They also tell the story of a generation that has great interest in humanity—an interest not usually possible until basic needs are assured.

The easiest way to bring music to the classroom is by way of cassette tapes. Teachers may record an entire song and use it in its entirety or use only parts of it. Marking the place on the tape where a particular part is becomes the problem. One cassette is large enough for recording several songs. If several songs are recorded on one tape, the most efficient use of the tape is to record songs that fit a category such as philosophy of life; male-female roles; differing views of love; crises; young love; wedding songs, etc. Several songs will be listed later under various categories.

Collecting music, organizing it, and preparing it for class takes a lot of time, not counting the time it takes planning the lesson and the generalization to be taught. Getting equipment together used to be a problem until the era of the cassette tape player. Using the music also takes quite a bit of time in class. It is not expected that teachers will use music very often. However, every bit of effort and every minute used in class is worth it. If you sensitize the students to the messages in music, they will begin to take over your job of collecting current music and noting teaching points. In fact, just for the objective of sensitizing the students, you may bring a radio to class to hear the songs of that very day. In most areas, there is a station that has popular music all day. Listen to a song or two and then cut off the radio and discuss

*Recordings or tapes of monologues are excellent for getting a discussion started. The anecdotes imply many stereotypes and beliefs which can be discussed at length as to where they came from and why they continue. Bill Cosby did an album called "Revenge" on RCA that included peer relationships, sibling relationships, husband-wife relationships, and many more. This record could be used to teach students to understand how they themselves feel about the use of revenge for self-preservation. If revenge is merely an extension of self-preservation, then where does the behavior change from self-preservation to self- and other-destruction? Children's records are a storehouse of materials on teaching values and principles of human behavior. The album which dramatizes Dr. Seuss's *Horton Hatches the Egg* and *The Sneetchies* is an example of a children's record for teaching such generalizations as this one: People tend to want what others have and those who have it do not want it after the others get it.

the songs. Turn the radio back on and listen to a few more. It does not matter what songs are on. The point is to discuss what one hears at that time. This technique could be used during the unit on understanding self or interpersonal relationships.

Youth Music

Never in the history of music have so many young people written, sung, played, and recorded music. The affluence of youth has given them the time, the education, and the electronic equipment with which to write, record, and play music. The lyrics in the songs have been a veritable history of the civil rights movement, existentialism, and disagreements with the Establishment.

Some disagreement between youth and their parent generation seems to be heightened by some youth music with its higher decibel count and covert messages. The staging or rendering of such music, being surprising to the parent generation to say the least, does little to help gain their acceptance of the music or the youth. However, when adults do begin to listen and when some of the youth age into the parent generation and infiltrate it with youth music acceptance, the understanding brought about by music is phenomenal. Witness the recent inclusion of nearly all kinds of music by the Boston Pops Orchestra.

Sources for Music

Although you can buy the records or tapes you need, there are other sources for music. Public and university libraries loan recordings. Radio stations sometimes discard recordings and may give them to you. Radio stations may also help you find a record and play it for you to record with your own equipment. Students themselves are a veritable storehouse of music. Not only do they have recent recordings, but many of them will also give their very own rendition live before the class.

Sometimes the words on a recording are not clear and copies of the words are needed for the class. Many of the current lyrics are printed in music fliers or magazines. Any music store could sell you these reprints. The top forty list of recordings will also keep the teacher informed about the recent popular music. In the June 1974 issue of *Mad* magazine there was a spoof on women's liberation set to the music of *My Fair Lady*.

Teaching Techniques

1. *To understand students' own beliefs and feelings about prison, about parents, about accepting people who have erred but who want to return to society, about the "Prodigal Son" notion, or about what they would do.*

Read the story below, "I'm Going Home." Stop reading the story just before the train reaches the tree so that the students will have to express what they really feel. Or play the record "Tie a Yellow Ribbon 'Round the Old Oak Tree" (Dawn on Bell label) which is essentially the same story.

I'M GOING HOME
(Author unknown)

As Tom sat on the train, anxious and apprehensive about what he might soon have to face, the man who sat next to him turned and said, "Son, you seem nervous and worried. Is there anything I can do to help?" Tom could not hold it back. He had to tell someone. He had to have a friend to share his deep fear even if it were just a stranger. "Mister," he said, "I just got out of prison. I won't make excuses, but one thing really haunts me about the mess I've made of my life and that's the way I broke my parents' hearts. They are old now and have lived in shame for all these years I have been in jail. I do still love them and I want to go home now that I'm out. I know you must think that takes a lot of guts for me to come home after all I have done to them. Well, I feel the same way about it."

Tom paused a few seconds in his story. He looked out at the bleak, bare trees and thought of his tree—the one in his back yard. It was winter now and there was not a thing to be seen on the brittle branches, not even snow. "I wrote Mom and Dad and asked if I could come home. I wouldn't let them visit me in that crummy jail and so I haven't seen them for a long time. I was just too ashamed to let them come see me in there." Tom appreciated the way the man just sat there and listened. He couldn't tell whether he was shocked or sympathetic, but he was listening, and Tom felt he had to talk to someone to take up these last few minutes of agony.

"I told them they did not have to let me come home if they were too ashamed of me. You see, Mister, we live right by the railroad tracks and all the trains pass by our back yard as they come in. There's a big maple tree that hangs over our fence and into the railroad lot. Well, I asked them to tie a ribbon in that ole' tree if they were willing to let me get off." Tom let the alternative go unstated, but his pause spoke it all the louder.

"We're about there now, and—I'm scared to look. I can't blame them if they leave the tree bare. I don't deserve to have a home and the swell Mom and Dad I hurt so deeply."

He started to choke up and looked down to hide his shame. Neither man spoke at all for some time, and then the train began to slow down for the next station; it was Tom's home town.

(STOP AND DISCUSS)

A few tense moments passed and then the man next to Tom nudged him gently and said, "I think you can look now, son."

Tom struggled to look up. There was the tree, his tree, marvelously ablaze with hundreds of ribbons—red ones, blue ones, yellow, orange, and green. "I'll see you, Mister," Tom whispered, "I'm going home!"

2. *To become aware of one's own* **philosophy of life** *and to understand that others differ for varying reasons and that individuals vary somewhat from time to time.*
   a. Play a medley of about five songs that show different philosophies. Play the medley twice. Ask each student to write a word or two about each philosophy and to rank the five as they fit the individual student's philosophy from most like me (1) to least like me (5). Then draw a chart on the board to get a profile of the class. If there are thirty-five students in the class, the profile may look like this:

	First Choice	*Second Choice*	*Third Choice*	*Fourth Choice*	*Fifth Choice*
Song #1	8	4	9	4	(10)
Song #2	(14)	6	8	7	0
Song #3	3	3	1	(18)	(10)
Song #4	0	2	(12)	6	(15)
Song #5	(10)	(20)	5	0	0
	35	35	35	35	35

Discussion:

(1) Even though the largest frequencies in any one block have been circled to show which song was chosen most often, this profile does not give a rightness or wrongness; it merely shows where various people are or which songs were most suited to certain individuals.

(2) Ask the students to think to themselves why they ranked the songs they did. Then ask them to reveal some of their thoughts, if they would.

(3) Further the discussion by bringing in these generalizations:
   (a) One's philosophy is his guide for his behavior.
   (b) A philosophy is learned through past experience or through modeling others.
   (c) A philosophy varies somewhat through time and experiences.

   b. The following songs are suggested for giving a philosophy of life. Select from these or from older or more current ones.

SONGS	PHILOSOPHY
"Bridge over Troubled Water" (Simon and Garfunkel)	Kind, charitable, helping concern

SONGS	PHILOSOPHY
"Climb Every Mountain" (*Sound of Music*)	Courage, faces things, looks for challenge
"Diamonds Are a Girl's Best Friend" (Marilyn Monroe, *Gentlemen Prefer Blondes*)	Security, materialistic
"Everybody Has the Right to Be Wrong" (Frank Sinatra)	Tolerance, forgiving
"Everything Is Beautiful in Its Own Way" (Ray Stevens)	Positive outlook, tolerance, recognizes beauty
"Gentle on My Mind" (Glen Campbell)	Carefree, irresponsible
"He's Got the Whole World in His Hand"	God-centered, religion
"I Want to Teach the World to Sing" (The New Seekers)	Understanding, love, cooperation
"I Want to Be Free" (Jimmy Rodgers)	Carefree, irresponsible
"I'll Walk with God" (Mario Lanza, *Student Prince*)	God-centered
"The Impossible Dream" (*Man of La Mancha*)	Courage, integrity
"Is That All There Is?" (Peggy Lee)	Negative, cynical, unshakable
"It's Not Easy Being Green" (Frank Sinatra)	Self-contentment
"I've Got to Be Me" (Sammy Davis Jr.)	Individuality
"King of the Road" (Roger Miller)	Carefree, irresponsible, nonmaterialistic
"My Way" (Frank Sinatra)	Integrity, individuality, courageous
"People" (Barbra Streisand)	Interested in and cares for others
"Put a Little Love in Your Heart" (Andy Williams)	Loving, concern for others
"Raindrops Keep Falling on My Head" (B. J. Thomas)	Grit, determination, optimism
"That Lucky Old Sun" (Frankie Laine or Ray Charles)	Hard work, God-centered, Protestant ethic
"What Are You Doing Sunday?"	Casual, irresponsible

SONGS	PHILOSOPHY
"A Working Man's Prayer"	Hard work, family, hope, trust in God, overcoming hardship, Protestant ethic
"Candy Man" (Sammy Davis Jr.)	Ever-loving provider

3. *To become aware of the* ***beliefs and customs*** *perpetuated by popular music.*
   a. Assign the students to listen to the current music and answer some of the following questions. Assign this activity in groups and have them give a report and concert.
      (1) How many different ways is love interpreted?
      (2) How are male and female roles defined and reinforced?
      (3) How do people meet depression (blues)?
      (4) How is a need for people or interaction shown?
      (5) What are some illustrations of certain theories of personality? ("You're Nobody Until Somebody Loves You," "People")
      (6) What causes love to change?
      (7) What are some of the recurrent problems in life?
      (8) What parent-child problems are discussed?
   b. Play some records of various eras and correlate with the social customs of those times. Compare the parents' and grandparents' eras as exemplified by their music. Discuss the effect of the social era of the grandparents on the parents and eventually on you.

Pictures*

Pictures are sometimes more valuable than the words of role playing because the meaning is caught instantaneously. The manipulation of pictures in teaching some generalization in relationships is similar to the manipulation of words or postures. When teachers want the students to gain insight through induction, they must give them several illustrations. The illustrations or examples sometimes are written, sometimes are spoken, sometimes are acted out, but sometimes they are shown through pictures.

Since people have different learning styles, pictures may be the very way some students learn best some of the time. In fact, there are some relationships insights which are actually learned best through pictures.

*Many of the suggestions in this section were given by Marilyn Karmel (student), Department of Child Development and Family Relations, University of North Carolina, Greensboro, N.C.

Part of the problem is to have the right pictures at the time that they would be the best method. Start a collection now. After reading how pictures may be used, teachers will be more aware of how almost any picture can be used. Obviously, if the pictures are to be shown in front of a group they must be large and clear in detail; however, don't overlook the possible use of smaller pictures by individual students or shown in an opaque projector.

The objectives which are taught well through pictures are (1) the understanding that there are many perspectives to a situation; (2) the expression of one's own feelings or values; (3) the awareness of one's own hierarchy of roles; (4) the understanding of the cultural stereotypes; and (5) the development of a deeper understanding of a topic. Almost all of these objectives may be taught through the pictorial essay, the incomplete story, the pictorial differential, or cartoons.

The Pictorial Essay

Just as photo-journalists do, assemble pictures which tell a story and arrange them on a long foldout so that they may all be seen at once. Pictures may be collected to illustrate the many perspectives of one or more of the following topics. To understand subcultural stereotypes and many other perspectives of a topic are objectives for these collections.

1. Ways of expressing love
2. Women in America
3. Men in America
4. Families
5. Parents (mothers and fathers)
6. Grandparents
7. Best friends
8. Anger
9. Jealousy
10. Intergenerations
11. Jobs
12. Communication

Example: Perspective of Women in America

1. Women are culturally conditioned to accept the homemaker role even when they work outside the home.
2. Women come in all sizes, shapes, and personalities.
3. Women take both the expressive and the instrumental roles, i.e., the nurturing and managerial roles.
4. The appearance or behavior of women may be more associated with social class than American culture.

(Use with such chapters as 11. Intergenerational Relationships, 13. Human Sexual Identity, 10. Communication, and 12. Interpersonal Relationships.)

The Incomplete Story

The objective here is also many-faceted. The students are shown a picture which is ambiguous, and they each have to tell a story about (1) what went on before, (2) what is happening now, and (3) what will happen next. They will learn that people see things differently, that each one sees the story in light of his own background and wishes, and that things are not always what they seem.

Teachers may use one large picture for the whole class or one picture of any size for small groups. They should look intently at the picture for several minutes and write some notes on the three aspects noted in the above paragraph. (Use with such chapters as 9. Understanding Human Behavior and 10. Communication.)

Show a picture of a single individual and ask students to study the facial expression, the posture, the hands. It is said that second to the face, the position of a person's hands expresses emotions, especially those of anxiety and tension. When the students talk about the picture, they are essentially empathizing or talking about themselves.

A Pictorial Differential

The term "pictorial differential" is taken from the idea of a semantic differential* (Osgood, Suci, and Tannenbaum 1957) in which a concept is described by selecting a point on several bipolar continua. The pictorial differential can be used when there are enough pictures on one concept so that the students could arrange them in an order along some continuum from one extreme to the other. There will be no "right" arrangement except in the students' own minds.

The objective is to help the students become aware of their own value system or their own hierarchy. A pictorial differential can also help the students understand that people see things differently and that there are many perspectives according to the conditioning of the individual student. Pictures could be collected to illustrate one or more of the following topics:

1. Any emotion from its constructive to its destructive aspect (from anger used to stop a devastating act to anger used to devastate).
2. Roles of men and women.
3. Masculinity or femininity (from least masculine to most masculine, *not* from most masculine to most feminine).

*Osgood et al. explain "differential" as the title given to the exercise in which one differentiates (makes a selection from) among a set of descriptive terms so that the selection describes the person making it.

Cartoons

Most cartoons are pointed, almost piercing, illustrations of relationships situations. Cartoons with their captions can be used to start discussions, to illustrate a point, or to get the students to take a serious look at why they thought the cartoon was so funny.

To guide the learning experience ask the following questions:

1. At what generalization in society is it aimed?
2. Is there truth in the cartoon?
3. Do you agree or disagree?
4. Why do you think it is so funny (or not so funny)?

Some of the cartoons which are based mainly on human relationships are the following:

Peanuts (Charlie Brown)
Dennis the Menace
Family Circus
The Better Half
Love IS or Happiness IS (You could collect these cartoons or buy the book *Love Is* and ask the students to challenge whether the cartoons illustrate love to them and why. Students may wish to draw their own and make another series illustrating what some other aspects of life are.)

(See the Chapter 17 on Differing Family Patterns for cartoon figures of future man.)

Other Sources of Pictures

Draw Your Own or Paint Your Own

Stick figures or a quick sketch on the board or on a large sheet of paper sometimes make a point more vivid than prepared pictures. A very accurate way of enlarging a drawing or cartoon is to project it on a large sheet of paper from an opaque projector and then trace the picture. If you paint, don't hesitate to bring some paint to class to show the feeling you put into your painting or to show what you were trying to communicate.

Reproductions

Pictures from different eras and different cultures (Mead and Heyman 1965) are excellent sources for showing changes in families. Artists have always been sensitive observers of human relations. Suggested artists are these: Norman Rockwell, Andrew Wyeth, Marc Chagall, Edgar Degas, Henry Moore (a series of sculptures on the family group), Rembrandt, Picasso, Renoir, Mary Cassatt, and Käthe Kollwitz.

Photographs

Slides, in particular, are very good for showing current relationships scenes. Many of these slides may be a decade or more old, showing progressions or changes in attitude. Students could make their own.

Summary

Music is a unique and little-used method for helping a person understand himself and others, but at times it is more valuable than other methods. The lyrics are as important as the music, for a few poetic words say more than a whole book does at times. The teacher must be very careful to teach the students that music is a medium for learning; otherwise, they may move into a stereotyped belief that music is for entertainment.

Pictures, too, have a special place in teaching about relationships. With so many different learning styles among the students, varied methods must be used. Even though it has been said that when a person does not understand words, he needs a picture, it should be noted that even a picture elicits different reactions and perceptions. These two methods are supplements that should not be overused but must not be overlooked.

The general methods of teaching family relationships included in this part of the book were the empathetic approach, literature, research, discussion, questions, role playing, simulation games and exercises, and finally music and pictures. Even though some examples of teaching techniques were included in each of these chapters, the nine chapters in the next part of the book are essentially filled with teaching techniques and are grouped according to areas and concepts of family relationships.

References

Mead, Margaret, and Heyman, Ken. *Family*. New York: Macmillan, 1965.

Osgood, Charles E.; Suci, George J.; and Tannenbaum, Percy H. *The Measurement of Meaning*. Urbana: University of Illinois Press, 1957.

Part Two

General Areas in Family Relationships and Techniques for Teaching

This book is intended to be used as a guide for teaching methods no matter what other book the teacher chooses for in-depth family relationships subject matter. Family relationships textbooks have traditionally been outlined by a normative chronological ordering of events in a family life cycle, but the outline for this Part was made from a different perspective. This perspective is essentially that family relationships operate on some basic generalizations about human behavior. The nine areas of family relationships presented in Part Two were selected for their pervasiveness and their relevance.

The first four chapters of Part Two–Understanding Human Behavior, Communication, Interpersonal Relationships in Any Family, and Intergenerational Relationships–deal with generalizations and teaching techniques that show how basic needs, communication techniques, age, and living together as a family affect relationships. The next three chapters present techniques to show how the generalizations about human behavior and societal customs operate in the specific areas of human sexual identity, money and work, and crises in families. To emphasize that families have changed and will change, even though the family itself will remain, two chapters are devoted to how and why change is needed. One chapter deals with single people, and Chapter 17 presents generalizations and teaching techniques about differing family forms.

The framework of each chapter is based on broad beliefs in the areas being discussed, and almost all objectives are written in terms of behaviors expected of the student. The generalization about a concept is often included in the objective. Techniques for teaching the various concepts and/or generalizations follow the objectives and, in many cases, the essence of the subject matter and references for further reading are included.

Chapter 9

Understanding Human Behavior

Human behavior is assumed to be the result of gratification of needs, some innatc and some learned. Certain needs seem to be basic to life—needs such as security, friends, sense of worth, new experience, philosophy of life, and some independence. The organization and intensity of these needs vary from person to person and from time to time within one person. This individual variation is a result of both internal makeup and external situations. People's perceptions of their needs and the external situation eventually affect their total behavior, including those perceptions and situations which determine their own self-images. As people see that certain behavior is an asset, they begin to continue that behavior and it then begins to have the status of a value. When it becomes a value, then it becomes a need and the behavior is self-perpetuating (Hall and Lindsey 1970).

This chapter is divided into four sections: needs, perception, self-image, and values. The interchange between the culture and the individual is seen throughout each of the four areas. Specific references are given throughout the chapter.

Needs

Teaching Techniques

1. *To apply the belief that everyone has* ***basic needs*** *(Murray and Kluckhohn 1953).*

   Using the following list of some basic psychological and social needs, show how advertisements or pleas or other persuasions are operating on these basic needs (Westlake 1969).

Basic Psychological and Social Needs

Security (being like others, freedom from want and anxiety) (Kagan 1972; Maslow 1954)

Friends (being liked and liking others and caring for them) (Maslow 1954)

Sense of worth (response and recognition) (Kagan 1972; Maslow 1954)
New experience (change of pace) (Kagan 1972)
Philosophy of life (guiding principles) (Maslow 1954)
Freedom and independence (Privacy and feeling of controlling self) (Kagan 1972; Maslow 1954)

Examples of Persuasive Statements (Add your own from current advertisements).

a. You owe it to yourself.
b. Four out of five people chose this one.
c. Try it; you'll like it.
d. We take care of everything.
e. There are no strings attached.
f. You can trust us.

2. *To understand that* **needs change** *from time to time, that the order of precedence of needs changes, and that the intensity of needs changes from time to time (Murray and Kluckhohn 1953).*
   a. Explain feelings and statements by the understanding of changing needs. For example, a man who has been married fourteen years says, "I don't love my wife anymore. She just doesn't excite me. She's not my kind. We have nothing in common."
   b. Predict what your family life would be like if your parents still had the same needs as they had when you were born. State what their needs and desires were then, and see if satisfying those needs and desires would be beneficial to you or to them *now.*
   c. State how your needs and desires of last year would fit your circumstances now.
   d. In order for the students to get some notion of their own hierarchy of needs or preferences, have them describe real situations in which they must make a decision which will affect them greatly–decisions such as leaving home, deciding to marry, taking a job, deciding to live at a certain place, etc. Although these situations are not mutually exclusive in that some or all of them could take place simultaneously, narrow the choice to one.
      (1) State the problems in the decision: cost, who will be hurt or benefited, efficiency, future, etc.
      (2) State your preferences in this particular situation if no one else were involved.
      (3) State the objections if only *your* preferences were to be considered.
      (4) Go through a private or counseling-type soliloquy using the preferences and the objections. State the preference and then say, "On the other hand . . ." and then state the objections.
      (5) After going through all the preferences and objections, come to

the most workable conclusion in which you get some preferences and make some concessions. Note the preferences on which you would not make concessions. This shows your hierarchy.

e. Read and discuss *Behind Every Face* by Fane and Fane (1970), a publication which includes three books about differing needs.

3. *To recognize when meeting one's own needs is interfering with meeting another's needs and so endangering or limiting a relationship.*

a. Write what you dislike about a certain person or a group of people such as a boy or boys in general, parents or your parents, teachers or your teacher, etc.

Whatever list is made will show as many of the writer's needs as it does the faults or needs of the person being written about. For example, the following list* of disliked behavior about boys by girls (Klemer 1970):

		Boy's Needs	Girl's Needs
(1)	They're conceited.	Recognition	
(2)	They're changeable.	Response	
(3)	They make too many sexual advances.	Recognition	
(4)	They call too late.		Security
(5)	They suggest the same old places to go.		New Experience

b. (Have everyone stand up.) Imagine yourself in a large party such as a school party for freshmen in order to get acquainted. As you stand there with a cup of punch in hand, what is your first desire? (After a few minutes, ask the following questions:)

(1) To look for a familiar face?
(2) To stand hoping someone will come to you?
(3) To think, but not move, about how you should introduce yourself?
(4) To go immediately to someone you don't know and begin talking?
(5) To get your old friends together and stay together throughout?
(6) To check continuously for people who do not have someone talking to them and go to them and introduce them to someone?

Encourage the students to express their feelings, fears and needs, and how they may help or hinder relationships. Ask them to express

*From pp. 80-81 in *Marriage and Family Relationships* by Richard H. Klemer. Copyright ©1970 by Richard H. Klemer. Used by permission of Harper & Row, Publishers, Inc.

whose needs they were meeting as they decided what to do. One way to encourage the timid is to suggest that they can make the first move when they realize that the others are probably feeling the same way and would welcome someone's coming to talk with them.

4. *To apply the generalizations that (a)* ***mutual need meeting*** *is a pleasant combination; (b) two flexibles help each other fit; (c) some people are inflexible, forcing you to make all the changes; and (d) two inflexibles can't fit together.*

Make two puzzle pieces from fifteen or twenty (if you have thirty or forty students) six-inch squares of a variety of materials, from cardboard to paper, from stiffly woven cloth to loosely woven cloth. Shuffle the pieces. (Make sure that there are at least two or three pieces that won't fit, no matter how flexible; in other words, leave their matching pieces out.) Pass these puzzle pieces out to the class members and ask them to find their partners. The students will noisily try to fit the pieces. They will stretch the flexible ones and will be disappointed when their inflexible ones won't change. They will feel the joy in flexibility; they will feel the frustration of inflexibility. Those students without a partner will feel the impact of no one to fit them no matter how flexible their puzzle piece is.

Ask them to reveal some of their feelings and to transfer the feelings in the exercises to real-life situations.

Creative compromise is that situation when two people are flexible enough to make brand new plans when neither one wanted exactly what the other one wanted.

a. People like each other better when the puzzle pieces fit—when they meet each other's needs. (Great joy when partner was found.)
b. There are many people who can meet your needs. (Several pieces and spaces alike.)
c. The more flexible the person, the more easily he can stretch to fit or meet the needs of others (soft foam).
d. Some people only appear flexible (hard foam).
e. Some people can change to fit the situation (fit a soft foam puzzle piece to an odd fitting piece). It's easier for some people than others to change (easier for foam than paper.)
f. If a person has to change too much, he loses his own identity (tear up a puzzle piece to fit unusual hole).

Perception

Teaching Techniques

1. *To understand that* ***perception is truth*** *to the individual and that the perception, not just the facts, must change in order for any change in*

behavior to occur (Rogers 1961). Thomas (1917) said, "If a situation is defined as real, it is real in its consequences."

a. Use the classic problem of presenting the students with four boxes (small as matchboxes if necessary) and asking them to construct a corral and barn.

   Give them several minutes to work. Probably no one will construct the corral and barn because of a perceptual set.

   Then tear or cut the boxes into their component parts–four sides and a bottom–and give them the same construction problem.

   Note the difference in ability to change behavior when the perception changed from "boxes" to "flat rectangles."

   Discuss this changed perception and its effects on their behavior.

b. Using the above introduction to change in perception, use a drop-in-the-basket technique of analyzing and discussing the following case. (Each time a new piece of information is added, the perception, and subsequently the action or behavior of the student changes.)

THE CASE OF MIKE

Mike, at eighteen years of age, has just been ordered by his grandmother to pack his clothes, gather his possessions, and move out of her house. He does not know where he can go. (What are your perceptions of the situation at the moment?)

He finished high school two months ago and has an excellent job as assistant manager of the sports department in a department store. He has recently purchased a compact car and will have trouble paying for both his car and an apartment of his own. (What changes have occurred in your perceptions? Describe Mike the way you see him. Speculate on what the grandmother is like.)

Mike is the oldest of four children. His parents divorced when he was ten years old, and he lived with his mother, who remarried, until he was fifteen. Then after his father remarried, he went to live with him. When his father separated from his stepmother a year later, he came to live with his grandparents. (How has this changed your perception? What questions do you want answered now? Have you any clues from what you know about people which would help you understand why his grandmother ordered him to leave her house?)

The grandfather has always been a heavy drinker but not an alcoholic. He is a typical traditional male who believes in working, paying his bills, ruling the house and wife, doing only the "masculine" work, and having the privilege of playing poker and coming and going as he wishes. (Does this affect your perception or begin to solidify your picture of Mike or either of the grandparents? What other questions need answering?)

The grandmother has worked almost all her life except for the time out to have two children. Although she complains about her husband's drinking and her having to do all the work around the house, including mowing the yard, she eventually goes ahead and does it. She also owns her own car and comes and goes pretty much as she pleases. They all work at different hours and shifts; therefore, regular meals together are almost unheard of. She just keeps some food cooked, the laundry done, and the house and yard in fair shape. (Is your perception changing any now? Does your changed perception change what you would expect Mike to do?)

During the year or more that Mike has lived with his grandparents he has worked part-time at the department store, and therefore he has barely had time to get his school work finished, let alone do anything in the house and yard. What little spare time he does have, he has to work on his motorcycle or his 10 speed bicycle or take his girl out. (Has the former perception changed measurably? What happens when we draw conclusions on too little evidence? How do our stereotypes and own perceptions about life affect our decisions?)

Since there is no garage, Mike has had to store his extra bike parts in the bedroom which has become quite crowded, especially when he has neglected to hang up his clothes or put anything else in order. When his grandmother has asked him to clean up the mess or at least bring his dirty clothes out, he has yelled at her to mind her business. He has minded his own business, and he hasn't wanted her butting into his. He, in fact, has come and gone as he pleases, also. He has begun to stay out very late at night and then more often all night. She has not known where he was. Finally she tells him she cannot take the mental and physical anguish of his insults and the extra work he puts on her. (What would you tell him now? What would you tell her now? How did the situation grow to these proportions? Was it an inevitable situation? How did your perception change with each new bit of knowledge? What else would you have to know to make other changes in your perception and therefore your behavior?)

Note: Another way to teach how perceptions affect one's behavior is to give half of the students the whole case to begin with and read the case in parts to the others. The half that had read the case in full would be instructed to withhold comment but to record their observations and thoughts about how too little information affects perception.

2. *To evaluate the effects of perceptions.*
   a. Show the students a picture which will elicit differing perceptions from the students and discuss the reason for the differing perceptions. If the students begin to think in terms of "right" and "wrong" perceptions, remind them that a perception is never right or wrong except as it elicits behavior that is considered right or wrong by the cultural standards. What action would you as observer take? Why? On what basis would you take this action? Would your action be beneficial to anyone? How?
   b. Show the film "Up Pill, Down Pill" to elicit various perceptions about the use of pills for controlling one's spirits.
3. *To understand that accusations become a part of one's perception about others and to apply this understanding to one's use of circumstantial evidence and hearsay.*

a. Read excerpts of Guy de Maupassant's "The Piece of String" (reprinted in the Literature chapter).
   (1) Discuss how false accusations never really are removed from anyone's perceptions.
   (2) What are the implications of accusing or being accused without evidence?

b. Using the empathetic approach, describe some situation in which a person has been accused and you are using the principle that once a person is accused, it is difficult to overcome the accusation because what is learned first has less interference (Skinner 1953). Continuing to use the empathetic approach, describe how that person must feel. The following are some sample accusations that people have had to suffer through:
   (1) The man was suspected of embezzling company funds, but no conclusive proof was found that he either did or did not.
   (2) The girl was accused of lying, but it was never proven that she had lied.
   (3) The woman who was accused of being inept was suspect from then on, even though many people came to her defense.

c. Read the following and discuss:
   "J. B." by Archibald MacLeish (1957-60), a play showing how the Biblical character Job was misperceived and how he misperceived God's plan.
   All My Friends Are Going to be Strangers by Larry McMurtry (1973), a book showing how perceptions change friends to strangers.
   "The Vacation" by Joe A. Porter (1972), a story about the misperception of family and neighbors when the father wanted to have a unique vacation.

4. *To understand that* ***perceptions*** *of people may be gained* ***by*** *the* ***association*** *of someone with certain persons, things, or events.*
   a. Where do these sayings gain their strength?
      "Birds of a feather flock together."
      "Water will seek its own level."
      "People become more alike the longer they live together."
   b. Play the following game of associations. Divide the class into four sections. Have one section present words one at a time such as "blue jeans," "beach," "backyard," "car," "drink," "pink," "black," "yellow," "bikini," "boots," or "bare" and have the other three sections make associations of (1) people, (2) ideas, and (3) things, respectively, as each stimulus word is presented. This exercise illustrates the principle of association in that the qualities of one

person are taken on by the other person according to the beliefs one has. When the class is divided into designated areas, the students will see that there are many perceptions about any one concept. This is a good lead-in to a discussion about *misperceptions* about people because of associations.

5. *To understand that* ***perceptions*** *of others may be gained* ***through stereotyping****, a process of both generalization and discrimination (Skinner 1953).*
   a. How do these sayings gain their strength?
      "You expect that of their kind or ilk."
      "It is just like that kind to do that."
      "Just like a woman."
      "Just like a man."
      "People do revert to their basic nature when under stress."
   b. Although stereotyping is an efficient way of thinking, it could also be disastrous when one is defining the expectations of a person. Set the stage by giving these examples of discrimination and generalization.
      (1) Two distinct genders of the human species may be discriminated—male and female; when the characteristics which were used to *discriminate* these two genders are known, the characteristics may be *generalized* to every other male or female. The discriminating characteristics are the primary and secondary sex characteristics which are physical in nature. However, there is great variation in these characteristics.
      (2) Five relatively distinct regions of the United States have been defined, e.g., North, South, East, Midwest, and West; when one has knowledge of the characteristics which were used to *discriminate* or define these regions, particularly the people who live in these regions, these characteristics may be *generalized* to every other person in a particular region. However, there is great variation in these characteristics.
      (3) Two accepted and legally distinct maturity levels of people have been discriminated—adult and child (major and minor); when one knows the characteristics which were used to *discriminate* these two maturity levels, the characteristics may be *generalized* to every person in the two levels. However, there is great variation in these characteristics.

   After reading these three examples of discrimination and generalization as they cause one to stereotype people, ask the students to make up examples of their own, such as races, religion, socioeconomic levels, families, neighborhood, etc. From this discussion show

how stereotyping is efficient and yet damaging if the great variety of characteristics is not considered before making a judgment.

Self-Image

Teaching Techniques

1. *To become aware of one's own image of oneself.*
   a. Rank the following characteristics from "most like me" to "least like me"

Apathetic	Anxious	Plain looks
Calm	Sense of humor	Sensible
Honest	Leader	Lonely
Wasteful	Convincing	Creative
Cheerful	Sure	Saving
Dependable	Loving	Good looks
Apprehensive	Energetic	

Then rearrange the characteristics to describe two other people, and speculate on whether this would be the arrangement those other two people would have made. Speculate on how you think someone else would rank these characteristics of you.
Note that all these rankings and speculations were done by you; no one else saw them and no one else ranked you. What you have just put on paper is your image of yourself.
(Only in classes where the students know each other well and where they are aware of the importance of ranking each other should you ever allow them to rank each other.)

   b. Read this quotation: "This above all, to thine own self be true; and it must follow, as the night the day, thou canst not then be false to any man." (From Shakespeare's *Hamlet*, Act I, Sc. 3.)

Discussion Questions

(1) What is complete honesty?
(2) Is it more honest to tell all for cathartic exercises ("to get it off one's chest") or to use discretion?
(3) How can one be true to oneself?
(4) Is it more true to do as one pleases or to know one's desires and at the same time know how far one can go?

   c. Read this quotation and consider the implications of knowing one's qualities: ". . .I was not slow to discover that I lacked the qualities needed to play the brilliant role of which I dreamed; both my good qualities and my defects proved obstacles. I was not sufficiently virtuous to command respect, but I had too much integrity to adapt myself to all those petty practices then necessary for quick success. . . . When by chance I have been obliged to speak in a bad cause or to take a wrong path, I have immediately found myself completely bereft of talent as well as enthusiasm. . . I should have made a very mediocre and clumsy rascal. . . . I also discovered that I completely lacked the art of holding men together and leading them as a body. It is only in a tête-à-tête that I show any dexterity, whereas in a crowd I am constrained and dumb" (Tocqueville 1949).

d. Role play the situation in which one person in a pair is instructed to tell all his or her good qualities and the other person is instructed (privately) to respond in either of two ways: (1) encourage the person or (2) reject the attempt of the other person.

Any of the following pairs might be used (either one of the pair may be the first speaker):

Parent and son or daughter
Man and woman
Peers
Student and teacher
Niece or nephew and uncle or aunt

Discussion Questions

(1) What are your strong points, abilities, things you do most comfortably, or things which are easiest for you?
(2) What are the hardest things you've ever done or the most distasteful things or things you cannot do, but people expect you to?
(3) When do you do the things you dislike to do, and why?
(4) How do you feel about saying "No" when you know you are incompetent or only mediocre?
(5) How do you feel about people calling on you because "you do it so easily"?
(6) How can you explain to people that you choose some of your activities for some personal gain and therefore these activities may, in the end, be more useful to others?

2. *To understand that one develops a self-image by evaluating oneself against others' standards (Cooley 1964).*

a. Role play the following:
(1) The part of the son or daughter who is telling all his or her good qualities to his or her parent(s).
(2) The part of the parent who is telling all his or her good qualities to a son or daughter.
(3) The parts of niece and aunt; two peers; student and teacher; son

who has been successful in a field different from what his father wanted; girl and boy, in which one person of each pair tells his or her own good qualities.

b. Compare the connotations of the words as they are used other than to describe body build and speculate on the unconscious effect on a person's self-image.

(1) Short
On the short end of the stick
Caught short
Short changed
Short of the mark

(2) Tall
Stand tall
Head and shoulders above
Tall in the saddle

(3) Average
Just average
Above average
No more than average

(4) Skinny
Skinny serving of food
Bare bones of a report

(5) Fat
Dead weight
Excess baggage
Waste

c. Many people are referred to as chronic "losers" because they aren't accepted anywhere. *Newsweek* magazine featured "Games Singles Play" (16 July 1973), in which it was said that the fervent push for happiness has again shown an attrition rate which is higher than hoped for. Read the whole article or just the excerpt below and discuss how the "losers" were really people who were measuring themselves by others.

> Therein, it seems, lies the dark side of the singles world. There are players who score and those who strike out, yet for both a sobering degree of loneliness and *tristesse* seems to be built into the rules. It is no revelation that the physically unattractive and socially maladroit find the singles game a never-ending round of rejection. But what does surprise is the prevalence of unhappiness among the very singles who appear ostensibly to be living the Mary Tyler Moore life (p. 57).

d. Describe on paper or orally what a camera would see if a picture

were taken of you now. Describe what a camera would see if a picture were taken of another person in the class.
For example: The hair is just below the shoulders. It is loose. It may not have been combed. The lips are apart, but not smiling. Then describe the picture from a judgmental point of view and explain why these particular critical words entered the picture. For example: That long hair is a tangled mess; probably hasn't been washing or combed in weeks.

e. Show "Johnny Lingo," a film about a South Seas Island girl who thought she was homely until her husband purchased her for a higher price than any other girl on the island had ever been purchased.

3. *To understand the complexity of factors affecting self-image and behavior; among these are body build, inherent activity or energy level, intellectual capacity, reinforcement of behaviors, and situations one happens to encounter (Hollister 1968).*

   a. Note several people who have one of the above characteristics in common and then compare the other characteristics to see the impact that the other characteristics have had on this one singled-out characteristic.
   For example:
   Characteristics of three men: Besides the commonality of inherent high intellectual capacity, other characteristics of these three are listed:

	Person 1	Person 2	Person 3
(1) Body build:	Tall, slim	Tall, muscular	Average height, overweight
(2) Reinforcement	Rigid	Rigid	Very lax
(3) Situations encountered:	Stable home life	Reared by one grandmother	Stable home life
(4) Energy level:	Slow	Moderate	Active

   Discuss how these various aspects of a person's life interact to make his personality what it is. Although rigid reinforcements of behavior may cause some people to rebel, some other aspects, such as the good self-image of the tall muscular person, may have overcome any rebellion he may have felt by the rigid rearing of his grandmother.

   b. Present the following outline of how self-esteem is affected by making transparencies of each separate number or draw illustrations on the board as you present the ideas.

BASIC EMOTIONAL NEEDS*

(1) We each need to feel:
+loved, cared about
+valued, respected
+significant, worthwhile
+safe and secure
+that one belongs and is accepted

(2) Our emotional needs are met by experiences that evoke within us the feelings of being cared about, valued, significant, safe, accepted, such as:

close friendships
satisfying work
loving relationships
goal achievement

(3) Experiences that meet emotional needs and help to build our self-image (one's sense of self, picture of who we are).

Rewarding experiences help build a positive self-image.

Defeating experiences help build a negative self-image.

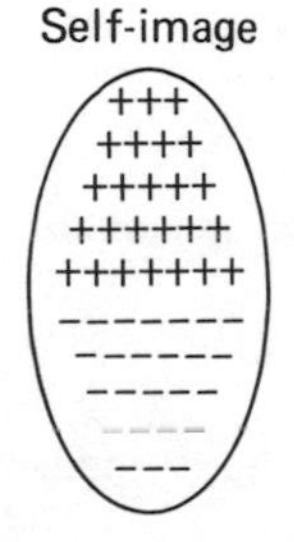

(+) = I am lovable, accepted, secure, valued, etc.

(-) = I am not liked, inadequate, unsafe, etc.

Most of us have some positive and some negative feelings about ourselves.

(4) How we feel about ourselves (our self-image) affects how we feel about others (how we relate).

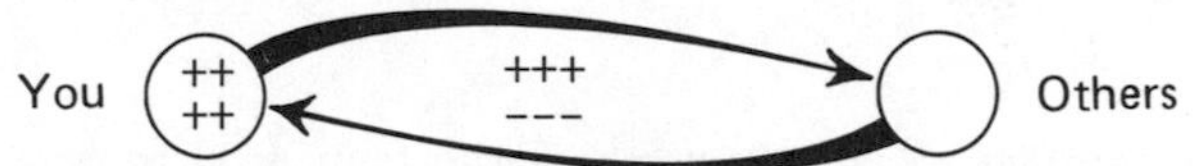

People who feel good about themselves tend to feel good about others—and communicate it—and often win a positive response. A negative self-image often leads to negative relationships and responses.

*Adapted from *Basic Emotional Needs* transparencies by William G. Hollister Chicago: National Congress of Parents and Teachers, 1968. Used by permission of the author.

(5) Our self-image is built in our interactions with significant other people in our lives.

Mother, father	++ / --	child's developing self-image
Teachers, youth leaders, peers	++++ ++++ / ---- ---	expands and elaborates
Peers, spouses, bosses, children	+++++ ++++++ / ------ ----- ---	to form the adult sense of being a person

Need-meeting experiences and relationships reinforce and reconfirm our positive self-image.

(6) Inadequate meeting of emotional needs may create emotional learning-behavior problems.

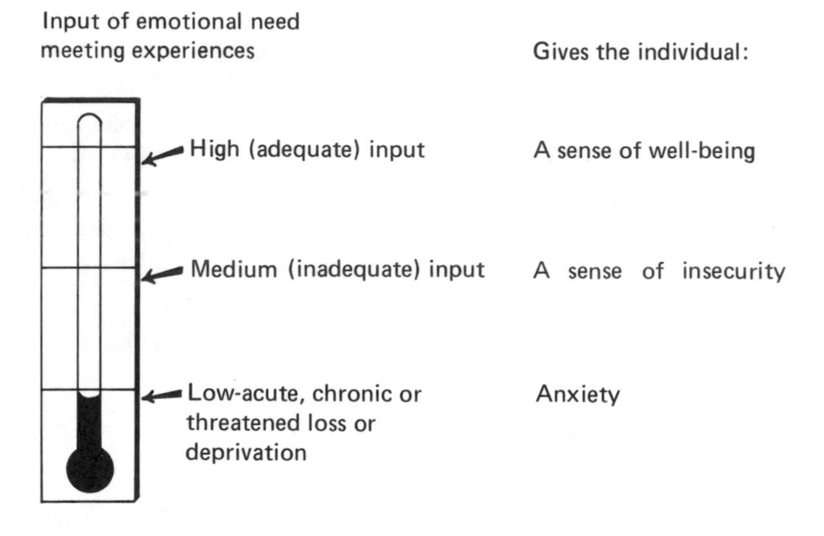

Important signals: Pain means the body is in trouble. Anxiety means deep insecurity and emotional trouble.

(7) Anxiety appears in several different forms.
   (a) In anxiety attacks, feeling weak or apprehensive, sweating, trembling, etc.
   or
   (b) Hidden behind anxious behavior—behavior that covers up or shows insecurity
   or

(c) Hidden and converted to nervous tension

Deprivation of basic emotional needs (real or threatened) causes anxiety.

(8) All these forms of anxiety can be
- –mild, moderate, or severe
- –transient, brief, or chronic
- –inconsequential or very disabling

(9) Depending on:
- (a) How much stress there is on the person
- (b) How well one's emotional needs are being met
- (c) How strong one's sense of self has been built

THE PERSON

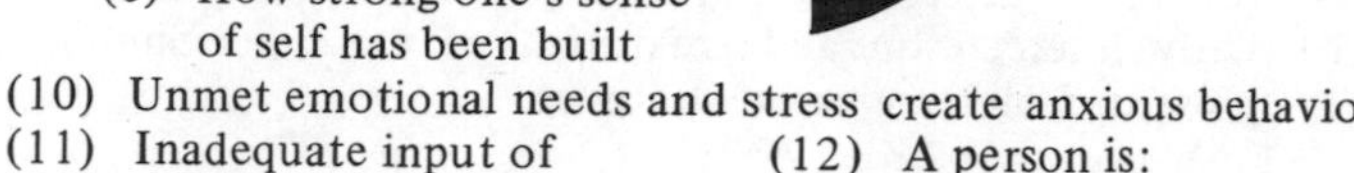

(10) Unmet emotional needs and stress create anxious behaviors.

(11) Inadequate input of
- --love
- --safety
- --acceptance
- --recognition

plus stresses:
- --demands
- --pressures
- --conflicts

help create

(12) A person is: overwhelmed and unable to cope with his feeling and the stresses–gradually and unawaredly slips into poor behavior.

(13) Fighting others
aggressive
hostile
controlling
bossy
blaming
bullying, etc.

Flight from others:
evasive
run away
shy
withdrawn
over confronting
dependent, etc.

or

To help
Don't attack the behavior
Attack the causes.

(14) Some people get nervous tension when they are anxious and insecure. Tension (or strong nervous impulses) pours down their inner (autonomic) nervous system.

Producing:

First:
Changes in organ function

Second:
Tissue damage if tension is prolonged.

Possible consequences

Asthma
Ulcers
Colitis

Coronary problems
High blood pressure
Sexual problems

(15) Acute or prolonged anxiety creates emotional illnesses.
  (a) The neuroses—fear, obsessions, hypochondriases, hysterias.
  (b) The psychoses—major depressions or escapes from reality in delusions.
  (c) The character disorders—deeply twisted personalities.

(16) Early interception and treatment of these persons might have prevented such major breakdowns.

(17) Help prevent emotional problems by providing adequate resources and experiences to help meet children's emotional needs.

(18) Good emotional needs inputs

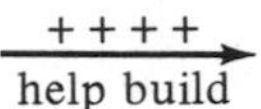

Stronger personalities, a more positive self-image, a greater capacity to love, to cope with stress, and to relate to others, and greater stability and security.

(19) Poor emotional needs inputs

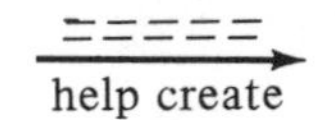

Anxious, insecure, dependent or overaggressive personalities. Anxious behavior or anxiety attacks, tensions that may lead to physical illness. Deep emotional illness.

(20) Self-image can be strengthened by providing experiences that meet emotional needs.

c. Using the following five generalizations about behavior, discuss the situations given below these generalizations (Kagan 1972):
  (1) Why people make excuses—It is difficult for us to accept responsibility for our own "cussedness"; therefore, we consciously and unconsciously blame others.
  (2) Why a person is not always the same—We act differently at different times and with different people because needs take on different order at different times.
  (3) Why parents and teachers are so demanding—For peace of

mind or security, people prefer to control whether it be through authoritarian means or through teaching self-discipline to others.

(4) Why men and women are different—People act according to what they have been taught and reinforeed to do.

(5) Why we can't believe the other person would do it—Our own perception is the most individual thing we have—it is like no one else's, but, when we realize that this is so, we are more likely to know why the other person does as he does.

Situation

A man sitting on the side of his bed in pain after a tremendous meal at a friend's house says, "I can't believe I ate the whole thing. I can't believe I ate the whole thing." Wife, half asleep in the other bed, says, "No, Ralph, I ate it." (Advertisement)

Situation

A girl finds herself two months pregnant and unmarried; her boyfriend is gone, and she has no money and is deciding what to do.

Situation

A girl who thought she was the only one loved by a certain boy finds she is one of many.

Situation

A boy who thought he was loved by the girl because she called on him to help her with her projects found she needed him for the projects, but she had not thought of love.

Situation

A grandmother gives her grandchildren money and privileges even when the parents disapprove.

4. *To understand that **behavior is caused** (unless now it has become habit) but that there are different causes for the same behavior of different people (Kagan 1972).*
   a. Compare people who play games or jokes to keep a light, witty conversation, as to their motives.
      (1) One person has learned that this makes others feel comfortable.
      (2) Another does it to cover up his own insecurity.
      (3) Another has learned that this is one way to make small talk and keep conversations going (See "The Cavalier Game" in Berne 1964).
      (4) Another does it to hurt other people by catching them in the joke.
   b. Compare people who are alone a great deal.
      (1) One prefers being alone in order to think through problems or situations.
      (2) Another is paranoid or thinks others do not like him.

(3) Another is unlikeable and is shunned.
(4) Another is timid.
(5) Another cannot afford to make friends because of his job.

c. Compare people who are one of the following: boisterous; sadistic; achievement-oriented; lackadaisical; solicitous; bitter; and many more. (You supply the varying underlying causes or have the students do this.)

Values

Teaching Techniques

1. *To assess one's own set of values (Simon et al. 1972).*

a. Designate a concept with a relatively strong emotional charge such as euthanasia, sexual intercourse under sixteen, legally limited number of children, trial marriage, or parental control after sixteen.

Draw a line on the board placing extreme views on each end of the line. Mark about five points on the line and number them. Ask each student to select the point which is where he thinks he stands on the issue.

Concept: Euthanasia

Absolute						Absolute
No	1	2	3	4	5	Yes
			Undecided			

Concept: Trial Marriage

Absolute						Absolute
No	1	2	3	4	5	Yes
			Undecided			

The points nearest the "absolute no" will be "no, except for . . ." and the points nearest the "absolute yes" will be "yes, but with reservations of . . ." No matter which number the student selects, ask him to finish the statements of "No, except for . . ." and "Yes, but with reservations of . . ."

In order to learn more about one's value system—that is, the organization of the total values—the students will need to have several of these concepts presented. After the students have placed themselves along the continuum for each of several concepts, ask some of the students to reveal their placement. After such a discussion, take one student who volunteers or use a hypothetical case and show that the student's total profile for all the concepts is an indication of his value system. Encourage each student to do the same for himself.

b. This technique is similar to that presented above. The exception is that under each concept there are several continua with opposites on the ends which are value judgments or feelings. This is called a semantic differential (Osgood, Suci, and Tannenbaum 1957).

The original semantic differential has seven points. You may select your own number.

Concept: Love

Good ______________________________ **Bad**
1 2 3 4 5 6 7

Warm ______________________________ **Cold**

Orange ______________________________ **Blue**

Exciting ______________________________ **Dull**

Productive ______________________________ **Unproductive**

Freedom ______________________________ **Prison**

You may use the same opposites for each concept or you may vary them as in the next example.

Concept: Jealousy

Good ______________________________ **Bad**
1 2 3 4 5 6 7

Useful ______________________________ **Detrimental**

Normal for Adults ______________________________ **Childish**

Beautiful ______________________________ **Ugly**

c. Read the story "I'm Going Home" reprinted in the chapter on Music and Pictures. Stop the reading just before the tree was reached and ask the students to finish the story explaining why they chose that ending. Their own values will be explicit in their answers.

d. Show a picture of some human interaction which could be interpreted in a variety of ways, and ask the students to respond individually on paper before group discussion. Such questions as "What is going on now?" "What preceded this?" "What will happen later?" are good for starting their thinking and for discussion efficiency. Pictures which have proven to be multi-interpreted show such interactions as the following:

A couple in a car
A group of young people in a parked convertible
A man with his arm around a young teen-age boy

A woman with a scowl on her face
An old man and old woman kissing
A person with his back to a group

The students' values come out as they describe the interaction as they see it. When students are willing to give different interpretations to the picture, their value of looking at many sides becomes evident.

The assessment of where people stand or what their values are seems to be easy enough. The difficult problem is in judging this value system. Evaluation is always done with a set of criteria such as the students' values in relation to others' values; students' values in relation to the behavior the values will influence, etc.

e. A very quick, simple, and fairly accurate assessment of values is asking the students to complete the following sentences about any concept.

Concept: Fifty-year-old Man

I think ____________________
I believe ____________________
I value ____________________
I want ____________________
I am willing to ______________

The same follow-up procedure is used here. Give several other concepts and ask students to respond. Ask the group to discuss, or ask people with opposing views to debate. And finally, describe a hypothetical student by his answers. Evaluation of the students' values are always in light of some specified criteria such as cultural values, peer group values, or optimum development of the person.

2. *To understand how* ***values gain or lose status****.*

a. Give several examples of a generalization and help the students see the similarities and differences among the examples so that they arrive at a generalization which explains the behavior in each example. Students have to be taught this inductive method; they do not automatically begin to compare examples and arrive at a general statement.

Read the following losses in status of certain values:

(1) The value of a large family is losing status rapidly under the influence of Zero Population Growth advocates.
(2) The value of neatness in dress lost some of its status in the 1960s under the influence of disdain for materialism.
(3) The value of stability in marriage is losing its status under the influence of less strict divorce laws, less criticism for divorced people, and the ability of single women to make a living.

(4) The value of chastity for women is losing its status under the influence of contraception, greater personal mobility, and lack of its being a prerequisite to marriage.

Before allowing reactions to or discussion about these statements, ask the students to look for similarities in the reasons for losses and to make a general statement which could explain why values lost status. The general statement they may give will be something like this, "When there is no longer a need for the holding of a value or the behavior, then the value loses status." They will arrive at this generalization usually after some specific prodding questions such as:

What was the original purpose of each value?

What were the consequences when the value or behavior was not adhered to?

What are the consequences now if the value is still held?

What are the consequences now if the value is lost?

These questions will give some specific substantiation for the loss of values. When students learn to analyze statements logically, they feel more comfortable with the final generalization. To challenge the brighter students, ask them to predict some value losses in the future based on the generalization that values lose status as the need for adherence to the value becomes less. If they need a starter, here's one:

> The value of ownership of single houses will decrease in status under the influence of increased benefits of attached houses such as permanent maintenance, playgrounds and parks, privacy with security, and reasonable cost.

The same technique of inductive reasoning can be applied to how values gain status. Actually, most of the statements made earlier can be altered to show the gain in status of small families, casual dress, and serious marriage.

b. Deductive reasoning is essentially the opposite of inductive reasoning in procedure. Instead of the examples being given first from which the generalization is drawn, the generalization is given first and is followed by examples. The students learn by being taught how the examples are alike and different and then applying the original generalization. Teaching by deductive reasoning is used for efficiency and in cases where the students would not have the background to induce their own generalizations. Areas best taught by deductive reasoning are those which are new to the student, such as in theories of human development or history of the family or principles of human behavior.

Generalization about Loss of Status of a Value

When a cultural value begins to lose status, it does not lose its status with everyone at the same time because it is difficult to give up conditioned beliefs even if they are no longer efficient.

Examples

(1) A girl who does not have a date will hesitate to call a boy even if it means both that girl and that boy stays home, and even though the other girls whom she knows do make initial contacts with the boys.

(2) Paying cash for everything may have at one time meant a person was known to be very honorable, but the same practice now could create a person's not being known at all. Yet some people still prefer to pay cash.

Generalization about the Gain in Status of a Value

A value begins to be more accepted the more one is exposed to the acceptable or nondestructive behavioral manifestations of it.

Examples

(1) The value of longer hair styles for men gained status as people saw that the hair itself was not the culprit or the reason for destructive behavior.

(2) The value of individualism in a marriage gained status as neither men nor women were threatened by role reversals or differing schedules.

3. *To understand that **values fluctuate in rank order**.*

What was most important yesterday or last year may not be as important today but may return to "most important" status later on. Why? Because people have differing needs at differing times. People are criticized sometimes because they change their minds. A person who is too changeable too often is difficult to work with because we operate on our expectations from others. When that expectation is not the same, we have to change our way of acting.

When students learn that values do fluctuate in rank of status within each person and that it is a common occurrence and, in fact, a self-preserving act, they are not as worried about their own and others' fluctuations. Some stability of rank order of values, however, is necessary for security.

Under what circumstances would the following values be your most outstanding or leading guide for your behavior?

Friendly, courteous approach to fellow workers

Thinking freely, almost daydreaming, with no overt sign of being busy

Calling home to let someone know you'll be late

Chatting with someone in order to get better acquainted

Generalization

The rank of status a value holds depends on the needs at the moment as well as the long-term outcome of the behavior.

4. *To understand how **values guide behavior** (Rokeach 1968; Simon et al. 1972; "Value Clarification" 1972).*

   Ask the students to write what they would do in the following situations. After they have finished, ask them to think why they said they would do that particular thing. Their answers to the "why" will vary from simple expediency answers to statements of their values.

   What do you do when:

   a. You find a dollar bill on the street?
   b. You find a dollar bill in the classroom?
   c. You are given trading stamps?
   d. You are given a gift for no reason other than the person thinks you're very nice?
   e. You have a second invitation which is better than the first but both are at the same time?
   f. You have an invitation from your employer which conflicts with a prior invitation from your sister?

5. *To understand that **changing values of self** is not a mere decision.*

   In Mager's book *They Really Oughta Wanta* (1970) the notion is very clear that people do not do things because they "ought" to want to. They change behavior when the rewards (intrinsic or extrinsic) warrant the change. So is it with values. If valuing comes from believing because of past knowledge of the benefits, then to change a value, one must change the benefits.

   Have the students read the following list and select two actions which they might do and under what circumstances.

   a. Change jobs every year
   b. Change mates every year
   c. Give away all your money
   d. Compliment a hateful person
   e. Complete all unfinished projects
   f. Tell your strengths

   After they have selected, then ask them to consider how long it would take to feel comfortable in doing these activities. This process will show them the difficulty in changing a value.

Summary

The objectives and teaching techniques in this chapter are based on the assumption that human behavior is a result of gratification of needs, some of which are innate and some of which are learned. It is also assumed that the level of these needs varies from person to person and from time to time. How needs change in addition to the problem of trying to meet others' needs while meeting one's own needs is illustrated in the teaching techniques. Needs are influenced by perception, self-image, and values, and all four of these affect human behavior.

This chapter on human behavior preceded the other chapters in this part of the book because one's understanding of human behavior affects the understanding of the various experiences among people in different settings. This understanding is essential to becoming more adept in communication, the subject of the following chapter.

References

Berne, Eric. *Games People Play*. New York: Grove Press, Inc., 1964.

Cooley, Charles H. *Human Nature and the Social Order*. New York: Schocken, 1964.

Fane, Arthur, and Fane, Xenia. *Behind Every Face*. Boston: Ginn and Company, 1970. (Includes three books: *A Changing Person, A Challenge of Success, A Family*)

"Games Singles Play." *Newsweek,* 16 July 1973, pp. 52-58.

Hall, Calvin S. and Lindsey, Gardner. *Theories of Personality*, 2nd ed. New York: John Wiley and Sons, Inc., 1970.

Hollister, William G. "Basic Emotional Needs." Chicago: National Congress of Parents and Teachers, 1968. (Transparencies.)

Kagan, Jerome. *Understanding Children*. New York: Harcourt Brace Jovanovich, 1972.

Klemer, Richard H. *Marriage and Family Relationships*. New York: Harper & Row, 1970.

MacLeish, Archibald. "J. B." In *Broadway's Best*. New York; Doubleday, 1957-60.

McMurtry, Larry. *All My Friends Are Going to be Strangers*. New York: Pocket Books, 1973.

Mager, Robert F. *They Really Oughta Wanta*. Palo Alto, California: Fearon Publishers. 1970.

Maslow, Abraham H. *Motivation and Personality*. New York: Harper and Row, 1954.

Maupassant, Guy de. "The Piece of String." *Yvette–A Novelette and Ten Other Stories*. Freeport, New York: Books for Libraries Press, Reprinted, 1971.

Murray, H. A., and Kluckhohn, C. "Outline of a Conception of Personality." In *Personality in Nature, Society, and Culture*, 2nd ed., edited by C. Kluckhohn, H. A. Murray, and D. Schneider. New York: Knopf, 1953, pp. 3-52.

Osgood, Charles E.; Suci, George J.; and Tannenbaum, Percy H. *The Measurement of Meaning*. Urbana: University of Illinois Press, 1957.

Porter, Joe Ashby. "The Vacation." In *The Best American Short Stories 1972,* edited by Martha Foley. New York: Ballantine Books, 1972.

Rogers, Carl R. *On Becoming a Person*. Boston: Houghton Mifflin Co., 1961.

Rokeach, Milton. *Beliefs, Attitudes and Values*. San Francisco: Jossey-Bass, 1968.

Simon, Sidney B.; Home, Leland W.; and Kirschenbaum, Howard. *Values Clarification: A Handbook of Practical Strategies for Teachers and Students.* New York: Hart Publishing Co., 1972.

Skinner, B. F. *Science and Human Behavior.* New York: The MacMillan Co., 1953.

Thomas, William I. "The Persistence of Primary-Group Norms in Present Day Society." In *Suggestions of Modern Science Concerning Education,* by H. S. Jennings, et al. New York: Macmillan, 1917, pp. 159-197.

Tocqueville, Alexis. *Recollections.* New York: Columbia Press, 1949.

"Value Clarification" (entire issue). *Forum.* New York: The J. C. Penny Company, Inc., Spring/Summer, 1972.

Westlake, Helen Gum. *Relationships: A Study in Human Behavior.* Boston: Ginn and Co., 1969.

Suggested Films

Johnny Lingo (1970, 30 min.). Brigham Young U., Provo, Utah.

Up Pill, Down Pill (1970, 13½ min.). BFA Educ. Media, 2211 Michigan Ave., Santa Monica, Calif.

Chapter 10

Communication

Teaching about communication involves four factors: (1) knowledge of concepts about communication, (2) knowledge of the dynamics of communication, (3) increased ability to communicate, and (4) some skill in diagnosing and effecting improvement in communication. Each of these four factors will be presented briefly below. Methods for teaching communication in specific family areas are also included in the following chapters.

Concepts About Communication

Communication is that process by which any message is passed from one person to another person. It is said that a person cannot *not* communicate because some message always gets through. The words used to send the message are accompanied by gestures, tone of voice, facial expressions, and variations in volume. These nonverbal aspects are called meta-communication. They portray or give away the connotations of the actual words that are used. The message received may also be altered because of the interpretations of the verbal and nonverbal message made by the receiver because of some past interpretations. Messages are innocently distorted as they are conveyed from one person to another (Klemer 1970; Waltzlawick et al. 1967).

Teaching Techniques

1. *To understand that **various messages** are communicated in any transaction between people.*
   a. Note the varying interpretations that might be made from these statements. The interpretation will be affected by how the receiver views the sender as well as by the words that are said.

      "I can't believe I ate the whole thing."

      "I'm going out."

      "I may or may not be back."

"It will benefit us more if you will sit at the table with these other guests rather than at the head table at the banquet."

"You must have rocks in your head."

"You're the best I've ever seen at that job."

b. Using the students' interpretations or the ones given below, give illustrations of how both the sender (talker) and the receiver (listener) may have interpreted the statements differently according to each one's own needs of the moment. For the statement, "You're the best I've ever seen at that job," the sender may have meant, "You really are good, but I'd better make it sound better to keep you working," whereas the receiver may have understood it to mean, "I'm really good. I just got a big compliment. I'm the best. I'm better than the others." Why might these two people have had different meanings from the statements? Assume the sender had experienced the following just prior to the statement. The sender had a rush order come in and he was in great need of excellent work. The statement may then have meant he was pushed and tense and was more willing to go a little to extremes in his encouragement.

Assume the receiver had had the following experience prior to the statement. The receiver had seen some of the other people turn out some very good work and was concerned about his own. The statement from the sender could have come through to mean that the receiver could quit worrying and not be so anxious and maybe relax a little now.

c. Read the following statement and get class reaction (or print it and post it during the study of communication).

> I know you believe you understand what you think I said, but I am not sure you realize that what you heard is not what I meant (author unknown).

2. *To understand that **some people mean exactly what they say** and that nothing else should be read into the statement.*

Use some of the statements above and discuss how the receiver can distort the meaning when nothing more was intended than the absolute meaning.

The statement, "It will benefit you more if you will sit at the table with these other guests rather than at the head table at the banquet" probably meant just that. But if the receiver thought he was being pushed out, the relationship between the two people would be altered.

3. *To gain experience in awareness of the duality of the **denotations and connotations** in communication.*

a. Divide the class into groups of three: one sender, one receiver, one observer. Have the sender tell something. The receiver may respond to the sender. The observer is to note the totality of the message and tell the sender and receiver his interpretation. The receiver and sender each then tells what he thought he said and heard. Some of these experiences would be helpful to relate to the whole class for further discussion.

b. Divide the class into pairs. For variety, ask one or more pairs to perform for the entire group. The sender would tell something and the receiver would respond by telling what he heard, including the meta-communication. The sender would respond by telling how accurate the interpretation was.

c. A class discussion could follow each presentation. After about two or three presentations before the entire class, the other students could participate in the exercise as individual pairs.

4. *To be aware of and to be able to interpret nonverbal communication (meta-communication).*

a. Have a student (or the teacher) make one of the following statements and ask two or three students (not necessarily the whole class) to *describe* the meta-communication and *interpret* the meaning of the statements accordingly.

"I'm so glad you came." (Stretched smile, cursory pat on the shoulder)

"I can't eat lunch with you today as we had planned." (Pained look)

"Hey, where are you going?" (Demanding)

"Do you expect me to do all of that?" (Pleasant smile)

b. Request about five of the students to ask you (or another student) if you have seen a certain controversial movie. Each student should ask the same question in exactly the same way. Your answer would be either "Yes" or "No" each time the question is asked, but with each *yes* or *no* you should *imply* a different feeling as, "I wouldn't be seen there" to "I wish I had time to go" to "I enjoyed every minute of it" to "I didn't know it was showing" to "I didn't get turned on by it, but it was OK." Ask the students to interpret your answers.

c. Give partners a choice of certain messages to convey to the other *non*verbally. To begin with, the partners should not speak or touch, but later they may touch to convey the message. The answer should be nonverbal. Indicate one of these messages but don't speak. "I wish you would notice me more because I am a very likeable person and I think we could enjoy each other."

"You drive me wild when you won't speak up for yourself."

"You're really very nice and I would like to know you better."

"I need to talk to you desperately."

After a few minutes have the partners speak and let them discuss how well the message came across.

5. *To understand the **distortion in communicating** information as it is transmitted from the original source through several individuals to a final destination.*

From the class select six students to participate and send five of the six outside the room. The other will remain in the room with the rest of the class.

The teacher (or student) reads a message to the first participant: "I can't wait to report to the police what I saw in that accident. I must get to the hospital immediately. The truck, heading south, was turning right at the intersection when the sports car, heading north, attempted to turn left. When they saw that they were turning into the same lane, they both honked their horns but proceeded to turn without slowing down. In fact, the sports car seemed to be accelerating just before the crash."

The teacher reads the message to the first participant. Each participant is brought into the room one at a time. The first participant repeats what he heard to the second participant, and this exchange continues until all but the sixth participant return to the room. The sixth participant becomes the policeman, and after the fifth participant repeats the story, the policeman writes it on the blackboard. The teacher then writes the original message, and it is compared with the policeman's message. Group discussion may follow with students (observers) reporting what they heard (Pfeiffer and Jones 1970, p. 14).

6. *To understand the **reasons** for a student's **own interpretation** of a scene.*

   a. Show a shadowed picture of a man with his arm on a boy's shoulders. Ask the class to describe in words what they see in the picture. Show them the title of the article from which the picture came. Ask them to describe the picture again. (Make up two titles such as: "A Boy Needs a Father" and "When One Leads Another Astray.")

Questions

What are the varieties of interpretations of the picture?

What are the differences in the first stories and the second stories?

Why do some of the stories change? Why do some of the stories stay the same?

What is the stereotype of an adult male homosexual? Is this basis enough to read into a situation something that is not there?

Why would an article on homosexuality portray a pleasant relationship between a father and his son?

What in your background caused you to project your particular feelings into this scene?

b. Show a picture of an angry or crying child.
   Ask the class members to describe what happened just prior to this picture and what will happen in the next hour.

Questions

What do these facial expressions show—that is, how many different feelings does crying express?

What other ways can the feelings enumerated by the class be expressed?

What words can express these feelings as well as the behaviorial display?

Does everyone express the same feeling with the same words or behavior?

Dynamics of Communication

Why can people not say what they mean? Why can people not take it the way it is meant? Four reasons will be presented. There may be a lack of ability, a lack of security, a lack of selectivity, or a lack of desire to communicate (Klemer 1970).

Teaching Techniques

1. *To understand how a* ***limited vocabulary*** *on the part of either the sender or receiver limits communication.*
   a. Read the following statements which include technical terms and ask students to interpret them.

      "When a person died intestate in the eighteenth century, the primogeniture rule was used in designating the recipient."

      "After one has read the taxonomy, the theory about hierarchy was not as absolute."

   b. Read the following statements which are full of colloquialisms (vary this to suit the colloquialisms in your area).

      "Put the *gear* in the *boot*." (Put the luggage in the car trunk.)

      "*Cook* the eggs while I *fix* the rest." (Finish cooking the eggs while I prepare the rest of the meal.)

2. *To understand the* ***effect of fears or lack of security*** *on communication.*
   a. Fear of saying the wrong thing comes from a background of being punished for saying what was either wrong or taken to be wrong. Ask a student to tell the class about some experience. Then ask him what concerned him as he talked (fear of mispronunciation, fear of being laughed at, fear of being misunderstood, fear of not being clear, fear of sounding stupid). Then discuss the ways in which these fears are conditioned.

b. Fear of starting a conversation with someone occurs (1) because that person might take it wrong, (2) because that person might take it as license to keep the conversation going longer than you had intended, (3) because of fear of starting an argument, or (4) because of fear of getting an unfavorable reply.

Give four people each one of the four roles described above without their knowing the roles of the others. Then ask one of the four to select one of the others with whom to start a conversation. Each person will react as his role describes: (1) take everything wrong, (2) keep talking incessantly, (3) start an argument, or (4) give unfavorable replies. After the point has been demonstrated, ask the observing students to discuss how a person tends to develop this type of response and why it has such an effect on the other persons in the conversation.

3. *To evaluate the communication based on the criterion of **selectivity**.*

a. Read the following situation and speculate on how selection of time and words affected the man.

> "I see now what I should have seen last night," Myra told the counselor. "But it's too late. It's just three weeks ago since Tod was told by the doctor that he had Hodgkins disease and probably had less than a year to live. Last night he sat up crying in bed. I was still half asleep when I asked him what was wrong. 'Oh, my darling,' he said, 'I'm so worred about what will happen to you and the children after I'm gone!' I just didn't think, I guess, because I said to him too quickly, 'Oh, we'll be all right, darling. I can take care of the children!' It didn't seem to help him a bit. Now that I have thought it over, I know why."*

b. A child rushes in from school on a hot day and the mother says, "What did you do at school?" His answer will more than likely be, "Nothing much," or "Same old thing." If the same question was asked after he had some food or even as he was being tucked into bed, the answer might be a little more tolerable: "We began studying the Northwest Pacific."

A selective question may fire an interesting answer which communicates a great deal. "What was the worst thing that happened today?" The selection of the unusual question gets attention in that the child feels you really want to know and are not just making conversation. Usually an impish look comes over his face and he lets you in on some very wild things. Indicate why the timing was as important as the question.

4. *To understand that a person may **lack a desire to communicate** because*

*From p. 203 in *Marriage and Family Relationships* by Richard H. Klemer, Copyright © 1970 by Richard H. Klemer. Used by permission of Harper & Row, Publishers, Inc.

he is not motivated or that he may desire to communicate but lacks the ability or the courage.

Play a record of a comedian such as Bill Cosby ("Revenge" on RCA) and discuss several things such as his motivation to communicate as an entertainer and some students' desires to communicate as comedians. Have the students who would like to be comedians find out why the other students would not like to be. The reasons will bring out conditioned fears, feelings of inadequacies, family backgrounds that were quiet, and feelings that what they have to say is unimportant.

Skill in Communication

Knowledge of communication concepts and understanding of the dynamics of communication must be transformed into skills of communication. Application does not automatically follow knowledge and understanding. It is an entirely different learning process; therefore, if skill in communication is a goal, opportunities for application must be included in the teaching. Many of these exercises should be assigned for out-of-class work.

Teaching Techniques

1. *To say exactly what you mean and to mean exactly what you say.*
   a. Practice in class by having each student tell something meaningful to another and have the one listening tell what he heard.
   b. Ask students to keep a mental or written note on how many times other students had to ask them to repeat themselves or how many times the listener did not understand, shown by his doing something different or by turning the conversation to another topic.
   c. Practice in class by having each student tell another to do something and have the one listening do exactly what he was told. If the message was misinterpreted, the talker must try again.
2. *To be able to hear both the denotative and connotative meanings of a communication.*
   a. Give some of the students the following messages (half of them if you have a small group). The students should not use the words. They should beat around the bush, but the meaning should be there:

      "I don't need to study for this exam."
      "My parents just got a divorce."
      "I'm pregnant."
      "I hate some people."

      The other students are to be observers for the connotative meanings and discuss what they saw and heard.
   b. Each class member is to keep notes on times he has discriminated between denotative and connotative messages.

3. *To become* ***a responsible sender*** *(some things are better left unsaid).*
   a. Ask two or three of the students to tell their partners some bad news. Use either approach of being responsible or irresponsible.

      "Your roommate (or brother) just called to say that your room has been burglarized."

      "The test scheduled for day after tomorrow will be given tomorrow."

      The class will observe the responsibility (or lack of) taken by the sender not to frighten, threaten, or worry the receiver.
   b. Each class member is instructed to keep notes on how each one has handled a situation outside of class when the receiver needed to have the blow of the message softened or when the message might have been damaging to another person.
   c. Students are asked to keep a record (or remember past experiences) of two things: the times they chose not to tell all the facts and the reasoning for not telling all at that particular time. Without revealing what was not told or what was "sugar coated," encourage students to reveal their reasons for withholding to bring out these generalizations:
      (1) People stereotype or categorize people for efficiency and a particular incident told without understanding on the part of the receiver may label or categorize the sender to his detriment.
      (2) The receiver may lose confidence in the sender if he reveals his anxieties.
4. *To become* ***a responsible listener.***

   Along with being responsible for not telling what other people confide in you, the listener has another responsibility to provide the permissive atmosphere necessary for the other to feel free to talk.
   a. Ask all the students to write something on a piece of paper that would require a very responsible listener for them to tell that written message. Then ask them to write another message which would not require as much trust in the other person. These messages are to be placed in a box. One person at a time then draws out one message and proceeds to reveal this information to one or more class members who provide a permissive atmosphere.
   b. To understand that there is as much responsibility on the part of the listener to make the speaker secure as there is for the speaker not to alarm the listener, have the students pair off (or in any small group) and read the following quotation of Dinah Maria Mulock Craik twice. (Mimeograph it and give to each student.)

      As Dinah Maria Mulock Craik, an English novelist of the nineteenth century said:

> Oh, the comfort, the inexpressible comfort of feeling safe with a person, having neither to weigh thoughts nor measure words, but pouring them all right out, just as they are, chaff and grain together, certain that a faithful hand will take and sift them, keep what is worth keeping, and then with the breath of kindness, blow the rest away (quoted in Klemer 1970, p. 214).

Ask one of the pair, or group, to act as speaker and one to act as listener. The speaker is asked to tell one of the most foolish things he ever did. The listener is asked to listen to the words, the intent, and the facial expressions and to watch the body movements while at the same time applying the thought in the quotation. After the story is told, the speakers are asked how they felt while telling the story and whether or not they thought the listener responded with acceptance. Then ask the listeners how well they think they responded.

After this session, reverse the roles, but ask the speakers to tell a story of something they are proud they did; in fact, encourage bragging. Repeat the discussion session. Ask them also to discuss differences in ability to brag or to laugh at self. Some of the generalizations which might evolve are these:

(1) People who listen provide a therapeutic session for others.
(2) People learn to listen by practicing listening.
(3) People communicate more than they mean to say.
(4) People who are in an emotional state say disorganized things.
(5) It is usually easier to tell a foolish thing than to brag because we've been punished for bragging.

5. *To be able* ***to select the right words****, the right* ***timing****, and the right* ***place*** *in which to communicate.*

a. Set up the following role-playing scene. Select students to play a boy of fifteen and his mother and father. Give the boy this instruction: Ask your father for five more dollars to buy some equipment for your bicycle. Give these instructions to the father: Your money is already allocated, and there is nowhere to get it except by putting off the payment of something. You may never have done this in your life, and you don't believe in it. Give these instructions to the mother: You think your son should work for his money like his father did.

The observing students are to note the selectivity used by each of the three role players.

b. Select four people—one to play the part of the father and the other three each to play the part of his child. Send the three players of the children out of the room. (Tell each of them privately he is to ask for a motor bike.) Explain that the father will listen to a previously made tape of some boys and/or girls downgrading fathers. The father listens to the tape. Class should watch his expression and note how what he has heard affects his answer to his child. Bring in the first player (sixteen years old) who asks in his own way to have a motor bike. After enough conversation has occurred to show the effect of the tape on the reaction of the father, cut the scene. Call in the second child who will ask the same question but in his own way. Call in the third player.

Questions to the Class

(1) What examples of communication skills were exhibited by the father? By each of the players?
(2) Ask the father how he felt during the tape and during the three conversations with the children. Ask him if he changed his tactic from one child to the other and why?
(3) Ask the three children what their strategies were in confronting the father.
(4) Ask the first two children if they would change their strategies after hearing the first.
(5) Ask the class what they would have done differently from what the father or the children did.
(6) Can communication skills be learned? Where would you use to advantage your knowledge that better communication has the factors of ability, desire, selectivity, and security?

6. ***To evaluate one's own skill in communication.***
Duplicate the following checksheet for the students to use in self-evaluation. This checksheet may be used as an outline for a project in improving communication.

Self-Evaluation and Progress in Communication

Date	Describe present skills by noting actual situations in which you have used them	Describe a situation in which you have tried new skills in communication

Diagnosing Communication Problems

To make a glib statement, "If they would only communicate," does little toward helping others to communicate better. You must be able to identify the specific communication problem or problems. Is one person refusing to listen to the other? Why? Is one person using an overflow of words and a wall to keep others from getting in to them? Is one person expecting the other to hear all his troubles without being affected? Is one person making an attempt to misconstrue communication? Is the subject one that would be better left uncommunicated?

Teaching Techniques

1. *To identify the communication problem.*
   a. The following situation illustrates the communication problem of lack of selectivity. Read it to the class (or duplicate it and use it as an evaluation device).

   Jeff, age ten, was belligerent and crying. His favorite friend was going home after staying with him a month.
   Jeff (with tears in his eyes): John is going away. I'll be all alone again.
   Mother: You'll have lots of other friends.
   Jeff: I won't like them.
   Mother: Act your age.
   Jeff: Oh, Mother! (Growls)
   Mother: You are ten years old and still a crybaby.
   Jeff gave his mother a disgusted look and ran out slamming the door behind him.

   b. Use a modified version of The Minnesota Couples Communication Program (Miller et al. 1972) to teach students how to diagnose communication problems. Use the song "Do You Love Me?" from *Fiddler on the Roof* to show the four styles of communication: (1) small talk, (2) accusative, (3) factual, and (4) inner feelings. Style two has high risk in that it can raise the ire of the listener. Style four has high risk because it leaves the person vulnerable unless the listener is nonexploitive.
2. *To study and clarify where communication is strongest and to identify communication problems in a family in order to begin to understand its dynamics.*
   Have each student draw a sketch of the family with the student in the center and the other members revolving around the student. Use circles for children and triangles for parents. Draw an arrow from the student to each family member and an arrow from each family member to the student to indicate the strength of communication. A large arrow means a strong feeling, a thin arrow means a moderate feeling, and a wiggly arrow means conflict. Show the following diagram and discuss possible reasons for the type of communication based on age and sex (Lindquist 1968).

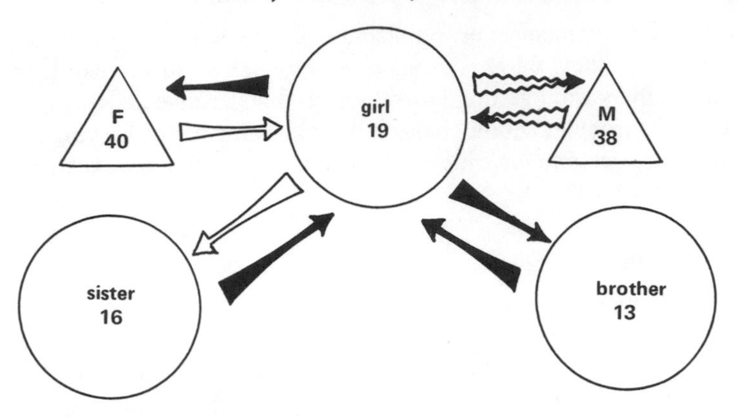

a. What are probable reasons for the types of communication?
b. What are the probable types of communication between other family members?
c. Under what circumstances might the conflict areas become less conflictual?
d. Is it possible or even necessary or even desirable to have strong lines of communication with everyone?

After each student has drawn a sociogram with himself in the center, have him draw a separate sociogram for each member of the family with that member in the center. Students are to study the sociogram for the entire family to begin to understand more about the dynamics of the family by asking the questions above about all the relationships between various family members.

Another question for further thinking and insight is this one: How do you think another member of your family would have drawn the lines of communication and why? If possible have others in your family draw these sociograms as they see them and compare. This exchange could start some communication in a family. Hopefully the student would be selective in the timing of asking others in the family to participate.

Discrepancy in Communication

The concepts of transactional analysis (Berne 1961, 1964; Harris 1967; James and Jongeward 1971) are appropriate for teaching people to understand the discrepancy between two people attempting to transact a message. Briefly, the beliefs are that people respond from any one of three different parts of the person: (1) a "playful or pity-me child," (2) a "rule-enforcing or pious or nurturant parent," or (3) a "rational or logical adult."

These three parts of the person from which responses come are believed to have had their beginnings in childhood. They are conditioned sufficiently to remain throughout life. Both the "playful child" behaviors and "pity-me child" behaviors are appropriate even in adulthood when the situation warrants them. The "rational adult" and the "rule-enforcing or nurturant parent" parts of a person also had their beginnings in childhood and have continued into adulthood. These "adult" and "parent" parts were probably first learned from imitating and identifying with parents.

Behaviors from all three parts are appropriate at times even in adulthood. The problem in communication occurs when one person is speaking from one part such as his "pity-me child" part wanting a reciprocal "nurturing parent" response but getting an unexpected "rational adult" response. The conflict occurs because of the unexpected response. The communication stops because neither is getting what he wants.

Examples of working transactions between two adults are given below:

1. Same level (reciprocal messages and communicating).

   Adult-Adult comment and Adult-Adult response

   "We need to go to the grocery store." (Rational adult)

   "I can go when I finish mowing." (Rational adult)

   Parent-Parent comment with Parent-Parent response

   "We should already have gone to the grocery store; what will people think?" (Rule conscious, punishing parent)

   "I know it; I'm ashamed that we've waited so long." (Rule conscious, punishing parent)

   Child-Child comment with Child-Child response

   "I know we need groceries but I don't want to go." (Playful child)

   "I don't either; maybe we'll be the first ones to live on love." (Playful child)

2. Transactions between two people on two different but reciprocal levels, yet communicating.

   Parent-Child comment with Child-Parent response

   "Why don't you look after those children?" (Punishing parent)

   "You're always picking on me." (Pity-me child)

   Adult-Parent comment with Parent-Adult response

   "I know you think it's not right, but under the circumstances I had to give the boy a chance to play with the others. (Rational adult)

   "Your job is to protect him." (Rule-enforcing parent)

   Child-Adult comment with Adult-Child response

   "He wanted to play with the others and I had to let him." (Pity-me child)

   "You were only doing what you thought was best." (Rational adult)

3. Transactions which are *not reciprocal* and therefore *non-communicating*.

   Adult-Adult comment with Parent-Child response

"I've had several people ask me to go, but I'm not sure I should go." (Rational adult)

"You should know what to do." (Punishing parent)

Teaching Techniques

1. *To understand the concepts of* ***transactions from differing levels.***
   a. Read the above illustrations to the class and have them write different comments and responses for discussion.
   b. Have the class members enact some transactions.
2. *To recognize* ***transaction difficulties*** *within this conceptual framework.*
   a. Have students determine the levels on which spontaneous transactions are made.
   b. Have two students discuss some controversial topic and ask the class to analyze the exchange by showing the fluctuation of levels of responses from time to time.
   c. Have three or more students discuss some controversial topic and ask the class members to observe and determine the levels of transactions between any two people of the group.
3. *To analyze communication difficulties by* ***using the transactional analysis framework.***
   a. Play a tape-recorded conversation about some issue between a couple who have relationship difficulties and analyze the conversation.
   b. Present two written conversations, one that shows a relationship difficulty which is really communication difficulty and the other which shows incompatibility–not communication–as the difficulty. Have the class determine which conversation has communication difficulty and which one does not. Then discuss the communication difficulty.

Case #1 (Incompatibility as the difficulty)

"Do you want to go to the ball game Saturday?"
"No, I really don't care to go."
"Why not?"
"I don't like baseball, but you can go."
"I want you to go; you haven't been with me all season."
"I don't like baseball; I never have."

Case #2 (Communication as the difficulty)

"Do you want to go to the ball game Saturday?"
"Do you want me to go?"
"Certainly, or else I wouldn't have asked you."
"You don't usually ask me; why are you starting now? Do you feel guilty?"

"No, I don't feel guilty. I just think you ought to go."
"Maybe I will and maybe I won't."

4. ***To understand and analyze the maturity level of messages between a marital pair.***
The following simplistic approach (not a therapeutic approach) for analyzing transactions between a marital pair is adapted from Eric Berne's *Transactional Analysis* (1961). Have several pairs of students enact the following scenes. After each transaction have the class make a decision about the level of maturity of the statements—"playful or pity-me child," "rule-enforcing or pious parent," or "rational or logical adult."

Examples

Partner 1: "Where's the toothpaste?" (Adult)
Partner 2: "How should I know?" (Child)
or "It's in the cabinet." (Adult)
or "You've always thought I hide it." (Child)
or "It's where you last put it; why can't you look?" (Parent)
or "Where in the sam hill is the toothpaste?" (Child)
or "I can't ever find the toothpaste after you've used it." (Parent)
or "Have you seen the toothpaste?" (Adult)
Partner 1: "Would you like to go out for dinner?" (Adult)
Partner 2: "Why are you asking?" (Parent)

Summary

Communication is easier when a person combines an understanding of human behavior with skills of communication. The techniques selected for this chapter were chosen to teach about communication in a variety of settings. Sometimes family situations were used. Many techniques for using communication skills to enrich interpersonal relationships are included in several other chapters in this book. The next chapter on intergenerational relationships shows the use of both understanding human behavior and communication.

References

Berne, Eric. *Games People Play*. New York: Grove Press, Inc., 1964.
——. *Transactional Analysis in Psychotherapy*. New York: Grove Press, Inc., 1961.
Harris, Thomas. *I'm OK–You're OK*. New York: Harper & Row, 1967.
James, Muriel and Jongeward, Dorothy. *Born to Win: Transactional Analysis with Gestalt Experiments*. Reading, Massachusetts: Addison-Wesley Publishing Co., 1971.

Klemer, Richard H. *Marriage and Family Relationships*. New York: Harper & Row, 1970.

Lindquist, Rita. "Teach Sex Education as the Fourth 'R'." *What's New in Home Economics* 32:39-41, 1968.

Miller, Sherod; Nunnally, Elam W.; and Wackman, Daniel B. with Brazman, Ronald. *The Minnesota Couples Communication Program*. Published by the Minnesota Couples Communication Program, 2001 Riverside Avenue, Minneapolis, Minn., 55404, 1972.

Pfeiffer, J. William, and Jones, John. *A Handbook of Structured Experiences for Human Relations Training*. Vols. 1, 2, 3, and 4. Iowa City, Iowa: University Associates Press, 1971-1974.

Waltzlawick, Paul; Beavin, Janet H.; and Jackson, Don D. *Pragmatics of Human Communication*. New York: W. W. Norton & Co., 1967.

Chapter 11

Intergenerational Relationships

In this chapter specific teaching techniques will be suggested to lead parents and youth to a better mutual understanding through open communication. A basic premise is that parents, grandparents, and youths will each contribute to the others' understanding and growth; therefore, many of the activities will involve multiple generations.

Kingsley Davis (1971) wrote a classic analysis of parent-child conflict. He identified three universals and four critical variables peculiar to modern culture which remain relevant. They will form the basic outline for this chapter.

The birth cycle differential is the first universal that Davis proposed to account for intergenerational conflict. This idea is that parents will always have a different historical framework from their children because of occurrences during the twenty-to-thirty years of parental life preceding procreation. The second universal is that the rate of socialization proceeds at a rapid pace in childhood and adolescence and then begins to decrease with age. Thus, adolescents are absorbing more of the present world at a faster pace than their parents or grandparents. The third universal is that intergenerational physiological, psychosocial, and sociological differences are the result of this birth cycle and differential socialization.

The preceding universals are fairly consistent across all cultures and tend to produce adult-youth conflict. Some societies have little conflict, however, whereas others are seething with dissention. What are the determining factors in the appearance or lack of conflict in a society? The critical factors determining the actual occurrence of conflict are (1) rate of social change, (2) extent and complexity of the system, (3) degree of cultural integration, and (4) velocity of movement. Teaching techniques will be suggested for guiding

*This chapter was written with Carol McLester (student), Department of Child Development and Family Relations, University of North Carolina, Greensboro, N.C.

students in the understanding of each of the preceding constants and variables.

Students should gain a thorough understanding of generational differences. Then the empathetic method should be used as a technique to teach the students to apply their knowledge to increase intergenerational communication (Smith and McLester 1973). Suggestions will be made for culminating activities which stress the empathetic approach to intergenerational understanding. Through application, learning which may have taken place superficially will be firmly established.

Introduction

The introduction to a unit of study should be a stimulus to fire the imagination of the students. They should begin to identify with the concepts to be studied and should begin to be able to answer the question, "What does this concept have to offer me?"

Teaching Techniques

1. *To stimulate the students to clarify and define their personal concept of the generation gap.*
   a. Read the following in two or three parts, discussing the ideas that the students have at each *pause.* Permanently record the ideas to use later.

      A prominent New York lawyer has been ordered to resume support of his seventeen-year-old daughter, even though he thinks her "Hippie" life "stinks." (Pause.) "At some point," (said the family judge), "minors must have some right of their own views and needs for their independent and painful transition from minority to adulthood. (Pause.) This court absolves the daughter from bridging the generation gap any more than she has. (Pause.) The gap is not entirely the doing of the young, nor can it be bridged entirely by the children."

   b. Groups of students should list and study their definitions of generation and gap to formulate a definition of generation gap. Then combine the group definitions to form a class definition which may serve as a reference. The following definitions may be given to the class if dictionaries are not available.
      First consider some definitions of the word *gap*.
      (1) A break in a wall, hedge, or line of military defense, an assailable position.
      (2) A mountain pass.
      (3) A break in or lack of continuity.
      (4) A lack of balance.

Now consider definitions of the word *generation*.

(1) The group of living organisms which constitute a single step in a line of descent from an ancestor of the group of individuals born and living contemporaneously.

(2) The average period of time between the birth of parents and of their offspring.

(3) The process involved in coming into being.

c. See the movie "Future Shock" (1972) or read the book *Future Shock* (Toffler 1970) to learn some of the predictions for the generations of the future and to speculate on how present generations will react to the impact. There are twenty chapters in the book and assignments may be made to students or groups of students to read and report on one or two chapters (disassemble the book into chapters so that twenty people at a time may read one book). In class discussions establish factors from the film or book which may contribute to an understanding of generational problems. Record suggestions in a permanent way.

2. *To gain an overview of generational problems (Koller 1974).*

a. Combine all of the factors from the previous discussions to establish a framework for the remainder of the unit. See how close the class has come to defining the constants and variables identified by Kingsley Davis.

b. Assign a group of students to read the Kingsley Davis (1971) article. Ask the students to outline the article briefly. Ask them to compare their views of generational problems developed in class discussions with the outline of the Davis article.

c. Show these films to gain greater insight into the problems between generations:
"Ivan and His Father" (1971), "Trouble in the Family" (1965), and "Saturday Morning" (1970).

The Three Universals in Intergenerational Understanding

Birth Cycle—A Universal

The birth cycle is the span of time between the birth of one generation and its procreation. This twenty- to thirty-year span of time becomes significant only when coupled with differential socialization and rapid social change. Rapid social change will produce a historical milieu which is entirely different from one generation to the next. Teaching techniques will direct students' attention toward intergenerational differences aggravated by the time span between generations.

Teaching Techniques

1. *To understand that* ***stages of aging*** *have been definable by both biological and cultural means for centuries.*

   Read Jaques' soliloquy from Shakespeare's *As You Like It* and compare it with one or more of the following: Erikson's Eight Stages of Man (1963); Duvall's Family Life Cycle (1971); Time for Living and Dying in Ecclesiastes (all four of which are printed here). Compare these with the General Statutes of the State and Federal Government in order to show how ages have been used over the centuries to describe expectations, rights, privileges, and responsibilities.

JAQUES' SOLILOQUY ON THE SEVEN AGES OF MAN
FROM WILLIAM SHAKESPEARE'S *AS YOU LIKE IT*

All the world's a stage,
And all the men and women merely players.
They have their exits and their entrances;
And one man in his time plays many parts,
His acts being seven ages. At first the infant,
Mewling and puking in the nurse's arms.
And then the whining school-boy, with his satchel
And shining morning face, creeping like a snail
Unwillingly to school. And then the lover,
Sighing like furnace, with a woeful ballad
Made to his mistress' eyebrow. Then a soldier,
Full of strange oaths, and bearded like the bard;
Jealous in honour, sudden and quick in quarrel,
Seeking the bubble reputation
Even in the cannon's mouth. And then the justice,
In fair round belly with good capon lined
With eyes severe and beard of formal cut,
Full of wise saws and modern instances;
And so he plays his part. The sixth age shifts
Into the lean and slipper'd pantaloon,
With spectacles on nose and pouch on side!
His youthful hose, well saved, a world too wide
For his shrunk shank; and his big manly voice,
Turning again toward childish treble, pipes
And whistles in his sound. Last scene of all,
That ends this strange eventful history,
Is second childishness, and mere oblivion,
Sans teeth, sans eyes, sans taste, sans everything.

ERIKSON'S EIGHT STAGES OF MAN (1963)

Psychosocial Crises	*Approximate Life Stage*
1. Trust vs. Mistrust	Birth to toddler
2. Autonomy vs. Shame and Doubt	About two to four
3. Initiative vs. Guilt	About five to seven
4. Industry vs. Inferiority	About eight to twelve

Psychosocial Crises	*Approximate Life Stage*
5. Identity and Repudiation vs. Identity Diffusion	Adolescence
6. Intimacy and Solidarity vs. Isolation	Young Adulthood
7. Generativity vs. Self-absorption	Middle Adulthood
8. Integrity vs. Despair	Older Adulthood

DUVALL'S FAMILY LIFE CYCLE BY LENGTH OF TIME
IN EACH OF EIGHT STAGES (1971)*

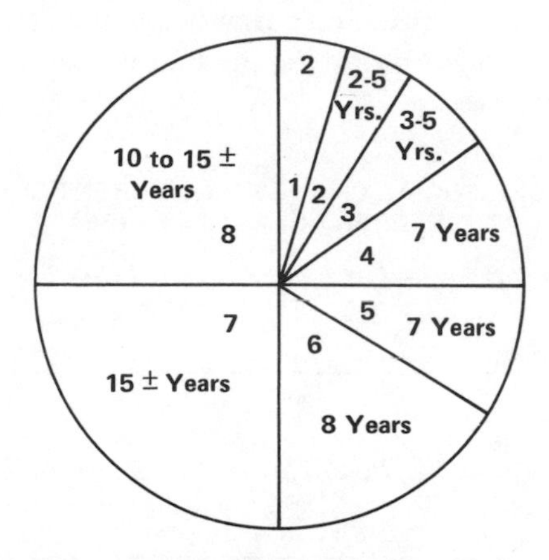

1. Newly Married Couples (without children).
2. Childbearing Families (birth to thirty months).
3. Families with Preschool Children (thirty months to six years).
4. Families with School children (six to thirteen years).
5. Families with Teenagers (thirteen to twenty years).
6. Families as Launching Centers (first child gone to last child leaving home).
7. Middle-aged Parents (No children at home to retirement).
8. Aging Family Members (retirement to death of spouses) (Duvall 1971).

ECCLESIASTES

To every thing there is a season, and a time to every purpose under the heaven:
A time to be born, and a time to die; a time to plant, and a time to pluck up that which is planted;
A time to kill, and a time to heal; a time to break down, and a time to build up;
A time to weep, and a time to laugh; a time to mourn, and a time to dance;
A time to cast away stones, and a time to gather stones together; a time to embrace, and a time to refrain from embracing;

*Adapted from Evelyn M. Duvall, *Family Development*, 4th ed. Philadelphia: J. B. Lippincott Co., 1971.

A time to get, and a time to lose; a time to keep, and a time to cast away;
A time to rend, and a time to sew; a time to keep silence, and a time to speak;
A time to love, and a time to hate; a time of war, and a time of peace.

2. *To demonstrate that parents and children are always at a different stage of development. This is called the* **birth cycle.** *According to the life cycle theory, how one reacts to life in each stage predicts what he will be like in each succeeding stage.*
   a. Draw the following figure on poster board or on the blackboard. If it is drawn on the blackboard, ask the students to copy it in their notes for later reference.

THE BIRTH CYCLE, SOCIAL CHANGE, AND PARENT-CHILD RELATIONS AT DIFFERENT STAGES OF LIFE*

Cultural Content Acquired at Each Stage of Life

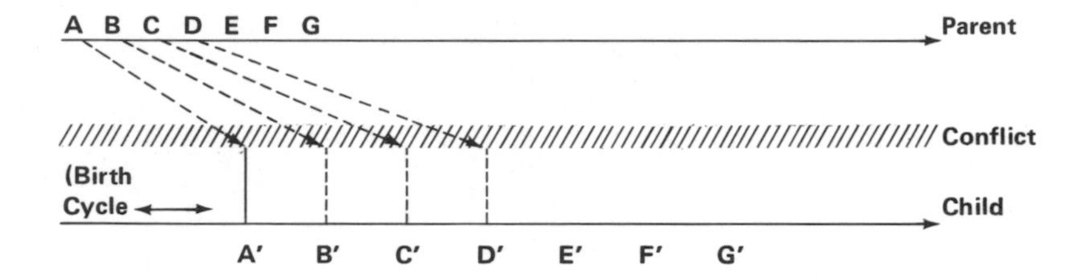

   The birth-cycle interval will remain constant, generations will always be at a different developmental stage, and relationships will always be subject to conflict. Ask students to make observations gleaned from this figure. For example: Though the birth cycle remains the same in total number of years, it occupies an increasingly smaller percentage of the total life span. After adolescence the span is reduced to a minimum part of the total life span and conflict consequently decreases.
   b. To illustrate and explain the notion of the family life cycle (Duvall 1971), give each student a sheet of graph paper on which he can mark off one vertical column of blocks representing the years his parents have been married. On the horizontal rows the student can mark off one row of blocks for each child born in his family beginning with the oldest. Using a different color in that row of blocks for each child, the students should color in that row

*From Kingsley Davis. "The Sociology of Parent-Youth Conflict." ASR, Vol. 5, August 1940, pp. 523-535. By permission of the American Sociological Association.

beginning with the year the child was born. This chart will give a very visible accounting of the student's own family as it attempts to meet the tasks in each stage in the family life cycle. It will also show how families differ from the average family and how many of the relationships problems stem from the parents' having to meet the tasks in too many different stages at one time. A not untypical family is shown below.

Years of Marriage

		1	2 3 4 5 6 7 8 9	10	11	12	13 14 15 16 17
	1						
Children	2						
	3						

Questions to help students gain insight:

(1) How does this family compare with the average family in Duvall's Family Life Cycle Chart?
(2) What are the probable ages of the parents at each year of marriage?
(3) What are the ages of the different children at each year of marriage?
(4) How many different stages of the Family Life Cycle is this family experiencing at one time?
(5) What are the conflicts of parents' needs and children's needs?

c. Survey (by interview) people of the students' parents' ages and older to find the songs which are remembered most from their youth to show that people tend to remember most fondly those songs which actually describe their present age, not their youth. For example, even though songs with a fast beat were very popular during their youth, middle-aged people tend to remember and prefer love songs whereas older people tend to prefer ballads which tell a story of life. Try some of the current songs with people of varying ages to get data (information) about various age groups.

3. *To understand that, because of the birth cycle, parents always have a **different historical perspective** than do students (Bengtson and Black 1973).*

Ask students to interview parents and to conduct searches in old newspapers and magazines to determine current events of their parents' youth. How could living through a depression or a world war affect your values and beliefs? What is current today which will have a lasting effect on adults and youth alike (Nesselroade and Baltes 1974)? How will the

Watergate scandal influence future perceptions of governmental credibility? Will this scandal be as relevant to future perceptions of children who were under ten years of age during the hearings of 1973? Will unborn children be relatively unaffected by this event since they will only read or hear about it historically?

Decelerating Socialization—A Universal

Organic factors, such as age, and social factors, such as less exposure to educational institutions, cause a decelerating rate of socialization (Lidz 1968). Childhood is a period of rapid physical and intellectual growth. Old age is a period of very slow physical and sometimes slower intellectual growth. Decelerating intellectual growth does not have to occur. When the world is changing rapidly, the youth, because of a lack of preexisting mental sets, are more able to incorporate the changes and to cope with them than are the aged. To facilitate communication, the young must accept the challenge of educating adults about what is currently important to youth. Adults must be willing to accept a role of student in addition to the traditional role of teacher.

Teaching Techniques

1. *To understand that the parent is expected to socialize his children but that he tends to apply inappropriate content from his own childhood.*
   a. Refer to Davis' birth cycle figure given earlier in this chapter. When social change is rapid, the cultural content of A will not apply to A′. The parent is placed in the uncomfortable situation of trying to apply knowledge gained in one era to an entirely different era. Discuss this inconsistency, listing problems of youth today in one column and problems faced by parents and grandparents in other columns. For example:

Problems Faced by Youth

Now	*20 Years Ago*	*40 Years Ago*
drugs	alcohol	smoking
sex	kissing on first date	jobs
futility		no hope

   Students should interview parents and grandparents to validate and expand their lists.
   b. Have a seminar on drugs (or another relevant issue) with multigenerational representation. First ask speakers (the police department usually has someone available) to present facts. Show a film on drugs; then let parents, grandparents, and students express feelings

with no interruptions. Tape the speaker's comments for use in class discussions, and ask students to determine why each speaker felt as he did.

c. Stage a debate on the issue of legalization of marijuana. Ask a set of three generations to argue pro and another set of three generations to argue con.

d. Invite a multigenerational panel to discuss "Codes of Dress–Today and Yesterday."

e. Choose other current, controversial newspaper or magazine articles and have students interview their parents and grandparents as to their opinions. The students' job is to *listen* and *record*, not to argue. Possible topics include foreign war and peace, the Equal Rights Amendment, or legalization of abortion. Students should discuss their findings in class and attempt to analyze them in the light of the historical perspective of the parents and grandparents.

2. *To become aware that **children have an influence on their parents**.*

a. Have the students interview their own or other parents to find out the changes they think children have made in their lives. When the students don't have the time to interview, have them write how they think they have influenced parents and compare their comments with the following findings from other interviews (Devor 1970).

"I'm stricter than I thought I would be."
"I'm beginning to like children."
"I don't want any more children."
"We watch 'Lassie' on TV instead of the late show."
"I am more open to people."
"I can hug people now."
"I'm more determined to do well in my job."
"We don't fight in front of the children."
"I have learned how to play."

b. Ask the students to describe the baby they would want to have including gender, size, and temperament. Then you describe a baby which is the antithesis of one student's description and pantomime handing the baby to the "new parent." Ask for the initial reaction to the baby. Then ask for other students' reactions which will lead into this generalization: A baby born with a highly active constitution will affect parents differentially according to their own anxiety level. For example, a set of calm parents, who are organizers, may be able to hold to a routine which can eventually make the baby calmer but never docile. A set of calm parents who expect others to set their own limits may be driven to distraction over the demands made by the child. A set of parents who are unsure about their own capabilities will probably become even more unsure as the baby demands his own way.

3. *To understand that* ***parents can change as children change,*** *but that it may be more difficult for parents to change ("When the Young Teach and the Old Learn" 1970).*

   a. Behavior modification works both ways. Children can change parents or other adults just as parents can change children. An essential ingredient in changing other people's behaviors is to know what is reinforcing to them. Have students list how they reinforce parents' behaviors: (1) deference to the parents at times, (2) producing well in some way, (3) asking parents' opinions, (4) complimenting parents, and (5) taking responsibility for one's actions. This list will vary tremendously with the variety of students. All suggested reinforcements must be accepted, for it is they, the children, not you the teacher, who know what reinforces their parents' or their adult friends' behaviors.

      Have students set up several situations in which certain behaviors of parents or other adults are to be changed and plan how the students could carry out one of these. (For example: The adult behavior of treating the children as if they didn't have valid opinions is to be changed to the adults' listening to the children's points of view. Listening is different from surrendering to the children; it is the same as getting other adults' opinions before making some drastic move which affects all people concerned.)

   b. Have a group of adults indicate what they think is distasteful to them about children's dress, actions, ideas, etc. As these adults list the things they dislike, ask them why they dislike each thing. The answers may be that the distaste comes from associations with something unacceptable in the past. A typical list with former associations is this:

Disliked characteristics	Past associations
1) Child who doesn't perform to his ability	1) People who won't work, leaving work for others to do
2) Patched or dirty clothes	2) People who couldn't afford better or were too "lazy" to clean up
3) Children who are experts or know quite a bit more than the parents	3) People who outshone them in their own childhood

   Gather the same information from children about their dislike of adults, and similar past associations will come forth. If both groups, especially if they are unrelated, could express these dislikes and associations, then a greater understanding and change would occur.

c. If the students in class are under twenty-one years of age, have them talk with someone fifteen years old and younger about some current ideas and issues. (If the students are eighteen years old, have them talk with twelve year olds.) The students are to register the feelings they got from the discussion in an effort to understand how their parents or other adults feel. This assignment can involve an individual or a group of younger people might be brought to the classroom (Steiner 1970).

d. Discuss the adages "You can't teach old dogs new tricks" and "Bring up a child in the way he should go, and when he is old he will not depart from it." Remind the students that, even though behavior in succeeding stages of the life cycle is predictable from earlier stages, various influences from within and without the person can change his behavior.

Intrinsic Intergenerational Differences—A Universal

Physiological, psychological, and sociological differences complicate intergenerational relationships and make communication more difficult.

Physiological differences between parent and child vary throughout life. In our accomplishment-oriented society, interage competition places the organically superior youth at a distinct advantage.

Psychosocially, adults in general tend to be more realistic than youths are because of their experiences. Youths may press for action whereas adults, whose ideals have been tempered by experience, may stress thought before action. Age can cause people to become more tolerant and to have a greater perspective, and in turn it may be the basis for their realism and caution.

From a sociological perspective parents in our society encourage independence of their children but demand obedience. The total authority of parents over their children must be relinquished, but the sequential transition from total dependence of the newborn to total independence of the child when he reaches adulthood is a difficult one for parents and child. In addition, youths tend to place hopes on the future whereas the aged place their hopes vicariously on the youth (Hansel 1969; Mead 1970).

Teaching Techniques

1. *To become more aware of the **physiological differences** between parent and child throughout life.*

   a. Show the film "A Changing View of the Change of Life" to show the change in hormones as a cause of mental depression and figure change in women.

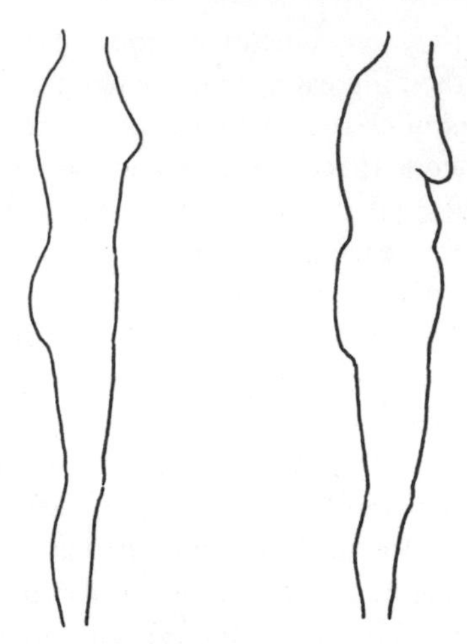

b. Draw these two figures of women on the board and ask which one belongs to the students.
Point out the basic changes as dowager's hump, sagging breasts, small waistline, protruding abdomen, extra fat pad at top of hips and flat derriere. Discuss the causes of the changes as a possible result of a lack of estrogen, a lack of exercise, and a poor diet.

Questions

(1) What is the cultural norm concerning a youthful, well-formed figure?
(2) Which of the two women might have the most resentments?
(3) How do resentments affect one's social relations?
(4) Are cutting remarks, pressures, refusals, etc., a cover-up for jealousies?
(5) Could mothers resent daughters because of their figures?

2. *To compare* ***psychosocial stresses*** *and strains of the parents' youth with their children's own youth.*
   a. Run a film that is old enough to have been seen by the students' parents when they were students (such as "This Charming Couple" 1950), but turn on the sound *without* the picture. You may tell the students that you want them to listen to the words without the picture for various reasons: to feel the impact of the words of their parents as youngsters; to keep from being influenced by dress.
   b. Short stories of the era of students' parents reveal the problems of those times. Read a short story to the class or assign one for them to read.
3. *To make some judgments about actions toward* ***people in the older generation who feel alienated*** *when they are no longer needed.*

Pose the following situation to see what the students' immediate reaction would be. Then point out through questioning why people react differently.

A couple with no children are living with the husband's parents while their new house is being built next door. Just prior to the completion of the house, his father dies. The husband is an only child. (1) Should the couple move to the new house and the mother stay in her house? (2) Should all three of them move to the new house? (3) Should all three of them stay in the old house? (4) Why–in general? (5) Why–in your case? (6) Why–in certain cases? (7) What division of labor (role responsibilities) would you make? (8) What are the underlying generalizations on which your answer is based?

Suppose it had been the father who lived the longest?

Suppose there had been brothers and sisters?

Suppose there had been children?

Suppose this event had taken place after the couple had been married less than one year? Two years? Five, ten, fifteen years?

4. *To compare* ***differing social*** *and educational* ***levels*** *of the parent and grandparent generation and to judge the threat on relationships.*

 a. Show how religious teachings affect adult children's feelings about parents as the adult children move up socially. Compare the following religions as to their position of parents and the elderly: Judeo-Christian; The Code of Hammurabi.

FROM: *EXODUS*

Honour thy father and thy mother: that thy days may be long upon the land which the Lord thy God giveth thee.

He that curseth his father, or his mother, shall surely be put to death.

FROM: *THE CODE OF HAMMURABI*

If a craftsman has taken a child to bring up and has taught him his handicraft, he shall not be reclaimed. If he has not taught him his handicraft, that foster child shall return to his father's house.

If a son has struck his father, his hands shall be cut off.

If a man has determined to disinherit his son and has declared before the judge, "I cut off my son," the judge shall inquire into the son's past; and, if the son has not committed a grave misdemeanor such as should cut him off from sonship, the father shall not disinherit his son.

 b. Compare the following social levels as to certain behaviors about generations (Schulz 1972):

Upper Middle

Parents and children are both important. Parents are striving to hold on or move upward. Children are expected to be high achievers and are given every opportunity. Grandparents are not as important since these families are actively seeking mobility upward and away from older generations who may have been from a lower social class.

Middle

All three generations are important. Children are of central concern since they are the ones who could possibly move upward through better education and jobs. Families do not have enough money to ignore the help from the older generations.

Upper Lower

All three generations are important and are needed. Children are expected to comply to rules as do parents in their work world. Respect for adults is expected from children.

As social levels change, usually because of money and/or education, behavior changes. Old behavior is shunned and new behavior is accepted as one's own. The inner anxiety arises when the behavior being shunned is that behavior of one's parents and the shunning conflicts with the conditioned-in emotional feeling to honor one's parents.

The Four Variables Affecting the Universals in Intergenerational Understanding

Rate of Social Change—A Variable

Extremely rapid social change increases intergenerational conflict since the time interval between the births of one generation and the birth of their children becomes historically significant. Youth in slow-paced societies, although affected by the universal generational time gap, are more complacent than youth in a fast-moving society.

Teaching Techniques

1. *To examine* ***stable and nonstable societies*** *to determine the degree of parent-youth conflict.*
   Ask a group of students to read *Coming of Age in Samoa* (Mead 1949) and another group to read *The Good Earth* (Buck 1949). Ask the students to report findings related to cultural change and to youth's docility or rebellion. Class discussion should be directed toward comparing and contrasting the U.S. culture and youth to the Samoan and Chinese cultures and youth. Ask the students to compare the Chinese culture and youth of today (give a good reference) with its past culture.
2. *To determine whether* ***immigrant families,*** *who undergo the most rapid change of all, exhibit more parent-youth conflict than do middle-class Americans.*
   Play excerpts from the "West Side Story" record or see the movie and

discuss. Students should examine parents and youth to see what is happening to them with regard to communication and conflict. Compare various nationalities to see if there is a difference between differing ethnic groups. In many areas, students may discuss local ethnic groups.

Extent and Complexity of the System—A Variable

In the United States the social system has become very complex. This complexity is a result in part of the diversity of backgrounds and the extent of the landmass. Recently, public communication systems and franchised retail markets have narrowed some of the differences in that more people know what more people are doing. This communication has been true especially in the last generation and a half. Travel has also become easier and is being done by some people in all age groups. These factors, influencing increased communication, have had a much greater impact on today's youth than they had on today's parents in their own youth.

Teaching Techniques

1. *To illustrate that* ***mass communication and travel*** *has only recently become available to the majority of the population.*
   a. Students should poll parents and grandparents to determine the age at which they were first introduced to radio, television, and daily newspapers in the setting of their homes. When did they see their first movie? Compare the parents' ages with the ages of the students when they were first exposed to these means of communication within their own homes.
   b. Examine the system used to elect the president of the United States. The electoral system was established because people had no way of knowing about the candidates. They chose people to vote for them who could determine the best candidate. Because of wide television coverage today, the electoral college may be outdated.
2. *To understand why older generations are "caught" in the* ***adult-work world*** *and must conform.*
   a. Read and discuss excerpts about the time in life people can be the objector with little to lose.
   b. Discuss jobs which provide nothing but a livelihood. The jobs are monotonous, repetitive, with no intrinsic reward or intellectual stimulation. How many parents and grandparents are caught in such jobs? Why do they continue to work at such jobs? How would students feel about such jobs? What type of work do the students hope to do?

Degree of Cultural Integration—A Variable

The security one feels about his role or identity as an adult is greatly determined by both his childhood socialization and the rewards for that role after he reaches adulthood. The tremendous changes in adult roles make it doubly difficult for a young adult to be moving easily into adult life roles. First of all, what he was taught as a child may not be the accepted role when he becomes an adult (the changing roles of men and women, for example). Second, the traditional roles of parents are being usurped by experts. Presently the lack of an integrated approach among the experts, the institutions, and the people is hindering the ability of people to move from childhood to adulthood or to find a satisfying adult role.

Teaching Technique

To understand the effect of experts' advice on the self-concepts of parents, how experts have invaded the traditional role of mother without helping her feel a part of the transition.

Read and discuss the following article:

POOR MOM, DONE IN BY EXPERTS*

Contrary to popular belief, Mother's Day, which this year falls next Sunday, was not written into the Constitution by the Founding Fathers. It is a 20th Century phenomenon, first proclaimed by President Wilson in 1914. Its purpose was a noble one, to honor motherhood. At the time, improved maternal and child health care were beginning to lower national death rates. It was also the dawn of an era in which American childcare would be professionalized, thereby making mother's influence less and less important.

The first White House Conference on Children, for example, was called by President Theodore Roosevelt in 1909. The Children's Bureau was established. And it was in the early part of the century that pediatrics and obstetrics became recognized medical specialties. Psychology arrived as an academic discipline. Mandatory birth registration was introduced in many states, and the first systematic attempts to study child development got underway. The professionalization of motherhood was part and parcel of a new faith in "scientific" methods that dominated the American scene.

This professionalization of childcare, though probably necessary and beneficial, had the unfortunate side effect of putting mother down. The glory went to an ever-proliferating army of experts—pediatricians, social scientists, counselors, nutritionists, etc.—who fractured motherhood and defined it in terms of their own specialties and professional interests. What is sadly ironic is that Mother's Day was invented at precisely this moment when Mother was on the way to becoming at best a para-professional. All that remained for her was to follow the experts' prescriptions. No longer a certified "pro" at anything, mother no longer knew best.

There had been advice books for mothers during the 19th Century, to be sure. But these were written by "ladies" and ministers, not Ph.D.s and M.D.s. The message in those days was that mother was indispensable and supreme as the guardian of the home against the spiritual and material onslaughts of the outside world.

Alas, the message for the 20th Century mother became: "Let us, the experts, tell you how you should do it." The pitch was that there is only one "right" way to bring up children; to deviate from it was to court disaster. The new science of child development was too insecure, too interested in building its prestige, to leave anything to mother's unlicensed judgment.

In 1905, a pediatrician noted the "general ignorance and helplessness of the young mother who knows little or nothing regarding the essential hygience (sic) of early life." In their famous study, "Middletown" (1920), Robert and Helen Lynd quote a properly brainwashed mother: "I realize that I ought to be half a dozen experts, but I am afraid of making mistakes. . . ."

The U.S. Government Printing Office's all-time best seller, "Infant Care," warned in its first edition in 1914: "The rule that parents should not play with the baby may seem hard, but it is without doubt a safe one." This arrogant prohibition was softened in later editions as was another dictum of the 1914 era: "After baby's needs have been fully satisfied, he should be put down alone and allowed to cry until he goes to sleep." No rocking or lullaby allowed. Mother would just have to listen to baby cry; the experts remained at a safe distance.

What was left for poor mother to do? She was cowed by the "new" professionals who, eager to impress their colleagues, ignored any potential harm to mother's confidence, a process that reached its zenith in the 1940s with the popularization of Freud. Millions who had never read Freud at all were subjected to interpretations by the few who had misread him. If mother made a wrong move, her child would be damaged for life, while she was left in a state of irreparable guilt. By the time Dr. Spock entered the scene, mothers were so intimidated that they were often unable to benefit fully from his common sense, which in fact aimed at restoring mother's self-confidence.

In the 1950s Philip Wylie introduced the term "momism" into American culture and vocabulary, a pejorative for a dominating mother–source of all evil. The slander never ebbed, as witness Mother Portnoy.

Women's Liberation sensed the dissatisfaction of many American mothers, but responded in the standard American fashion: Because mother gets no financial remuneration is proof positive that motherhood is not recognized as a bona fide job. Thus, another triumph for the idea of the "professional."

No doubt childcare and medical experts have done much to improve the physical safety of child-bearing and child-rearing. But the new science has dramatically reduced the skills and activities that a mother can pass on to her children, particularly her daughters, because she is afraid of being old-fashioned, of handing down obsolete or unscientific practices. And modern medicine supposedly has lessened the need for maternal nursing skills, mother's bedside manner being replaced by penicillin and television.

No one would advocate a return to the "good old days," even if that were possible. But Mother's Day seems a fitting time to remember that each "scientific" advance brings new problems along with benefits. Mother's Day, quite apart from its commercial exploitation, carries with it an admission of our national guilt. After putting mother down as an obsolete anachronism in life or as a dominating monster in literature, we put her on a nostalgic pedestal for a day.

Mother's Day will not rid itself easily of its aroma of hypocrisy until women, when asked to state their occupation, can once again write "Mother"—without any apology to the experts.

Velocity of Movement—A Variable

There are some who say a generation is only five years rather than twenty to thirty years because of the speed with which ideas are generated. In this way, a generation is defined as a generation of attitudes or beliefs and not a mere generation of physiological human beings. The differences in a family may as easily be between siblings of five to ten years age differences as between parents and children. There is definitely a difference among some adults of short age spans.

Teaching Technique

*To understand that because of the velocity of movement within our society there may be **a shorter generation time span**. The generational differences in a family may as easily be between siblings of five to ten year age differences as between parents and children.* Students should read newspaper headlines of today and of ten and twenty years ago. Youth's commitment makes headlines whereas apathy does not. The "beat" generation of youth operated with a "keep cool" philosophy. The "hippie" youth tended to be "with it," involved and committed with regard to social issues. Who was making the headlines twenty years ago? Ten years ago? Today? What was making the headlines?

Empathetic Approach to Intergenerational Understanding and Communication

Generations may get together through confrontation, constructive argumentation, and negotiation or exchange. Persons who understand generational differences are in a much better position to negotiate. The empathetic approach can facilitate understanding (Smith and McLester 1973). Every bit of knowledge gained in this unit of study will be utilized by students to understand parents, grandparents, and younger brothers and sisters.

Teaching Techniques

1. *To demonstrate that intergenerational conflict is aggravated by **differing meanings given to words** and events by the generations.*
   a. Read this quotation: "In conversing with teen-agers, parents envy

the United Nations those earphones which give instant, simultaneous translations."

Then make some statements commonly made to parents by teen-agers such as:

"You don't trust me!"
"Everybody is doing it!"
"O.K. I'll listen; say it!"
"But you promised last week!"

Have a panel of three or four students act as the interpretive earphones and restate what the teen-ager meant. The other class members are asked to comment on why these garbled messages came through.

b. Using the generalization that preexisting mental sets color perceptions of external events, ask students to look at (or imagine looking at) a picture while wearing colored glasses or while looking through colored cellophane. Different parts of the picture will become more obvious depending on the color of glasses worn. Essentially, the birth cycle causes parents to look at the world through glasses which are colored differently from the students' glasses.

c. Tell the story of the six blind men and the elephant. Discuss, relating the story to differing perceptions of young and old.

2. *To analyze* ***preconceived notions*** *that parents, grandparents, and teens have about each other which inhibit open communication.*

a. Hand students lists of words and phrases that describe the older generation and ask the students to put a *P* by the words that apply to their parents, to put a *G* by the words that apply to their grandparents, and to put an *O* by the words that describe most other adults. Students could make up their own lists. A representative list may include such things as:

old-fashioned	modern
bossy	democratic
not understanding	understanding
stingy	generous
out-of-touch	with it

Let the students make a list of words or phrases that their parents would use to describe them. Students should take the list home to ask parents to check the ones with which they agree. Parents may add additional words or phrases. For example:

irresponsible	responsible
untrustworthy	trustworthy
careless	careful
headstrong	

Conduct a class discussion about the ensuing lists. Discuss questions, such as: Do students perceive their own parents and grandparents in the same way that they see most other adults? Do students accurately predict what their parents think of them? If a student perceives his parent as being stingy, how might he approach the parent to get money? Suggest several ways. If a student perceives parents as being generous, how might he approach the parent to get money? Discuss other words and phrases in this same way until students begin to see how preexisting mental sets can affect attempts to communicate.

b. Careful listening facilitates intergenerational communication, yet we react to a statement before we understand the speaker's meaning.

Ask a parent to communicate a feeling to a teenager, or role play this situation. The teenager may react only by interpreting exactly what the parent has said. Continue until the teenager can interpret the message to the satisfaction of the adult. Repeat with the teenager being the sender of the message. This process may be likened to a mirror which only reflects the message which hits it. Teens and parents should practice this message-reflection technique at home.

c. Hostility eliminates free expression of ideas. Therefore, a hostile person may tune out the message of the sender. Invite students and parents to name techniques that are used to tune out messages from the other person.

Parents may send children to their rooms when communication gets touchy. Both parents and children may just not listen to each other. Teenagers may start an argument to avoid talking with parents. Avoidance of eye contact or set facial expressions may limit communication. Interruptions inhibit communication.

d. There are two generation gaps for the generation in the middle (Carlson 1970). Role playing may be used to give students the feeling of the dilemma of their parents. Use this situation to introduce the topic or to emphasize it.

Situation

A sixteen-year-old boy has just told his father he wants to move out and live elsewhere. The father responds with surprise and indignation and the doubt that the boy could make it alone. The boy leaves in a huff. Immediately the grandfather enters and proposes to his son that he and his family come to live with the grandfather.

Questions

(1) Why does the boy want to move out?
(2) Why does the father hesitate to allow it?

(3) How does the father feel when the grandfather suggests he live with the grandfather?
(4) What is the similarity in the two sons' feelings?
(5) What is the dilemma of the father that neither the boy nor the grandfather has?

e. Read and discuss "The Breadman" by Mary Heath (1972), a story about a second marriage in middle adulthood.
Read and discuss *The Centaur* by John Updike (1963), a book about a father through his son's eyes.

f. Do the following role playing to show that people act the way they do because of the way we treat them. Send three people out of the room. Then ask the remaining people to describe what they expect from a 26-year-old, a 56-year-old, and a 76-year-old. Have them list typical questions asked of each age in small talk. Bring the people outside the room in one at a time. The people in the room will then begin to treat that person and talk to that person as if he were one of the ages. The person brought in will not know the purpose of the discussion, but each one will take on behaviors of the age placed on them.

3. *To apply the theory that how one reacts to life in each stage predicts what he will be like in each succeeding stage. (The* ***Developmental Task Theory*** *states that it is difficult for a person to meet the tasks or problems of his present stage in life if he has not successfully satisfied the tasks or requirements of the preceding stages.)*

a. Use Erikson's Eight Stages of Man (printed earlier in this chapter) which is also based on the theory that success in one stage encourages success in the next stage, to show how the uncertainties, successes, and failures of childhood and young adulthood affect the behavior and feeling of older adults.
(1) Have students predict their own behavior as a grandparent.
(2) Challenge the following statements:
"Overlook him; he's just old."
"When they're over 30, they've had it."
"Don't promote anyone over 45."
"Mandatory retirement age should be 60."
"I feel sorry for old people."

b. Present parts from the play *I Never Sang for My Father* (1970) to stimulate discussion about adult children and aging parents.

Questions

(1) Ask the persons playing the father and the son how each felt merely by playing the parts.
(2) Why do fathers hang on to authority?

(3) What is the difference in a father or a mother being the widowed one with respect to needs?

(4) What plans can people make about their aging parents which keep neither generation from controlling the other?

4. *To apply the notion that* ***parents' behavior*** *may be* ***a result of their children's behavior.***

Role Playing

Select three people to assume the role of a parent. Seat them at the side. Give the following statements to several students in the class who will walk up to the parents or stay in their seats. Each student will express the statements below with strong emotion. The parent role players will react silently, but emotionally, to the expressions and later will express their feelings to the class.

Statements (Call them tirades or anything.)

"You're just stingy; you're selfish!"

"I don't ever get anything!"

"Everybody has one but me!"

"I heard you had to get married, too!"

"Why are you so hard on me?"

"Momma (pause), what would you say if I told you I didn't really spend the night at Aunt Martha's?"

"I don't care! I'm not going to college!"

"You know, Dad, it's like you always said—a guy has to believe in himself!"

"What did you do when you were my age that makes you so suspicious of me now?"

"I wish you'd get off my back. It's a round in court every time I get back. 'Where did you go? With Whom?' . . . . It's my life, so let me do what I please!"

"You've ordered me around all my life, but this time it's going to be a different story."

"I want to be an individual—not a carbon copy of you; so quit telling me how to dress, how to wear my hair, etc. . . ."

"I'm getting sick and tired of your reading my mail and listening in on my phone calls, reading my diary, etc."

"If I hear 'when I was your age' one time more, I am leaving home for good."

"You're so money motivated, Dad; that's not the most important thing in life. Bob and I are getting married right after high school graduation."

"You are so old-fashioned; science has perfected birth control. Don't worry. I won't disgrace you by getting pregnant."

"I've seen you drunk before. What's wrong with my taking a drink now and then?"

"You let Margie date at 15; just because she had to get married, you're punishing me by not letting me date until 18. I think you're both crazy!"

"He's 40; his health has started failing."

"His mind is very dull . . . he's 60."

"It is awful to be old."

Questions (First ask the parent role players and the child role players how they felt.)

(1) How does a parent (or anyone) begin to react when these situations are constantly facing them?

(2) Is it possible that parents could be more "human" if children were complimentary once in a while? The question is, how can children make parents better people? (Gray 1974)

Before students can have more rewarding relationships with people in other generations—younger and older—they must be aware of (1) certain universal, unchanging factors such as the broad stages in the life cycle and the decelerating rates of socialization as well as (2) the lasting effects of the current environmental factors on people in each stage of the life cycle.

It is necessary to remember that generational conflict may be as much from attitudes as from age. There is often a pronounced disassociation even within the same generation. Specific techniques to be used in bridge building intergenerationally and intragenerationally include:

1. clear communication
2. confrontation
3. constructive argumentation
4. appropriate exchange or negotiation.

As in other family relationships intergenerational and intragenerational conflicts must be faced and resolved. Confrontation, however, must occur or growth cannot occur.

Summary

Intergenerational relationships and conflicts are as value-specific as they are age-specific. The age differential and the historical period in which one grows up are two factors that cannot be changed, yet they do affect the way two people of different generations interact. However, when a high learning rate continues through adulthood and when both generations keep up with current thought, intergenerational relationships are complementary. Stereotypes are questioned and exercises are suggested in this chapter that permit students to gain some skill in better intergenerational relationships.

Although married couples are usually in the same generation age-wise, their conflicts may be based on some of the same conflicts between generations—differences in values. The next chapter discusses methods for teaching about relationships in marriage, living together unmarried, love as interaction, and coping with marital conflict.

References

Anderson, Robert. *I Never Sang for My Father.* New York: New American Library, 1970.

Bengtson, Vern L. and Black, K. Dean. "Intergenerational Relations and Continuities in Socialization." In *Life-Span Developmental Psychology: Personality and Socialization,* edited by Paul B. Baltes and K. Warner Schaie. New York: Academic Press, 1973.

Buck, Pearl. *The Good Earth.* New York: J. Day Co., 1949.

Carlson, Duane R., ed. *Generation in the Middle.* Chicago: Blue Cross Assoc., 1970.

Davis, Kingsley. "The Sociology of Parent-Youth Conflict." In *People as Partners,* edited by Jacqueline P. Wiseman. San Francisco: Canfield Press, 1971.

Devor, Geraldine M. "Children as Agents in Socializing Parents." *The Family Coordinator* 19:208-212, 1970.

Duvall, Evelyn M. *Family Development,* 4th ed. Philadelphia: J. B. Lippincott Co., 1971.

Erikson, Erik. *Childhood and Society.* New York: Norton, 1964.

Gray, Farnum. "Little Brother Is Changing You." *Psychology Today* 7:42-46, 1974.

Hansel, Robert R. *Like Father, Like Son—Like Hell.* New York: The Seabury Press, 1969.

Heath, Mary. "The Breadman." In *The Best American Short Stories 1972,* edited by Martha Foley. New York: Ballantine Books, 1972.

Hechinger, Grace. "Poor Mom, Done In By Experts." *The Wall Street Journal.* May 10, 1973.

Koller, Marvin R. *Families: A Multigenerational Approach.* New York: McGraw-Hill Book Co., 1974.

Lidz, Theodore. *The Person: His Development Throughout the Life Cycle.* New York: Basic Books, Inc., 1968.

Mead, Margaret. *Coming of Age in Samoa.* New York: New American Library, 1949.

____. *Culture and Generation Gap.* Garden City, New York: Natural History Press, 1970.

Nesselroade, John R., and Baltes, Paul B. *Adolescent Personality Development and Historical Change: 1970-72.* Monograph No. 154, vol. 39. Chicago: Society for Research in Child Development, 1974.

Schulz, David A. *The Changing Family.* Englewood Cliffs, New Jersey: Prentice-Hall, 1972.

Smith, Rebecca, and McLester, Carol. "Empathetic Intergeneration Education." Toronto, Canada: Paper presented at the annual meeting of the National Council on Family Relations, 20 October 1973.

Steiner, George J. "Parent-Teen Education—An Exercise in Communication." *The Family Coordinator* 19:213-218, 1970.

Toffler, Alvin. *Future Shock*. New York: Bantam Books, 1970.
Updike, John. *The Centaur*. New York: Alfred A. Knopf, 1963.
"When the Young Teach and the Old Learn." *Time*, 17 August 1970, pp. 35-40.

Suggested Films

A Changing View of the Change of Life (1970, 25 min.) Association/Sterling Films, 600 Grand Avenue, Ridgefield, New Jersey 07657.

Coming Home (Intergenerational) (1972, 84 min.) National Film Board of Canada. 1 Lombard Street, Toronto, Ontario M5C 1 J6, Canada.

Future Shock (1971, 50 min.) McGraw-Hill / Contemporary Films, 1221 Avenue of the Americas, New York, N.Y. 10020.

Ivan and His Father (1971, 13½ min.). Churchill Films, 662 North Robertson Blvd., Los Angeles, CA 90069.

Saturday Morning (1970, 88 min.). Columbia Pictures, 711 Fifth Avenue, New York, N.Y. 10022.

This Charming Couple (1950, 19 min.). McGraw-Hill Book Co., 1221 Avenue of the Americas, New York, N.Y. 10020.

Trouble in the Family (1965, 90 min., 3 reels). National Educational Television Film Service, Indiana University, Bloomington, Ind. 47405.

Chapter 12
Interpersonal Relationships In Any Family

There are many kinds of families, including the married pair who has no children or who has biological or adopted children; the one-parent family (widowed or divorced parent, adoptive single parent, or unwed mother or father); the blended family which is any combination of remarried people and their children, several generations in one house, or a communal family; and the unmarried pair living together. The same human relationships problems occur in any type family and are based on each person's self-concept, his conditioned beliefs, and the situation.

The teaching techniques presented here may include people from any family although one of the above types of families is used in each illustration.

Factors Affecting Relationships After Marriage

Interpersonal relationships are the same in some ways and yet different in other ways after two people marry. Spouses still have the same childhood conditioning and needs they had prior to marriage, but marriage changes the situation. The one specific and tangible change is the legality of the situation with all its duties and responsibilities both explicit by law and implicit by culture.

There are several factors in marriage which affect interpersonal relationships that are not spelled out by law and are little discussed by culture. Four will be discussed here. One is the factor of constancy which leads to satiation or boredom as well as loss of privacy and independence after marriage. Adding to this constancy is society's pressure against outside companionship, particularly with the opposite sex, which leads to a loss of stimulating interchange. Constancy, however, can also be security.

Another factor, which seems to be unexpected, is the change in relative bargaining power after marriage. Associated with this change in bargaining power are the expectations of role behavior. Some people are very surprised to learn that their spouses expect *not* to carry out some traditional role such as manager of the house. The person who determines the roles may have the greatest bargaining power, however. If the wife works full-time and makes as much or almost as much money as the husband, she may have more bargaining power to make the decision about who will manage the household than if she does not work.

Another factor is the exploitation of one spouse by the other and vice versa under the guise that in marriage people are expected to perform certain duties. The comment that "I am taken for granted" results from this lack of appreciation. Two other exploitative behaviors are expecting achievement on the part of the spouse without building up that spouse's self-concept and unnecessarily using the spouse's time and energy. Interpersonal relationships are also different after marriage because of a fourth factor—that of conflicting expectations and unexpected expectations.

The following teaching techniques are designed to enlighten students about some of these aspects of interpersonal relationships in marriage and the family.

Teaching Techniques

1. *To understand the reasons, particularly* ***satiation and exploitation****, for sexual problems after marriage.*
   a. Report the following statement as a description of sexual attitudes of young married people.

      "When we were having sexual relationships prior to marriage, we found it to be exciting and never once was there a time when neither of us had an orgasm. Now, I don't know what to think. Many times I don't want intercourse or cannot reach orgasm or I seem to have to lost my ability to get him aroused."

      Ask students to suggest various reasons for the change. Some reasons they might or might not bring out are these:
      (1) They are not yet adjusted.
      (2) They are not suited to each other.
      (3) They are using too little variation.
      (4) They have begun to resent something in the other.
      (5) They may be tired from working.
      (6) They may just be bored with being together so much.
      (7) They may expect more from intercourse than is physically possible just because they are married.
      (8) They may not be as eager to please as before.
2. *To investigate the ways people try to meet some basic needs of* ***privacy and independence*** *in marriage.*
   a. In studying the development of needs, it is found that union and

dependence at infancy (Ausubel and Sullivan 1970; Sears, Rau, and Alpert 1965) are precursors for privacy and independence later. How do the following statements show a move to meet privacy and independence needs?

(1) A wife and mother who looks forward to reading after everyone is in bed.
(2) A wife who "piddles" around rather than working when everyone gets out of the house.
(3) A husband who "tinkers" in the garage.
(4) A husband who goes "fishing."
(5) A wife who goes "shopping."
(6) A wife who will not let anyone in the kitchen.
(7) A husband who goes into his shell.
(8) A wife who "cuts people out."

b. Tell this story to the class.

I went to visit a student, and as I went onto the porch, I saw the grandmother rocking and staring out into space. I spoke but she didn't speak, and therefore I knocked on the door. The student came to the door and I went in. We talked with the mother for nearly an hour and then I left. Later I asked the student how her grandmother was and why she didn't speak. With great enthusiasm she told me that her grandmother was taking her "quiet hour," and no one ever interrupted another person's "quiet hour." In fact, each person in the family had the privilege of taking a "quiet hour" each day with the assurance that no one would disturb him.

3. *To become aware that there may be a loss or gain of prestige when someone is called only by a role name.*

a. Think of everyone in your family and the various names they are called.

(1) When the name is a role name as grandmother or aunt, do you tend to see them as roles more than as individuals?
(2) Are any of your family members called Mr. or Mrs. or Miss? Why? Do some people prefer this?
(3) Do some of them prefer a role name? Why?
(4) How have you changed the names you call relatives as you have grown older?

b. What are the different names you are called? By whom? Why? Would you like to change any of them?

c. Tell this story.

A young mother who lived in the house with her mother-in-law chose "Mama" for the name her child should use. Why? If she had chosen "Mother," then the grandmother would have chosen

"Mama." The grandmother was forced to use "Grandmother." What happened was that both are called "Mama" and the grandmother is called "Grandma" at times.

d. Most people have to play several family roles in their lifetime and many of them simultaneously. The problem lies in having to play a role for which one does not feel comfortable whether by choice or by force. Discuss some of the roles played for which one is unsuited.
   (1) The older son who must take the part of father to the younger children and husband (in responsibility) to the mother when the father is either gone or ineffective.
   (2) The daughter who must take the part of the son who was never born.
   (3) The grandmother who must take the part of the mother who leads a life of her own.
   (4) The husband who must take the part of the father to the wife who never had one or who had one who was ineffective.
   (5) The child who must try to fulfill the dreams of the parent who never had the opportunities the child is given.

4. *To understand that* ***excessive attachment*** *to another person limits one's choices and activities.*
   a. Ask for three people to play the parts of a father, an eighteen-year-old daughter, and her boyfriend. Tie a ten- to twelve-foot rope around the girl's waist and give the end to the father who stands to one side. The boy and girl make plans to do a variety of things and attempt to do such activities as going out, hugging, going to the beach, and many more. As the father hears the plans, he either tightens the rope or lets go according to his wishes and fears. The daughter holds back or fights the knotted rope as she wishes or fears. The boy helps the girl, walks off alone, or fights the father as he wishes or fears.

Other Situations

The parts could be these roles: (1) a wife attached to a former husband as she and a new husband try to make a new life; (2) a mother attached to her children as her husband attempts to get her to come with him; (3) a father attached to his job as his family encourages him to pay attention to them; (4) a mother attached to a memory of her parents as her husband tries to get her to think for herself (Satir 1972).

   b. Ask for four to five volunteers for this situation. The players are any members of a family. Give each member a string or rope for the connection between him and each of the others. The problem here is to ask one of them to leave the group. (Then after he has gone, ask one more to leave.)

Note how he handles the situation.

(1) Does he drop all strings and walk out?

(2) Does he ask the others to give him their end of the string and keep the string?

(3) Do some of them make him drop their ends whereas others give up their string to him easily?

(4) Do some of them refuse to drop theirs and resist his dropping theirs?

(5) Are the strings tossed away or pocketed for later use (Satir 1972)?

5. *To experience the feeling of having* **excessive demands** *made at one time. Since no one can stay in this position long, a move has to be made (Satir, 1972).*

a. Ask five students to volunteer for family members: mother, father, twelve-year-old son, eight-year-old daughter, four-year-old son.

Situation

The father (or mother) has just returned from work. Each wants the father's (or mother's) attention immediately.

Simulated Situation

Father (or mother) stands in the middle and each of the other members grasps the parent somewhere–leg, arm, body, hand–and pulls gently until there is tension. Then freeze in the tension pull. (The parent will begin to feel stretched and off balance. He will make some attempt to keep his balance.) Encourage him to act in some way verbally or physically to get out of the stranglehold.

Discussion

(1) Ask each person how he felt, particularly the one in the middle.

(2) What happened as the one in the middle got loose?

(3) He could knock everyone loose or he could push everyone loose or he could just collapse (as a person would who uses illness to get away.) He could bribe or beg or call for help. He could tell them how he feels and ask them to give him time and he will listen to each as well as to have some time of his own.

(4) Note that the same *physical* feelings will occur when a person is being pulled verbally more than he can stand. The same guilt feelings will occur if someone got a stronger push away than he intended.

(5) Describe many situations in which one family member is "pulled" further than he can give.

  (a) Married daughter who is pulled by her parents, her children, and her husband as well as her job.

  (b) Child who is pulled by his playmates, his schoolwork, his parents, and his own wishes.

(c) Mother whose food is boiling over, the telephone ringing, her child hurt, and her husband calling.

(d) Define the pressures on you and how you can handle them.

b. Role play the following situation:

Situation

Husband too involved in job.

Wife: (Answering telephone) "But, you must come home for dinner tomorrow. It's Junior's fifth birthday and I'd planned to have a special surprise desert. (She's eager that he be there because of the son.)

Husband: (Concerned, but eager to finish a plan for a contract to be submitted next week)

Points

(1) Jobs are important, but so are families.

(2) A family and a home can be one of the reasons that a man can advance in his job.

(3) Sometimes a man needs to be helped to see the necessity of giving attention to both job and family.

6. *To understand that conflict is more likely the greater the* ***number of people in a family.***

a. Show the class the algebraic formula for finding how the number of relationships increases as each family member is added (Bossard 1945).

x = number of relationships

y = number of people

$$x = \frac{y^2 - y}{2}$$

If there are two people in a family, there is *one* relationship only.

$$x = \frac{2^2 - 2}{2}$$

$$x = \frac{4 - 2}{2}$$

$$x = \frac{2}{2}$$

$$x = 1$$

If there are four people in a family, there are six relationships.

$$x = \frac{4^2 - 4}{2}$$

$$x = \frac{16 - 4}{2}$$

$$x = \frac{12}{2}$$

$$x = 6$$

Five: ten relationships
Six: fifteen relationships
Seven: twenty-one relationships
Eight: twenty-eight relationships
Nine: thirty-six relationships
Ten: forty-five relationships

b. Show these additional relationships by use of people and strings. Start with two people and have each hold a string between them. Add one person to the group and put a string between the new person and each one in the group (now three strings). Add one person more and put a string between this new person and each of the other three (now six strings). Continue until there are about six people in the group (fifteen strings).

c. To make this concrete showing of relationships even more realistic, you might use different sizes of string (even rope or knitting yarn) to show different strengths of the relationships between certain people. Some strings can be very weak.
Then have some of the students tug on some of the strings to show the effect of the strengths. Some of the weaker threads will break, some will get tangled, and some will get dropped. Use everything that happens to illustrate the dynamics.

For example

(1) Show that relationships can be strangling by tying the string around one's neck.
(2) Show that relationships get taut by tightening the strings.
(3) Show a relationship in which one wants to tighten his relationship or manipulate the other person and the other fights back or gives a little.
(4) Some relationships are cut and later retied (actually cut this one with scissors). When the relationship is cut, the family falters.
(5) It is everybody's responsibility to keep ties workable, not just the parents'.
(6) Parents may need to help untie a child who is strangling, yet hold onto their own relationship.

Questions

(1) To the family group: How did you feel as more and more people were added to the group? How did you feel when some of your strings were tied to another or were cut?
(2) To the audience: What special feelings did you get as the group

became larger? Where did you want to step in and help? Where did you want to say that this tie isn't like the ones in your family?

Some General Statements about Large Numbers of People Involved

(1) The more people there are, the more involved the relationships are.
(2) When one relationship gets too tight, the others sometimes also suffer.
(3) When one person pulls to tighten a relationship, the other person sometimes needs to be flexible.

7. *To understand that the power to dominate is determined by such factors as physical beauty, amount of education, job status, and the presence or absence of children, and to understand that the better* **bargaining position** *can fluctuate from one partner to the other at various times in the marriage (Blood and Wolfe 1960).*

   a. Select a married couple you know well. What is the status of power? Put a + or − under the columns Husband and Wife across from each attribute according to which has the bargaining power.

Factors	*Husband*	*Wife*	*Explanation and Comments*
Physical beauty		+	But he is big and tall
Amount of education		+	But he is smarter
Job status	+		He is an executive; she is a teacher.
Children		+	Because of fulltime maid and his willingness to share all of the work
Verbal fluency		+	Generally, yes, and in her field, but not in his
Common Sense	+		More down to earth
Problem-solving ability	+		Has more perspective

   b. Using the same chart above, discuss a couple whose relative bargaining power changed and note why and what the consequences were.

   c. To establish individual student views of male and female rights to be out at night and the change in bargaining power, read and discuss the case of John and Eloise, and in the same class period read the case of Marian and Alex. Note the difference in how the students react to John and to Marian as they both carry out their jobs. It is usually assumed that Marian has no right to work at night, but that John does.

THE CASE OF JOHN AND ELOISE*

"John is ruining our marriage!" Eloise said. "I work hours preparing a nice dinner for him, and he's never on time to eat it. The worst part about it is that he doesn't even call me to let me know that he'll be late. He could be on time every night if he wanted to. He just doesn't want to. He doesn't love me enough. I know he'll tell you that he's a salesman and can't get up and run out of his prospect's office when suppertime comes, but 90 percent of the time that isn't so, and the other times he could at least call me. All he thinks about is himself. When he does get home and the dinner is cold or burned, he complains.

"He wasn't that way before we married. He had the same job, but he was almost always on time for our dinner dates. I'm just not going to put up with his selfishness any longer. I'm tired of begging him, and I'm tired of screaming at him; now I'm going to leave him."

John had a somewhat different version of the same story. "If Eloise told you that I can't get home for dinner every night right on the minute, she's right," John told the counselor. "She knew when I married her that I was a salesman. I have to be where the client is when he wants to buy, regardless of what time it is. She didn't make any fuss about it before we were married. She conveniently forgets about it now, but I was just about as late for our dates before as I am now. There were a couple of big differences then. In the first place, she wasn't cooking the meals. In the second place, it didn't seem to matter to her so much. She didn't give me the stuff she does now about her father always being on time! She and that perfect father of hers. He had a nine-to-five job and was never a minute late getting to the office and never a minute late getting home. Before we were married, she seemed to understand how I couldn't always figure out my time to the second. She even used to smile about it a little and call me 'Johnny-come-lately.' But after we got married she changed. Now she never smiles; she just screams.

"I admit that I'm not the best one about telephoning. Sometimes there isn't a phone around. But there's more to it than that. I feel like such a baby when I have to report to her every five minutes. The other fellows don't have to go running to the phone to call their wives. When they're late, their wives understand. My mother used to understand, too. Before we were married and I was living at home, Mother didn't nag me all the time. If I was a little late coming, she would just serve supper to the rest of them and put mine in the oven. In some ways I think my mother loved me more than my wife does. She wasn't trying to make me out like a bad guy all the time.

"I don't want a divorce; I love my wife and kids. But sometimes I think it would be better if she did get a divorce. She sure is making my life miserable the way it is."

*From pp. 175-176 in *Marriage and Family Relationships* by Richard H. Klemer. Copyright © 1970 by Richard H. Klemer. Used by permission of Harper & Row, Publishers, Inc.

THE CASE OF MARIAN AND ALEX*

"I'd been married to Marian for about seven years," Alex said. "She came from a home where she had a tremendously domineering father, and she was very much afraid of him. When he said she couldn't go out, that was that. For the first five or six years after we were married, she was pretty good about being a good wife. Whenever she went anywhere, she asked me if she could go. Sometimes it even seemed a little silly for me to tell a grown woman exactly what she could do.

"But then she got a job at a television studio. She is a very beautiful woman. At first I was all for it. I was pleased that my wife was so attractive. But pretty soon she began feeling very independent and staying out until all hours of the night. I began to scream and shout about her not coming in until two or three in the morning. Then she began to not tell me when she was going out. I'd get home and find that she'd left the kids at a babysitter's and gone off on some 'public relations' job. About the middle of the evening she'd call up and say she'd be home in half an hour. Then maybe at about two in the morning she'd finally get home. Since yelling at her didn't seem to do any good, I started trying to reason with her. That wasn't any better. She just told me that she'd do as she pleased.

"A couple of weeks ago I got so mad I moved out. I'd thought I'd show her. But now I'm wondering if I didn't make a bad mistake. She has shown no inclination to ask me to come back, and now she gets to go out anytime she wants to. Sure, I'm jealous. I don't know what she's doing out late at night. She says she's just either out with the girls or driving by herself. She says she wouldn't want any other man, and the way our sex life has been I don't think she would either. I think she hates men and sex too.

"What am I going to do? If I go back and tell her she can go out any time she wants to, I'll have lost face. Besides, I don't think that's what she really wants anyway."

When the counselor talked to Marian, she agreed that everything that Alex had said was right. "He used to carp at me and pick at me an awful lot. At first I tried to do better in every way he suggested. But I never could meet his expectations so finally I just stopped trying. Then I got my job. Everyone is nice to me down there, and I like the people, and I have a sense of achievement. Besides, it is very flattering to be told how nice I look. I'm not going to stop working now no matter what Alex does.

"Yes, it's true that I lie to him. The thing that set him off three weeks ago was that I waited until the last minute to tell him I was going out for an evening show. I told him I'd be home by ten, but I knew that I couldn't possibly be home before midnight. I was afraid to tell him that, because he would have hit the ceiling and been mad before I left and mad when I got home. When I finally did get home at three A.M., he was only mad once.

"Sure, I understand he doesn't like me out until three in the morning. But he goes out with the boys until all hours, why shouldn't

*From p. 181 in *Marriage and Family Relationships* by Richard H. Klemer. Copyright © 1970 by Richard H. Klemer. Used by permission of Harper & Row, Publishers, Inc.

I? Actually, I really think I want him to stop me, but to tell you the truth I don't know how he's going to. I'll leave him if he tries to use force. He did hit me once, you know.

"I don't know whether I'm glad or sorry he walked out, but in many ways it's nice to be independent. Yet in some ways I think I still need him. I wish he could find some way to solve this thing."

8. *To understand that an **equalitarian marriage** is one in which the decision making is joint at times and separate at times, but that the decision making is balanced.*

a. Draw several lines or continua, one for each area in which husbands and wives must make *decisions*. Put husband at one end and the wife at the other. Place a mark on the continuum according to whether the husband or the wife makes most of the decisions in that area. Summarize the placement of the marks to determine the extent of equalitarianism.

Area	*Who makes the decision–not who does the work*
Buying furniture	Husband ____________________ Wife
Insurance	Husband ____________________ Wife
What to do for entertainment	Husband ____________________ Wife
Menus	Husband ____________________ Wife
Children's discipline	Husband ____________________ Wife
Buying automobile	Husband ____________________ Wife
Buying house	Husband ____________________ Wife
Where to live	Husband ____________________ Wife
Housework	Husband ____________________ Wife
Yard work	Husband ____________________ Wife
Guests to invite	Husband ____________________ Wife

b. Discuss these points:

If a person is satisfied with the decision making although one spouse makes the large majority of the decisions, should he or she strive for a more equalitarian balance?

If one spouse makes most of the decisions and the other spouse is satisfied that this occurs, does this mean the decision-making spouse is satisfied with that position?

If one spouse makes most of the decisions and enjoys the position, does that give him the position of dominance if it is really the other spouse who has decided to give that right to make most of the decisions to the first spouse?

c. Challenge by debate: The greater the sharing of decisions, the healthier the marriage. Support for the above statement: When the decisions are shared because both spouses have input by virtue of their own intellect, strength, and desire, then the spouses are meeting their needs. Non-support for the debate statement: When the decisions are shared because one spouse thinks they should be when the other spouse does not have the desire to participate, then the spouses are not meeting each other's needs.

d. Discuss the possibility of a marriage in which both partners agree to certain responsibilities because they want to, not because of any preconceived notion of who *should* do it. First of all, assume each has equal ability—earning capacity, strength, background experiences in housekeeping, ability to procreate, ability in childcare, education, wit, etc. This discussion will inevitably have inputs about who "ought" to do what, what others in the neighborhood would think, as well as one's childhood conditioning. All of this discussion teaches the students how they have arrived at their beliefs and how custom is started. Keep the students on the question in point until they have come to some insight about the difficulties in this culture for having a truly equal partnership in marriage. You may have to throw in occasionally, "Suppose the couple were of the same sex?"

9. *To apply the* ***homeostasis theory*** *of social relations to the family. This theory states that there is a constant process of change in all parts of the social milieu in an effort to make a workable whole. As one part changes, other parts must change (Stagner 1968).*

a. Make a mobile frame with several places to attach cutouts of varying family members.
   (1) Attach husband and wife so that they balance.
   (2) Add one child, then two, but balance mobile by changing the parents also.
   (3) Replace first child with an older child and balance mobile.
   (4) Take one person away (death, divorce, extended separation).

   Every time a change occurs, all family members are disturbed. To replace balance, move some family members. All families who are still together are in balance, but what is the cost to each member to keep it?

b. Make some large stylized cutouts (with some adhesive backing) of different ages of people from birth to old age. Let the caricatures imply the developmental tasks of that age. Begin to make the stages in the family life cycle by placing the caricatures on the board. At first show the typical ages in the stages to give the students the notion of developmental needs of varying ages in typical stages. Then show some different families (thirty-five-year-old woman, thirty-eight-year-old man, six-month-old baby, sixty-year-old grandmother) and discuss the give and take to meet those varying needs.

10. *To understand that* **people change** *considerably every few years and that the person one marries will change several times in a married lifetime (Pineo 1969).*
    a. Tell students you know of a person who has (or that you have) been married four times and considering a fifth time and that you approve of it. (At first, they will look at you with disbelief mainly because you are a teacher of family relationships. They will inevitably question you, whereupon you will explain that a single marriage may be the same as having been married several times because people definitely do change in many ways.)
    b. Some people change more than others and often one stagnates as the other changes. Read the following case of Sally and Ronald.

THE CASE OF SALLY AND RONALD*

Sally and Ronald grew up together. They came from the same neighborhood in a small town, went to school and church together, and started going steady in high school. When the time came, they went off to the same college. By the time they were juniors, they decided that they could no longer wait to be married. After the wedding, Sally quit going to school and took a job as a typist so that Ron could complete his education.

In due course, Ron was graduated from college and admitted to medical school. Sally and Ron moved into a small housing project originally designed for low-income families. Sally, of course, continued to work, but she resented that, besides typing for eight hours a day, the household chores were largely her responsibility as well. In the few hours that Ron was home, he usually had some studying to do. Sally sometimes suspected that he could have done his studying at school, but then he would have missed the cafeteria conversation and the occasional bridge games with the other students.

Finally the great day came, and Ron was graduated from medical school and accepted as a resident at a nearby hospital. There was still very little money to spare, so Sally continued to work, but at long last she persuaded Ron to start a family. Before his residency was complete, they had a child. Sally quit her job and seemed to be very happy with her new life. Getting started in practice meant more lean years. Moreover, another baby was born. With two in diapers and a house to take care of, Sally was always tired. But she loved Ron and she believed Ron loved her.

Within a few years, Ron's practice began to prosper. In fact, before long, Sally and Ron had money for all the material things they wanted. At first Ron worked very hard to pay off the debts and to build up an investment income. After a while, however, he began to take an increasing amount of time off to play golf at the country club. Sally went to the country club once or twice, but she was a small-town girl

*From pp. 79-80 in *Marriage and Family Relationships* by Richard H. Klemer. Copyright © 1970 by Richard H. Klemer. Used by permission of Harper & Row, Publishers, Inc.

and felt out of place there. The women there talked about golf and bridge, neither of which she played. Ron kept urging her to try, but finally he gave up. With increasing frequency, he went to the country club by himself.

Meanwhile two more children had arrived, and Sally was busier with homemaking activities. At the country club, Ron met a great many people, including some attractive young divorcees who had grown up in the atmosphere of the country club. Sophisticated and charming, they had gone to elite Eastern women's colleges and seemed able to anticipate exactly what Ron wanted even before he himself realized it.

One day Ron came home and, in effect, said to Sally: "I have found that the women at the country club meet my needs better than you do. I've changed. I need someone who is gay and sophisticated. I am sure you wouldn't want to have me spend the rest of my life with you, knowing that I didn't love you. You are a good woman and would make some other man a good wife, but you and I no longer have common interests. I will always take care of you and the children financially, but I want a divorce."

11. *To analyze and evaluate family conditions as to why there are certain personal attitudes about one's family.*
    a. Make a tape recording of your family or have an outsider observe your family and describe what he saw—only what he saw or heard—not his interpretations. Interpretation gets into feelings and subjectivity.
    b. Have each family member keep notes hour-by-hour of where he was and with whom. One member compiles everybody's record by the hour. Members will note why they felt "left out" or "covered up in company" or "overworked."

       Were there many times when certain family members had time just for themselves? Were there times when no family member was available to contact?
    c. Make a list of all the jobs done daily by each member of the family.

       Were some members getting by without doing *any* household jobs? (Working a job should not let them out of all.)

       Were some members getting all the dirty jobs (washing dishes, carrying out trash, picking up clothes)?

       Were some members having all their personal needs taken care of by someone else?

12. *To apply the generalization that the **in-law relationships** being only a categorical type of relationship will flourish under the same circumstances as other relationships: When there is a need to be met, behavior will be undertaken to satisfy that need.*

    Have the students tell what they will or do call their mother-in-law or father-in-law. The various names will be these and probably in order:

Names	*Needs Satisfied*
First name	To be friends
Last name	To be respectful
Mother (last name) or Father (last name)	To be close but respectful
Mom (first name) or Daddy (first name)	To be close but respectful
Mother or Dad	To be very close
No name (just wait until they look at you to speak)	To be independent or uninvolved.

13. *To become aware of the **congruence of perceptions** between marriage partners.*
    a. Draw a picture of the most important thing you think is happening in your marriage at this time and one showing what you think your spouse thinks.
       (1) Describe your pictures to your spouse or have the spouse describe what he sees in the picture.
       (2) Compare drawings to see congruence or similarity of perceptions.
       (3) Discuss how congruence or lack of congruence affects marriage satisfaction.
    b. Present these research findings to the class for discussion (Luckey 1960):
       (1) The greater the congruence between your perception of yourself and the spouse's perception of you, the greater the satisfaction in marriage.
       (2) The greater the congruence between your perception of yourself and the spouse's perception of your perception of yourself, the greater the satisfaction in marriage. (Apply this to family members other than spouses.)
    c. Ask a male student to tell what he thinks a husband's role is and what a wife's role is.
       Ask a female student to tell what she thinks a husband's role is and what a wife's role is.
       Then suggest that these two assume the role of a married pair and present themselves to the class for premarital counseling. How would you counsel with this couple?

Woman: I think the wife's role is to keep the house clean and have the meals cooked. I also think she should make the home so that no problems exist when he comes home from work. I think he should provide well for his family and give them some freedom in spending the money. He should give his wife credit for keeping peace.

Male: I think the husband's role is to be head of the house and help make the decisions about the concerns of the family. He should provide most of the income even if his wife works. The wife should keep the house and keep the husband informed about what's going on. She should be a good bed partner.

14. *To become aware of the advantages and disadvantages of* ***cross-sex friends*** *after marriage.*

Read some excerpts from *Open Marriage* (O'Neill and O'Neill 1972) such as those below.* Discuss the suggestions in light of the human potential movement which suggests that we may be grossly limiting our potential while rigidly holding onto the exclusive monogamistic marriage.

If each partner is allowed to grow individually, in directions that he may find interesting and fulfilling but which his mate does not, if he is allowed to seek in others outside his marriage a response to those of his hook-up points that are not matched by his mate, then each partner will continue to grow and change, so that there will always be new things for his mate to discover in him. If discovery between two people is continuous, if each is always growing, then the fulfilling aspects of the relationship will never run their course. Thus couples who insist upon exclusivity, who continue to believe that any husband and wife can be all to one another, are in fact only insuring that their relationship will eventually cease to be fulfilling in a mutual way. To commit yourself to this ending, by accepting the traditional closed contract before you have ever begun, seems a tragic error, especially since it is such an unnecessary one. (pp. 169-170).

Open companionship works for the husband and wife who have already attained the degree of emotional security, independence and selfhood that we have been discussing throughout this book. Without a strong identity and the assurance of our value both to ourselves and to our mate, open companionship would of course pose a threat and so arouse jealousy. If you are insecure and depend upon your mate to fulfill all your needs, then you will experience a sense of loss when he shares himself with someone else, or even gives over large amounts of his time to a hobby or his career (p. 173).

Conditions under which open companionship of cross-sex friends works:

a. Establishment of priorities.
b. The third person must know about their openness to companions outside marriage.
c. To be concerned for the welfare of the outside companion.
d. Companions must be stable and independent.

e. Fully establish your relationship with your mate before trying outside relationships in any depth. (pp. 174-176)

15. *To understand the* ***myths about marriage*** *and the family (Lederer and Jackson 1968).*

As an introduction or as a discussion topic or as a review give the following list of myths about marriage and family (Crosby 1973) to the students, and ask them to mark each one as "False" or "Half-truth."

(F) a. A marriage relationship should fulfill all psychological and interpersonal human needs.
(F) b. Conflict is bad; marital conflict is worse.
(HT) c. Marriage can make unhappy people happy.
(F) d. Communication dissolves all conflict.
(HT) e. The trouble with marriage today is the legal-ecclesiastical tradition that undergirds it and defines it.
(HT) f. The main cause of marriage troubles today is the personality characteristics of the couple.
(F) g. Man by nature is a monogamous creature.
(HT) h. The trouble with marriage today is unrealistic societal expectations.
(F) i. Painless divorce would be a good thing for the institution of marriage.
(F) j. The family is in a state of breakdown and decay.
(HT) k. Children are good for a marriage.
(HT) l. Successful marriage should be a fusion of two identities into one.
(F) m. Legalizing marriage is the first step toward killing a relationship. (Crosby 1973).

Living Together Unmarried

Interpersonal relationships are based on some of the same factors of self-concept, meeting needs, and perceptions in or out of marriage. In marriage the constraints are circumscribed by the legal aspects, the constancy factor, the relative bargaining factor, and the exploitative factor. In a living-together unmarried arrangement certain other factors ensue which are different from the marriage situation or the single state.

One of the major problems is the persistent fear of some couples of being exposed. Even if some friends do know, there are sometimes some people such as parents and employers from whom the pair attempts to hide the arrangement.

Second, sometimes there is little security. The excitement of new experience, response, and newly found self-esteem sometimes wanes under the scrutiny of public opinion. In fact, within the relationship there is sometimes a threat of having neither an obligation nor a responsibility, and therefore there is a likelihood of one's walking out. There is also the realization that leaving any relationship is difficult, even without legal ties.

With both fear and lack of commitment added to the constancy factor, the relative bargaining factor, and the exploitative factor, the living-together arrangement has many obstacles (Berger 1971; Macklin 1972).

Teaching Techniques

1. ***To understand the accepted difference between being married and unmarried in one culture.***

   Read the following excerpts and discuss:

   > Men and women are careful to distinguish between marriage on the one hand and "common law," "shacking up," "living with" and other consensual unions on the other. There is, of course, a large overlap. The rights and duties which attach to consensual unions are patterned after those which attach to marriage and, in practice, some consensual unions are publicly indistinguishable from marriage. There are two principal differences. First, the rights and duties of consensual unions generally have less public force behind them. The result is that an act which violates both the marital and consensual union invokes a stronger sanction in the case of marriage. A second difference is that in consensual unions rights and duties are less clearly defined, especially at the edges. The result is that whereas everyone would agree that a given act stands in violation of the marital relationship, there could be—and frequently is—widespread disagreement as to whether the same act stands in violation of a consensual union. . . . A partner to a consensual union may explicitly point out the distinction between their own relationship and marriage in order to challenge the other's right or justification for his own behavior. Thus, one woman walked away in a huff from a man who was trying to get her to accompany him with the reminder that "*I'm your girlfriend, not your wife,*" and Leroy, at a time when he had been living with Charlene for several months, conceded that his rights were compromised by the fact that they were not formally, legally married. They had had an argument which brought their relationship almost to the breaking point. Later the same day Leroy left a note for Charlene which concluded: "I have decided to let you think it over until 6 P.M. Sunday. Until then, you can go where you want to, do what you want to, because like you said, I don't have any papers on you yet" (Liebow 1967).
   >
   > (Note: Charlene was in her ninth month of pregnancy.)

2. ***To gain some insight into reasons for living together unmarried.***

   a. Discuss living together unmarried as trial marriage from this standpoint: Marriage requires a crucial element that would be missing when living together unmarried: commitment.

"To live together without commitment is to confuse the test program with the action program" (Blood 1969, p. 58).

b. Compare by interview or case histories three couples to see the similarities and differences:
   (1) Unmarried couple dating each other exclusively, having sexual intimacy for about six months and undefined marriage plans (see case 6 in Crosby, 1973).
   (2) Unmarried couple living together for about six months with plans to marry later (see cases 11 and 12 in Crosby, 1973).
   (3) Married couple of about six months who may have had premarital sexual intimacy but who did not live together (see case 13 in Crosby, 1973).

3. *To gain some perspective about the variety of **attitudes about sexual relationships** between unmarried people.*
   a. The following descriptions show a variety of attitudes.
      (1) A couple who disdains the boredom of marriage may need to remember the struggle to find places for intimacy prior to marriage.
      (2) A man who has a strong childhood conditioning that sexual relationships without marriage are wrong will not be comfortable.
      (3) A man who has a strong professional goal which will take a lot of individual attention will be uneasy for fear of being led to marriage.
      (4) A woman who is comfortable with her own sexuality and achievement will not be insistent upon marriage.
      (5) A young boy who thinks sexual conquests are a mark of maturity.
      (6) A man or woman who thinks of sexual conquests and relations as communication.
   b. Read the "Fox and Swan" (L'Heureux 1972) in the Literature chapter to the class or assign it along with the other short stories and discuss the attitudes toward sexual relationships of unmarried people.
   c. Read and discuss the following case study (Crosby 1973).

THE CASE OF PAUL*

Paul is 20 years old, unmarried, and considers himself to be liberated from the binds of conventional middle-class morality.

"I made this appointment because I'm having trouble with a

*From *Illusion and Disillusion: The Self in Love and Marriage* by John F. Crosby, Case study 7, page 63.

problem," remarked Paul to the counselor. "I've had all kinds of girls . . . whores, pick-ups, townees, and some real nice bitches here on the campus. As far as I'm concerned the townees put out the best. They really know how to make a guy go out of his mind. Well, everything seemed to be going along fine until the other day. For some time now I've been dating this girl who I really like—kinda—and, well, she's a little bit different. I've had sex with her but when I did I had trouble getting an erection—Imagine that! Say, you aren't going to write this down or report me, are you? Like I was saying, this girl did something to me I can't seem to get out of my mind. I even started to feel jealous when she told me she had had sex with some other guy. The thing that really gets me though is that now I'm having trouble making it with townees. I don't seem to get very excited . . . and after it's over I get this empty feeling like all it amounted to was a lot of nothing."

On a subsequent visit to the counselor, Paul stated: "I never would have believed it but I think I've discovered there is more to sex than just orgasm. Late last week I couldn't make it with a townee. Hell! I just couldn't pull it off. Was I ever disgusted with myself. What would people think? The guys! Wow! So of course I told a pack of lies to the guys but inside I was miserable. Then the weekend—and that chick I told you about, the one who I got jealous about when I found out she had sex with another guy, well, we had the most fantastic weekend. We did everything—we ate together, went swimming, to the movies, studied together, went horseback riding, we really . . . (pause) we really opened up to each other . . . like it was great . . . I really emptied my guts to her and she to me. I never felt so close to another human being in my whole life. We had sex a couple of times and it was the greatest I ever had. For the first time in my life I felt I really *loved* a girl. We were so close."

Questions to Stimulate Discussion

(1) What is the difference in the reasons for sexual intimacy between the first girls and the last girl?

(2) What are some basic needs of people that sexual relations alone cannot satisfy?

d. Show the film *The Game* (1968).

This film shows how sex can be a game of conquest from peer group pressure among the very young.

4. *To understand why* ***sexual intimacy*** *eventually* ***changes some relationships*** *in one of three ways: to break off the relationship; to feel obligated to continue; to see sexual intimacy as an enrichment of many other intimacies.*

a. Discuss with the students why sexual intimacy sometimes causes a relationship to deteriorate by noting these attitudes by some people.

(1) Sexual intercourse is the goal or end.

(2) Sexual intercourse is separate and apart from other interactions and feelings.

(3) Sexual intercourse is an expectation.
(4) Sexual intercourse is to be engaged in at each encounter.

b. The feeling of obligation to continue may come from an old notion that when one engages in sexual intercourse, it is an exclusive, life-time activity; that is, conditional "oughts" take the place of making a rational decision.

How do these statements apply to the feeling of obligation to continue:

(1) You have a social responsibility not to encourage a deeper relationship than you are prepared to continue (Klemer 1970).
(2) Continuing a relationship because of a feeling of obligation may be meeting your needs to be the "good guy" who never lets a friend down more than it is a meeting of the needs of the other person.

c. There are some experiences of sexual intimacy in which sexual intercourse may or may not be included. If it is, it is only a part of the total experience but a part which enriches rather than ends it all. Read "Covenant" (Cherry 1972) and *Couples* (Updike 1968) to understand how some couples relate to each other without eliminating sexual intercourse but also without making it central to the relationship.

Love As Interaction With Others

Is love a need or are we taught to need love? If survival is the ultimate goal, we could say love is a need because our survival depends on other people. If we depend on other people for survival, we need to know how to relate to them. The feeling of love and the value of love arises out of the belief that it may be needed for survival although it is espoused in philosophical terms as a goal of humanity.

Whether we need love for survival or whether it is an avenue to reaching the goal of humanity, the fact is that many humans today believe there is a phenomenon called love.

The capacity to love is innate, but the ability to love is learned through experience, modeling, reinforcements, belief about self, sexual identity, and cultural expectations. The word "love" is lacking in differentiation of meaning in the English language with the result that it is being exploited and losing its full meaning (Crosby 1973). For example, how can we possibly "love" cake or baseball? To understand the varied meanings of love helps in understanding why the expected romantic love cannot be sustained in marriage, but also that it is not necessary as a constant diet.

The suggestions given here are intended as explanation for love as it is described in the culture and an enlightening of how it can be realized in any of us.

Teaching Techniques

1. *To understand that the foundations for the* ***ability to love*** *are set in children's childhood experience, modeling, reinforcements, belief about self-sexual identity, and cultural expectations.*
   a. What actual experience did you have in touching, hugging, giving, helping, and giving up for others in your childhood?
   Do you find it difficult now to touch people?
   Touch the student next to you. Touch the teacher. What do you experience? (Experiential and interaction theory)
   b. How do your parents show expressions of concern for each other, you, friends and relatives? Have you learned from your parents or others or vicariously through reading how to show love? (Modeling theory)
   c. What positive and negative reinforcements and punishments did you receive as a child for showing love for another? How have these experiences affected what you do or think now? (Reinforcement theory)
   d. Did you grow up with a belief that you are an acceptable specimen of humanity? If so, what are your attributes; if not, what do you *think* you lack? Do you think that if you do not get first place, you are in last place when in reality you are in the top ten? (Self-concept theory)
   e. Were you accepted and delighted with your own gender without being made to feel others wished you had been a boy (or girl)? (Psychoanalytic and reinforcement theories)
   f. How did your conditioning fit the cultural expectations of your childhood and now? (Field theory)
2. *To understand that if the* ***ability to love is learned,*** *then it* ***can be relearned*** *if it has been thwarted under reinforcing conditions; new learning, to be lasting, must have some reinforcement; inhibited behaviors can return in threatening situations.*
   a. Account for love affairs that are kindled between people whom no one thought were capable of love.
   b. Account for love affairs that "died" or marriages which became "devitalized."
   c. Account for married people or single adults who appear to be against love.
3. *To understand that the emotion and object of* ***romantic love is subculturally defined.***

a. Show a large series of pictures of boys, girls, men, and women from several subcultures, and ask students to select only those pictures which would fit the category of person they could possibly love in a romantic fashion.

After the students have chosen, find the following ranges of their choices: age range, facial appearance range, size range, clothing range, and any other characteristic which might circumscribe the culturally defined object.

b. Show a large series of the "LOVE IS" cartoons or captions of the cartoons and ask the students to select only those which designate their feelings about what romantic love is.

A variety of such statements are these:

(1) Love is helping her when you'd rather read.
(2) Love is losing your appetite when he comes close by.
(3) Love is solacing her when she's anxious.
(4) Love is doing your work and her work, too.
(5) Love is being dependent upon him to provide.
(6) Love is taking care of his clothes.
(7) Love is having an extremely rapid heartbeat when she looks at you.

4. *To understand that there are different types of love and that each type can be felt for the same person or different people in differing degrees and for all of them at the same time.*

a. Compare the following concepts of love (Crosby 1973).

Love for friends, equals; brotherly love; desire to communicate and interact

Love for mankind; for children; desire to accept others as humans without desire to manipulate

Love for physical release; desire to have human sexual contact rather than masturbation

Love for the opposite sex; drive to create and/or procreate; to communicate in the most intimate way possible; passion

b. Discuss the statement that "You can love more than one person at a time" (Blood 1969).

(1) Take each of the four types of love and substitute the type for the word "love" in the above statement.
(2) Why has our culture encouraged the idea of monogamous marriages, "one and only," and lifetime marriages? Weigh efficiency, security, stability against new experience.
(3) If you can love more than one person at a time, as is widely accepted in philos and agape, then why not in sexual and erotic love? (It is humanly possible, but cultural conditioning affects conscious and unconscious acceptance.)

5. *To understand that culturally conditioned needs for* ***sexual attraction*** *can be* ***used to manipulate*** *people.*
   a. Note the *use of* sexual attraction in the offices and plants of today's business world.
   Read Zetterberg's article (1966) to understand how this affects the interpersonal relations in business.
   Paraphrase
   There is an erotic ranking in every office. Every man or woman is viewed not only by their ability to perform their job, but also by their ability to attract the opposite sex. This ranking is done about each individual by all other individuals. The ranker sometimes suppresses the fact that he has made such a covert ranking. If a person has a higher erotic rank than a superior, he may lose a chance for promotion. If that person gets a promotion or recognition, his colleagues assume he got it on sexual attraction instead of merit. Many promotions have been denied on this count without the superior's or the person's conscious awareness. Some people use their erotic rankings to gain promotions and favors.
   There is a point in every emotion, even love, in which there is an "overcomeness" whereby the person loses control of himself and comes under the control of others (Simons and Reidy 1968; Zetterberg 1966).
   b. Note the not-so-subtle *use of* sexual attraction in today's advertising. It is said that business counts on the culturally conditioned need for sexual attraction and will continue to keep it a need so long as it makes selling profitable (Cox 1968; Packard 1957).
   c. Discuss the age at which children notice the sexual attraction basis and their interpretation. Also note the disillusionment and cynical comments about it later in life.
   d. Marriage in America has been based on the notion that the fulfillment of the need for sexual attraction is sexual intercourse that is acceptable only in marriage.
   How has this been a *manipulation* equally as subtle as advertising? In what ways have peers and adults said and implied that marriage is the expected place for fulfillment of sexual attraction?
   e. Some men and women have been *manipulated* by being taught to believe that only outside of marriage can the need for sexual attraction be fulfilled.
   Compare the cultural manipulation of people to marry and the counter-cultural manipulation of people not to marry—and for the same reason, that sexual fulfillment is the end in itself.
   f. Discuss how manipulation to the extreme can cause unusual sexual expressions.

Francoeur (1972) has described certain cultural attitudes toward sexual attraction and fulfillment as "hot sex" and "cool sex." The Puritans, in manipulating people to suppress sex, actually placed them in the position of negatively overreacting to sexual stimuli which is called "hot sex." The present-day trend toward "not getting involved" and sex as another activity is called "cool sex." Both of these extremes are explained by Slater (1970) as indications of the need to get involved. He called it need for community as against individualism and collective order.

6. *To examine marriage as a means for satisfying more needs than sexual gratification.*
   a. Discuss how you know when you have selected the mate most suitable for the experience of marriage.
      (1) If marriage is a commitment to each other, what commitments are involved? Human actualization for both (Satir 1972).
      (2) What differing aspects of love are necessary to meet the commitments?
      (3) What evidences does the prospective mate show that indicate he can help you become self-actualized (see the Introduction and Maslow 1954)?
      (4) What evidences do you exhibit that indicate you can help a person to become self-actualized?
   b. Critique the following research report (Knox 1970):
      A romantic conception of love tends to be more probable in late adolescence and the later years of marriage than in the early years of marriage.
7. *To understand and evaluate* ***behaviors*** *in any relationship* ***that encourage love*** *in any or all of its forms.*
   a. Interpret these metaphors:
      (1) To be successful, there has to be a planting of the seeds, cultivation, thinning, fertilization, good season, good soil, and replanting after harvesting. Sometimes hybrid seeds as well as differing methods of cultivation are found to cause an improvement.
      (2) When the plants are hardy, they can weather the storm.
      (3) There is a time to sow and a time to reap.
   b. Discuss the following ways to encourage love as given by some authorities.
      (1) Love is that relationship between two persons which is most conducive to the optimum development of both (Foote and Cottrell, 1955).
      (2) Love which grows into a lasting marriage needs both attachment and release. Release here is an expression of trust, respect, and

acceptance. If one partner is afraid to let go and tries to control the growth and creativity of the other, love will be strangled (Blood 1969).

(3) Basic elements which are characteristic of all forms of "productive love" are care, responsibility, respect, and knowledge. Care and responsibility denote that love is an activity rather than a passion (Fromm 1956).

(4) Love is the mutual emotional need to meet the other person's needs. (Love includes meeting other people's needs by applying human relationships generalizations.) (Klemer 1970).

c. How have these descriptions of mature and immature love changed from 1962 to now? Is there such a thing as immature or mature love? Do the descriptions of love given here include all four of the types of love? Where and how?

A COMPARISON OF SIGNIFICANT CHARACTERISTICS WHICH ENGENDER IMMATURE AND MATURE LOVE*

Immature	*Mature*
1. Love arises through the ideas of the one and only, love at first sight, and love wins out over all.	1. Love is an emergent experience which grows out of interaction with a realistic understanding of the relationship.
2. The love relationships are characterized by considerable ambivalence, with alternate feelings of attraction, indifference, or repulsion. Such feelings of ambivalence are frustrating for the person who feels ambivalent and perhaps even more frustrating to the person who experiences ambivalence in the partner. The person who is the one receiving the end of the ambivalence frequently develops considerable hostility and resentment.	2. The love relationship is characterized by relatively consistent feelings once the relationship has been established. Although the mature love relationship may be characterized by some ambivalence, it is seldom a pattern in the relationship, and when it is present it is usually related to some objective change in the relationship rather than inner doubts without foundation.
3. The love relationship is rooted primarily in sexual attraction. The concern is with personal, sexual satisfaction. A pronounced tendency	3. The love relationship is concerned with sexual satisfaction which is one aspect of the total relationship. Sexual involvement is not static but

*From *Marriage* by Herman R. Lantz and Eloise C. Snyder. Copyright © 1962, 1969 by John Wiley & Sons, Inc. Reprinted by permission of John Wiley & Sons, Inc.

Immature	*Mature*
for sexual involvement to remain static is present since the quality of the involvement is egocentric. The tendency here is for people to avoid evaluating their capacity to love and be loved, both of which have to be developed like other human attributes. To be able to love another human being consistently with completeness involves an emotional commitment and a high degree of personal integration devoid of the immaturities and personal difficulties discussed in the present chapter.	takes on more meaning as the relationship evolves since there is a pronounced tendency to be concerned with sexual and nonsexual needs of one another. The sexual involvement is much more relationship centered than egocentric.
4. The love relationship is characterized by considerable jealousy and insecurity with considerable fears regarding the continuance of the relationship.	4. The love relationship is characterized by mutual trust, feelings of confidence, and security in each other.
5. The love relationship tends to be exploitative with considerable using of each other for own ends.	5. The love relationship is oriented toward acceptance of each other as persons deserving dignity and respect. There is an absence of using each other as commodities.
6. The love relationship is characterized by considerable idealization based on fantasy, with marked tendency to distort the reality of one another and to fall in love with the distorted image.	6. The love relationship is characterized by an identification and pride based on the favorable qualities which have been developed and realized.
7. The love relationship is characterized by marked tendency to change the partner and to impose one's values on the partner without regard to the other's wishes.	7. The love relationship is characterized by the tendency to accept differences as potentially enriching the union.
8. The love feeling is characterized by sensing that one may be in love with more than one member of the opposite sex at one time. There is the case of a young lady who was	8. The love feeling is oriented toward a single member of the opposite sex.

Immature	*Mature*
engaged to a man who was employed in a community about a hundred miles from her home. The fiance' visited every weekend, and the young lady reported that she always had a wonderful time with him. Nevertheless she discovered that as soon as her boyfriend left, she began hoping that her phone would ring, in order that she would be asked out by another boy.	
9. The love relationship is characterized by overt competitiveness toward the other partner, as well as feelings of repressed envy, and the feeling that the achievement of one partner detracts from the desirability of the other. There is the case of the woman married to a public health officer. As a result of the husband's occupation he was called upon to speak at PTA groups frequently on the role of the family in maintaining proper health. His wife accompanied him on his talks and almost always whenever the man had completed his talk, the wife felt compelled to get up and add to her husband's comments. When she was through the husband felt it necessary to clear up some point his wife had made; and so they went on until the audience became bored. This kind of competitiveness characterized their marriage for several years. Finally the husband wrote a book only to discover that shortly afterward his wife discovered a need to write articles for ladies' magazines.	9. The love relationship is characterized by pride and identification with the achievements of each other. Thus as each member achieves something new, the other member has the feeling of sharing in the new achievement.

Coping With Marital Conflict

Conflicts between any two human adults, married or not, have some of the same bases and operate through some of the same processes. Marital conflicts differ somewhat, however, in that there may be much more involved and much more at stake. The conflict is an affront because of the former public statement and implication that the married pair entered into the partnership because they wanted to and because the cultural expectation is that they should be relatively satisfied throughout their married years.

Conflict is even more difficult in marriage because the partners have to live with each other during the conflict; they can't "go home" easily over every angered moment. Another aspect of marital conflict is that each partner knows all the vulnerable spots of the other and the possibility of an enormous harangue is there.

Handling marital conflict is more likely to be to the advantage of the marriage when people know more about their techniques, underlying motives, and the probable outcomes. Changing a person's coping behavior, however, has its problems if another coping behavior is not substituted. When a person has no way of coping, he is out of control, the result is not predictable, and therefore, even more devastating.

Teaching Techniques

1. *To gain some insight into the ways people manipulate other people, especially in a quarrel.*
   a. Illustrate the two quarreling techniques: (1) constructive–where only the topic of conflict is heatedly discussed, and (2) destructive–where the personalities are attacked in addition to the heated discussion of the topic of conflict.
   The scene can be the same for both. For example, the husband cannot find a matched pair of socks or finds the household check book in a mess or seems always to find his wife over at a neighbor's when he needs her. Or the wife may find no money was put into the bank to cover the checks or finds that her husband called in a neighbor to babysit when he was supposed to stay home with the children. One or both partners can play the constructive or destructive role. (The film *Handling Marital Conflicts* shows the constructive and destructive techniques.)
   b. Instead of playing the part of the destructive or constructive quarreler in the above role-playing scenes, play one of the following roles (Klemer 1970).
      (1) The person who exaggerates his strength, who dominates, orders, quotes authorities.

(2) The person who exaggerates his weakness and sensitivity, who is passively silent.
(3) The person who exaggerates his control, who deceives, lies, and constantly tries to outwit.
(4) The person who exaggerates dependency, who wants to be led, fooled, and taken care of.
(5) The person who exaggerates his aggression, cruelty, and unkindness, who controls by some implied threats.
(6) The person who exaggerates his caring and kills with kindness.
(7) The person who exaggerates his criticalness, who distrusts everyone, and who is blameful, resentful, and slow to forgive.
(8) The person who exaggerates his support, is oversympathetic, and refuses to allow those people he protects to stand up for themselves.
(9) The person who uses subtle pressure through tears, arm-twisting, withholding sex, or withholding money.
(10) The person who uses passive aggression through noncooperation, negativism, underenthusiasm.

c. Show thc film "Handling Marital Conflicts," an illustration of how one couple uses constructive quarreling and one couple uses destructive quarreling. Show it a second time to note the other manipulation techniques used.

d. If the students and community are mature enough, read excerpts from the myth *Lysistrata* in which the women stopped the wars by withholding sex from their men.

2. *To apply the generalization that satisfactory interpersonal relationships are achieved through accommodation, alteration, elimination, and aggression in varying degrees and varying combinations over time and that one method is not better than the other if one method works.*

a. Show one at a time three tubes of toothpaste squeezed in three typical ways: pressed at the top; pressed neatly from the bottom; and squeezed unmercifully all over. Ask students how they would react to each one if that were the tube squeezed by their partner. Ask how they would solve the problem if they did not like the way it is squeezed: by accommodation; by alteration; by aggression; or by elimination of the source.

The eternal argument over the way toothpaste tubes are squeezed is *eliminated* by buying each his own toothpaste tube. Other areas in which the source of a problem is eliminated is getting twin beds for active sleepers; two different chests of drawers; two different closets or two different clothes racks; two individual checking accounts, etc. Someone inevitably will claim that elimination of the source is bypassing the problem instead of solving it. But one method is not necessarily better than the other.

b. See Chapter 6 on Role Playing for a scene on spontaneous overt *aggression* as a means of changing a situation that accommodation had not previously changed.

c. See Chapter 9 on Understanding Human Behavior for a way to show how change in perception may be the alteration necessary for better interpersonal relationships.

d. Using the "Corner" game described by Berne (1964, p. 92), role play a situation in which one partner puts the other in a corner so that it is difficult to get out. Sometimes this is a doublebind.

Situation

Deciding where the baby will sleep.

Wife: We'll put the baby bed in our bedroom for a while.

Husband: Won't it be better for the baby to have a quieter place to sleep? Besides, I don't want a baby in our bedroom all the time.

Wife: But I won't be able to hear her if I don't. You wouldn't want her to suffocate just because I didn't hear her, would you?

Continue the role playing.

Discussion

(1) If the husband took the role of not wanting to do anything to look like a bad father, how do you think he felt? Would you have taken this role? Why?

(2) If the husband took the role of helping the wife see that the baby is better outside the bedroom (even if the bed is pushed into the hall or living room for the night), do you think he had ulterior motives or was he being very rational?

(3) If the wife holds her ground, what is the impelling force?

(4) What form of settling the argument finally ensued: accommodation, alteration, aggression, or elimination?

3. *To analyze the results of winning the "who's right" argument.*

a. These are situations in which the "who's right" argument has won:

(1) The daughter-in-law has just proven she was right about the mother-in-law's recipe.

(2) The husband has just proven he was right about not inviting the wife's relatives over for dinner.

(3) The mother has just proven she was right that the daughter's friend had to go home.

(4) The wife has just proven she was right about the car battery being in backward.

Ask these questions about the results of winning:
(1) Could the battered ego of the defeated make the relationship better?
(2) Could the defeated person love the winner more?
(3) Could the defeated person think of even more reasons why the winner was wrong?
(4) Is it an empty victory to be "right"?
(5) Could the winner get what he wanted?

b. Using the "Courtroom" game described by Berne (1964, p. 96), role play a situation in which the husband and the wife are telling a friend, a relative, or a counselor about a situation. Each one is attempting to get the listener to believe he is "right."

Situation

Dissention over spending money.

Husband: "Just let me tell you what Sue did yesterday! She went to the grocery store and . . . (role play this).

Wife: "Now, here is why I did it, but, anyway, it wasn't like that at all. He told me before I went that . . . and I assumed that . . . (role play this).

Listener: (To one of them) I think you're right.

Husband and wife continue but never concede and even attack the listener.

Stop the role playing at a high point, and tell the husband and wife to eliminate the listener and talk directly to each other to see what the outcome would be. Always stop the action at a heated place rather than letting it drag.

Discussion

(1) If one overpowered the other and "proved" he was "right," what was the effect on the other?
(2) If one pulled back realizing that proving "who's right" may hurt the relationship, did it in fact help the relationship?
(3) If the conversation changed, what caused the change?

4. *To apply the generalization that there are many ways to perceive a* ***conflict situation*** *according to one's own conditioning and experiences.* Collect sets of similar pictures of the same situations but with different poses, and put captions to the poses to indicate various reactions to that situation (or get one very ambiguous picture). Show the pictures and captions to the class for a discussion starter.

Examples of Situations and Captions

Title of the picture: Husband and wife facing each other.
Captions: "So this is it."
"I never really looked at you before. Ugh!"
"Who do you think you are?"

"I like you even if you do look like that."
"My, how you've changed."

Title of the picture: A mother-in-law and daughter-in-law.
Captions: "I'm glad I married into your family."
"I have to keep smiling to hide the tears."
"I wonder when she'll take those children and go home."
"To think, my son didn't really want to get married."
"I wonder how she liked her mother-in-law."

Collect a set and do not put captions. Have students put titles and captions to a set of pictures.

5. *To understand the enormous problem involved when a person is told, encouraged, taught, or reinforced to stop some coping behavior without substituting another coping behavior.*

One type of marriage has been described as "conflict-habituated" (Cuber and Harroff 1965), one in which there is an apparent need on the part of both husband and wife to communicate through continuous verbal (or physical) conflict. This conflict could be a result of one partner's need to play the part of the child and the other's need to play the part of a parent with both directing their conversation as if the other were rational adults (Harris 1967).

If in some way the couple are admonished not to use the "child" and "parent" accusations without being taught how to use rational thought and statements, they are left in a vacuum with the probable result of a breakup of the marriage. Heretofore they may have been managing very well because they have met their needs.

6. *To become aware that there are not really any new problems; people just have a lack of tolerance for old problems.*

Examples of Problems Which Remain the Same

a. Pecking order and bargaining power in groups or couples (traditional/equal)
b. Desire to express one's emotions and amount of control (men's inhibitions)
c. Jealousy as a motivator or strangler (women's lib)
d. Boredom (men's obligation to stay employed)

Divide the class into fourths and give them the following labels: one-fourth male traditionalists; one-fourth male liberationists; one-fourth female traditionalists; one-fourth female liberationists. In each group note some behaviors of people which would be classified as typical of your group.

Ask one "male traditionalist" and one "female liberationist" to volunteer for some role playing. Give the following information to the role players individually. Let the class know both bits of information but not the role players.

Male traditionalist: You have worked hard all day; you're hot and tired; you're hungry. You enter the house and find your wife dozing on the sofa. With all the disgust and ire you can transmit, say, "Haven't you even started dinner?"

Female liberationist: You have a comparable job to your husband's in an insurance firm. You have had an exhausting day, but you are *eager* to talk over a new concept in the insurance business as you relax a bit before dinner. You have been asleep five minutes when your husband enters.

People in the class may cut in and take the place of the role players as they have a desire to play that particular part. For example, a male liberationist might want to show how he would handle the part, etc.

As a shocker, send in a contrived ultra-liberal daughter to confront a very liberal mother to see if the mother can hold to her views of individual rights.

Questions to the Group

a. What were some of the most emotional comments brought out? Why?
b. Which couple was the least agreeable? Why?
c. Which couple was the most agreeable? Why?
d. What is happening in society today which makes us less willing to tolerate some of the old notions? Are we justified in not tolerating them?
e. Are the directions we are taking better than some of the traditional? Why?

Summary

Good interpersonal relationships depend on how well people mutually meet each other's needs. Since two chapters were given to understanding human behavior and communication, this chapter dealt primarily with those factors that affect people who are living together, whether they are a married pair, parents and children, or an unmarried pair.

The problems of the family include meeting role demands, too many expectations, power conflicts, changes in needs, and self-fulfillment. Even when people are living together unmarried, some of these same problems occur.

Love has been presented as it is involved in the interaction between people rather than as a state of being. The techniques encourage students to question some old notions and to see some new possibilities in definitions and actions.

When one is coping with marital conflicts, the skills of communication and understanding of human behavior are used extensively. Lack of coping shows either an inability to communicate or an inability to apply knowledge of interpersonal interaction.

Human sexual conditioning is also a factor in how males and females cope with conflict. The next chapter includes how human sexual identity occurs and how changes are being attempted in order to improve relationships.

References

Ausubel, David P., and Sullivan, Edmund. *Theories and Problems of Child Development,* 2nd ed. New York: Grune & Stratton, 1970.

Berger, Miriam. "Trial Marriage: Harnessing the Trend Constructively." *The Family Coordinator* 20: 38-43, 1971.

Berne, Eric. *Games People Play*. New York: Grove Press, Inc., 1964.

Blood, Robert O. *Marriage*. 2nd ed. New York: The Free Press, 1969.

Blood, Robert O. and Wolfe, Donald M. *Husbands and Wives*. New York: The Free Press, 1960.

Bossard, James H. S. "The Law of Family Interaction." *American Journal of Sociology* 50: 292-294, 1945.

Cherry, Kelly. "Covenant." In *The Best American Short Stories 1972*, edited by Martha Foley. New York: Ballantine, 1972.

Cox, Frank D. *Youth, Marriage and the Seductive Society*, revised ed. Dubuque, Iowa: Wm. C. Brown Co., 1968.

Crosby, John F. *Illusion and Disillusion: The Self in Love and Marriage*. Belmont, California: Wadsworth Publishing Co., Inc., 1973.

Cuber, John, and Harroff, Peggy. *The Significant Americans*. New York: Appleton-Century-Crofts, 1965.

Foote, Nelson, and Cottrell, Leonard S. *Identity and Interpersonal Competence.* Chicago: University of Chicago Press, 1955.

Francoeur, Robert T. *Eve's New Rib: Twenty Faces of Sex, Marriage and Family*. New York: Harcourt Brace Jovanovich, 1972.

Fromm, Erich. *The Art of Loving*. New York: Harper & Row, 1956.

Harris, Thomas. *I'm OK–You're OK*. New York: Harper & Row, 1967.

Klemer, Richard H. *Marriage and Family Relationships*. New York: Harper & Row, 1970.

Knox, David. "Conceptions of Love at Three Developmental Levels." *The Family Coordinator* 19: 151-156, 1970.

Lantz, Herman R., and Snyder, Eloise C. *Marriage*. New York: John Wiley, 1969.

Lederer, William S. and Jackson, Don. *The Mirages of Marriage*. New York: W. W. Norton, 1968.

L'Heureux, John. "Fox and Swan." In *The Best American Short Stories*, 1972, *1972,* edited by Martha Foley. New York: Ballantine Books, 1972.

Liebow, Elliot. *Tally's Corner.* Boston: Little Brown and Co., 1967.

Luckey, Eleanore "Marital Satisfaction and Its Association with Congruence of Perception." *Marriage and Family Living* 22: 49-54, 1960.

Macklin, Eleanor D. "Heterosexual Cohabitation among Unmarried College Students." *The Family Coordinator* 21: 463-473, 1972.

Maslow, Abraham H. *Motivation and Personality*. New York: Harper and Row, 1954.

O'Neill, Neva, and O'Neill, George. *Open Marriage*. New York: M. Evans, 1972.

Packard, Vance. *Hidden Persuaders*. New York: Pocket Books, Inc., 1957.

Pineo, Peter C. "Development Patterns in Marriage." *The Family Coordinator* 18: 135-140, 1969.

Satir, Virginia. *Peoplemaking*. Palo Alto, California: Science and Behavior Books, Inc., 1972.

Sears, Robert R.; Rau, Lucy; and Alpert, Richard. *Identification and Child Rearing*. Stanford, Calif.: Stanford U. Press, 1965.

Simons, Joseph, and Reidy, Jeanne. *The Risk of Loving*. New York: Herder and Herder, 1968.

Slater, Philip. *The Pursuit of Loneliness*. Boston: Beacon Press, 1970.

Stagner, R. "Homeostasis." In *International Encyclopedia of Social Sciences*. Vol. VI., edited by D. Sils. New York: Macmillan, 1968.

Updike, John. *Couples*. New York: Alfred A. Knopf, 1968.

Zetterberg, Hans L. "The Secret Ranking." *Journal of Marriage and the Family* 28: 134-142, 1966.

Suggested Films

The Game (1968, 48 min.). McGraw-Hill/Contemporary Films, 1221 Avenue of the Americas, New York, N.Y. 10020.

Handling Marital Conflicts (1965, 19 min.). McGraw-Hill/Contemporary Films, 1221 Avenue of the Americas, New York, N.Y. 10020.

How Close Can You Get? (1970, 10 min.). Churchill Films, 662 N. Robertson Blvd., Los Angeles, CA 90069.

Chapter 13

Human Sexual Identity

Identity by name, personality, behavior, and status in life are separate from, yet integrated with, a person's gender. Because people are designated at birth as male or female, they have a definite sexual identity. Although the genetic pattern is there, the culture reinforces one's human sexual identity. The criteria set up by the culture are such that substantial deviation is met with rebuffs. Presently the severe differentiations in sex roles of the past are being questioned. Still there are problems in being just a person first instead of being a *male* person or *female* person first. Since it may be difficult for some people to adhere to the cultural prescriptions for male behavior or female behavior because of many factors, these people may live out their lives in frustration. The question in the minds of many is, "Should the culture continue to reinforce such differentiation of the sexes?" Yet another question is, "Are we doing children an injustice if we don't reinforce culturally prescribed gender behavior?" Still other questions are these: "Is culturally acceptable human sexual identity important to a person's self-esteem? How is human sexual identity formed? What conditions in this society are beginning to be continued as a result of reinforcement of maleness and femaleness? Are the new goals of personal rights in this society being hampered by too strong adherence to gender differentiation?" This chapter gives some ways to consider the answers to these and other questions.

There are three ways men and women gain their sexual identity. The first way is by genetic makeup. Even genetic makeup is being questioned now that a different mixture of the so-called male and female chromosomes has been found in some human beings. For example, some people identified as male have more than one male chromosome (Money 1973). It is also believed that on these chromosomes there are specific genes which determine the primary gender characteristics, the genital organs, as well as the secondary gender characteristics, such as smooth skin, small muscles, and breasts for women. These genes determine a different muscular build and a beard for men. The production of a certain balance of male and female hormones is also believed to be determined genetically.

The second way of gaining sexual identity is cultural conditioning. The classification of gender at birth is the beginning of socializing the child as that gender. The comments, the reactions, and the expectations all start from birth and continue throughout life. Theories of reinforcement explain part of cultural conditioning.

The third way is psychological and is a very personal and individual phenomenon. This personal acceptance of gender comes from a combination of one's physical makeup, cultural conditioning, and the cognitive mechanism that allows human beings to conceptualize. Theories of identification and cognition explain psychological gender acceptance.

Comparison of the genetic, cultural conditioning, and identification theories enlightens most students that gender identification may not need to be so sharply defined.

Cultural Determination of Sexual Identity

Under the assumption that gender identity is culturally determined to meet the goals of the society, the major issue today is that too rigid bipolar demarcation lines of gender identification may be a hindrance to the future of this society. To study this issue, present teaching techniques for learning about (1) how the bipolar demarcation between the sexes occurs, (2) why the role differentiation is defined and reinforced, and (3) how the rigid differences are being restructured, with ensuing problems.

Teaching Techniques

1. *To understand the various mechanisms of gender identification.*
   a. Have the students state whether a person they know well is male or female, and then proceed to explain what evidence they are using.
      Immediately reinforce all answers because a person's *identity* as male or female is the crucial factor; that is, the *acceptance* of maleness or femaleness is really what makes that person male or female equally as much as any primary or secondary sex characteristics.
   b. Write on the board that the major irreversible difference between males and females is the male's ability to impregnate and the female's ability to gestate and lactate. Then ask the following questions:
      (1) In our society if a male cannot impregnate or a woman cannot gestate or lactate, are they immediately classified as the opposite sex? as neither sex? (of course not)
      (2) If a male chooses not to impregnate or a woman chooses not to

gestate, are they immediately classified as the opposite sex? as neither sex? (of course not)

(3) How has the ability to have children been reinforced as a top priority characteristic of femininity or masculinity then?

c. Read this to the class.

The following biological evidences of differentiation between the sexes can be changed or ignored if it is desired that a child should be brought up as the opposite sex.

(1) Chromosomal characteristics (combination of Xs and Ys)
(2) Androgenic (male) or estrogenic (female) hormonal predominance
(3) Evidence of ovaries or testicles
(4) Structure of internal reproductive organs
(5) Structure of external genitals

Divide the class into groups, one half to build a case for changing a biologically determined male to a female and the other half to build a case for changing a biologically determined female to a male. (This study may be used as an introduction to get at feelings, or later to study in depth the processes of decisions about changing the child's sexual identity.)

d. Tell this to the class to get their reactions.

(1) "The telephone rang and the other party said, 'The baby has been born!' and hung up. What is your next question?"
(2) The telephone has rung and "It's a girl!" comes through.

Ask the students to:
Give her a name
Give her a gift
Dress her for her first trip outside the house
Hold her in your arms
Teach her how to ride a tricycle
Teach her how to fight
Teach her what to do when other girls won't let her play with them (continue the list).

The students will give away their own views about differential conditioning techniques and values about roles even though some may think they are being very unbiased.

(3) "My father wanted a son," she said. What are the probable behaviors he reinforced in her? Will they make her a boy? Will they affect her femininity?
(4) (Have the class react as if they were parents.) Your ten-year-old son rushes in one day and says, "I found out I'm a girl!"

e. Indicate how these people are perpetuating or reinforcing a belief that having children and a person's sexual identity are connected.

(1) One man said, "They wouldn't have any children because they are selfish. I had four; I don't think only of myself."
(2) Another man said, "I have done my duty. I had four sons and seven daughters."
(3) A woman said, "I don't want any children."
(4) A man said, "It's none of your business how many children I have."
(5) A woman said, "If I didn't already have children, I wouldn't have them if I had it to do over."

2. *To understand **cultural conditioning of roles** and why role differentiation continues to be defined and reinforced by today's society.*
Margaret Mead (1949) said that men are culturally reinforced for their strength and their accomplishments in work to compensate for their lack of ability to bear children. She also said that when a society's men turn to housekeeping instead of fighting, the society declines. These references were from primitive, nontechnological cultures. Discuss the implications of these two statements with regard to the following societal changes in the United States:
a. There is less eagerness to enter into wars.
b. There is insistence on more group care of children under six.
c. There is greater acceptance of contraceptive measures.
d. There is apathy among men on the assembly lines; they want more creative endeavors.
e. There is an increase in the numbers of women working, particularly those with smaller children.

3. *To gain some insight into the **restructuring** of the rigid **male-female differentiation.***
a. Read these pairs of often-quoted, but almost contradictory, statements, and consider how the notions presented by the pairs have existed so long.
(1) Women have better finger dexterity.
Men make better surgeons than women.
(2) Women have equal or higher measured intelligence quotients.
Men make better surgeons than women.
(3) Men are less emotional than women.
Women work better under stress than men.
(4) Men must succeed.
"His expertise is only in writing; he isn't the athletic type."
b. Role play the following scene.
Wife (as she enters the door): "I've got some news! I have been promoted and offered a job with double my salary if we will move across the country. What do you think?"

Husband: (Ask several students to respond consecutively or use the cut-in methods. See Chapter 6 on Role Playing for directions.)

c. It has been stated that the "maternal leave" now granted to some women is undergoing another change—"paternal leave"—because fathers are important to the birth process and postpartum events. What do you *think*?
   (1) Is it the men or women who are demanding the change?
   (2) Has the increase in prepared childbirth courses, which includes mother and father preparation, had any influence on the demand for a change?

Relationship of Sexual Identity and Family Planning

Voluntary use of contraceptives by people when there is a positive correlation between pride in masculinity and femininity and the reproduction of children will probably not be sufficient to control population growth. A resocialization of the people not to want large families and not to associate having children (as well as sexual intercourse) with increased masculinity and femininity will be the most pervasive influence (Silverman and Silverman 1971). If an understanding of how socialization affects desires for children is taught to your students, they will be far more likely to be agents for resocialization.

Teaching Techniques

1. *To analyze the cultural influences on a person's desire for children.*
   a. Ask the students to add to the list of comments made to young married people about having children which both encourage having and punish for not having children.
      "When are you going to start your family?"
      "Do you have any children yet?"
      "Aren't you going to have any children?"
      "You don't have any children?"
      "When are you going to have a little brother or sister for your child?"
      "Are you going to keep all that money for yourselves?"
   b. Have students assume that they will have at least two children when they are between eighteen and thirty years old. Ask what positive thoughts enter their minds? Where did these influences come from? Start their thinking by reminding them of these pronatalist influences:
      Mother and child reverence in religions
      Doll play as children
      People asking females if they will marry more often than asking what they want to be when they grow up

Expectation of women to be good homemakers and mothers
Expectation of men to have children to prove masculinity

2. *To gain knowledge of **cultural influences** that are related to **smaller families** and to explore feelings in regard to them (Francoeur 1972; Veevers 1973).*
   Discuss whether or not the following behaviors are related to smaller family size.
   a. Equality of men and women
   b. Child welfare laws (which keep young children from working)
   c. Increasing desire for better standard of living
   d. Urbanization
   e. Women working outside the home
   f. Higher education
   g. Higher social status
   h. Availability of contraceptive and birth-control methods
3. *To analyze the **population problems** in the future.*
   Show this film and discuss the commission's recommendations. "Population and the American Future" (color, 60 min.)–Modern Talking Pictures (filmed version of the 1972 Report of the Commission on Population and the American Future).
   Some of the recommendations of the Commission that are relevant to resocialization of people to view sex roles apart from having children are reprinted below. Although the total report was not accepted by the President, the recommendations and report are affecting attitudes and legislation.
   a. Modify sex and family roles so that women "may choose attractive roles in place of or supplementary to motherhood (and be) free to develop as individuals rather than being molded to fit some sexual stereotype."
   b. End discrimination against women in education and employment, and give women equal access to all jobs, so that careers and more attractive work become more available to them.
   c. Modify content of schooling for both girls and boys to remove sex-role stereotypes and encourage varied life-choices and life-styles.

The Male Changes as the Female Changes

Would the male want to be different from what he is? Could he be different if he wanted to? What would he change if he could? What would females want him to change? Why?

The civil rights legislation has been directed toward women and minority groups, but the principle of homeostasis implies that there is change in all parts of a system; therefore, if women change, men must change whether they want to or not (Calderone 1972; Farrell 1971). Or could it be that because men have changed, now women can change?

Teaching Techniques

1. *To understand the effect of conditioned inexpressiveness of men.*
   a. Inexpressive single men have been categorized as either the playboy type (inexpressive but non-feeling) or the cowboy type (inexpressive but feeling) (Balswick and Peck 1971).
      Use this categorization to explain why the girl who expects inexpressiveness with feeling in males is surprised when her boyfriend is inexpressive but non-feeling.
      How do the two categories fit into the "I'm OK; You're OK" (Harris 1967) characterization?
      (1) Inexpressive, non-feeling is an example of "I'm Not OK; You're Not OK" (Harris 1967)
      (2) Inexpressive, feeling is an example of "I'm Not OK: You're OK" (Harris 1967)
   b. Compare two James Bond films, one prior to 1973 and one after 1973, to note that the inexpressive male has not changed, but the aggressiveness of the female has.
      1973 *Live and Let Die*
      1970 Goldfinger
   c. Read Koffend's *A Letter to My Wife* (1972) to see the devastating effect of the masculine mystique on a marriage.
   d. Discuss the following:
      If the family is changing from institution (the family as most important) to companionship (the relationship as most important), how will the inexpressive male survive?
      If an extramarital relationship with love is more threatening to the spouse than one without love, would an extramarital relationship of an inexpressive, non-feeling husband be more acceptable to the wife?
2. *To analyze conditioned role behavior of men.*
   a. Compare the behavior of the male and female in the LOVE IS cartoons and note the distinctly gender-oriented ways of expressing love. What explains the difference?
   b. Compare the behaviors of the male and female in the "Better Half" cartoons and note the distinctly different roles of the husband and wife even though both the male and female are victims.
   c. Apply the cultural lag theory (Ogburn 1922) to the needs of today's man and his culturally conditioned temperament. Cultural lag means that the social need is almost always several years ahead of the cultural preparation of individuals to meet the need.

Examples

(1) Men conditioned in an era of rugged individualism are having to live and work in organizational settings.

(2) Men conditioned in a dominant-husband society are having to live in a philosophically equalitarian society.

d. When someone is conditioned to believe and act a particular way, what is the effect of a change in the reinforcement? Frustration is a result of oscillating reinforcements. Stress is a result of not being reinforced at all. Trauma is a result of having an immediate reversal from positive reinforcement to punishment (Deese 1958). Discuss examples of how the traditional inexpressive male would react to oscillating reinforcement, no reinforcement, and immediate reversal from positively reinforcing traditional inexpressive behavior to punishment of the same behavior.

3. *To become aware of the changing roles of men and women.*

Role play the following:

a. *Situation*: Wife's job pays more.

Background: Both husband and wife have worked since they married except for a very short time when each of the two children were born. The children are teenagers now. The husband and wife who have both progressed in their jobs are each making about the same salary and are each having similar responsibilities in their respective jobs. The wife has always made a little more money than the husband.

Wife: She needs to break the news that she can be promoted and have a 50 percent raise in salary if they move from Greensboro to Atlanta.

Husband: He has rationalized his wife's making more than he all these years but has had ambivalent feelings about it.

Points

(1) Many men are recognizing the abilities of women and can feel pride in their accomplishments.

(2) Women are more often taking leadership roles in work.

(3) When a promotion is possible for a woman people are beginning not to say, "Well, you know she's married."

(4) Men are beginning not to feel less a man if they move because of their wives' promotions.

(5) Working wives can be as good wives and mothers as those who do not work.

b. *Situation*: The wife has a very good job but her husband wants her to quit work. She has supported her husband through graduate school. They were married immediately after each had graduated from college. They agreed that she would not work after he finished his advanced degree. She now does not want to quit. She is an executive secretary of a big firm, is an exceptional public relations person, and is rewarded both financially and personally for her work.

Husband: "When you quit work next summer, you'll have all the time in the world to relax and do all the things you've always wanted to do. I'll enjoy coming home to a beautiful, rested wife. I can't wait. What do you plan to do first?"

Wife: (Doesn't want to quit and would rather not think about being home doing "nothing.")

Points

(1) Women in good jobs get as much ego satisfaction as men do from their jobs.
(2) Women who are prepared for working, who have been conditioned to advance, and who have a strong sense of family management responsibility are eager to work.
(3) Some men can rationalize their wives' working while they were in school but not afterward.
(4) Some men think that all women want to do is to keep house.

c. *Situation*: The husband has a chance for promotion if he moves to another part of the country. His wife has a good job.

Background: This couple has been married for seven years. They live in the same town they grew up in. The wife has worked all the time except for six months two years ago when the baby was born. They have a very good arrangement for babysitting with her mother. The wife has advanced some in her job and is very happy in her present situation both at work and at home.

Scene: After dinner and after the child is in bed.

Husband: "There's a chance for me to be office manager if I move to Detroit. My salary will be almost double after two years. You could get a job easily, and the baby could be put in a day nursery. We'll have it made."

Wife: (She had been considering some home decorating, a local kindergarten for their child, and the possiblity of another child.)

Points

(1) Both the partners need to be achievement oriented in order for advancement to occur.
(2) Moving to another city is more difficult when the city is also out of the region one grew up in.
(3) Families tend to move because of the husband's, not the wife's job.
(4) In-laws are an asset most of the time, especially in caring for children.

d. *Situation*: The husband wants his wife to get more education and/or go to work, but the wife is reluctant.

Background: The couple married at the end of their sophomore year. She quit and went to work. He finished college and went to work. She quit work immediately. The two children are both in school now, and he is encouraging her to go back to school. She is enjoying her relative freedom and would prefer to continue her present role.

Husband: "Did you read that editorial in this morning's paper that I asked you to read?"

Wife: "What editorial?"

Husband: "The one about the new economic situation."

Wife: "No, I didn't have time. I don't understand that very well anyway."

Husband: (Encouraging her to stay abreast.)

Points

(1) Some men do want their wives to be intelligent and up-to-date.
(2) Some wives do like the role of homemaker and do not want to work.
(3) Women understand men better if they work.

Summary

Human sexual identity is affected by and in turn affects this society. However, when men and women are conditioned to identify as male and female with differentiated sex-role behaviors, changes in societal attitudes toward male and female roles are not easy to accept. The way a male or female thinks he or she should act affects nearly every area of family relationships.

Work and money are areas that are very personal and important to an individual and a family. Therefore, a whole chapter is devoted to work and money, and relationships as they are affected by differentiation in male and female roles.

References

Balswick, Jack D., and Peck, Charles W. "The Inexpressive Male: A Tragedy of American Society." *The Family Coordinator* 20: 303-368, 1971.

Calderone, Mary. "It's the Men Who Need Liberating." In *Marriage and Family in a Decade of Change*, edited by Gwen B. Carr. Reading, Massachusetts: Addison-Wesley Publishing Co., 1972.

Commission on Population and the American Future. *Population and the American Future*. Washington, D.C.: U.S. Government Printing Office, 1972.

Deese, James. *The Psychology of Learning*. New York: McGraw-Hill Book Co., Inc., 1958.

Farrell, Barry. "You've Come a Long Way, Buddy." *Life Magazine*, 27 August 1971, pp. 46-59.

Francoeur, Robert T. *Eve's New Rib: Twenty Faces of Sex, Marriage, and Family*. New York: Harcourt Brace Jovanovich, Inc., 1972.

Harris, Thomas. *I'm OK–You're OK*. New York: Harper & Row, 1967.

Koffend, John B. *A Letter to My Wife*. New York: Dell Pub. Co., 1972.

Mead, Margaret. *Male and Female*. New York: Dell Publishing Co., 1949.

Money, John. *Man and Woman, Boy and Girl*. Baltimore: Johns Hopkins, 1973.

Ogburn, William F. *Social Change*. New York: Viking Press, 1922.

Silverman, Anna, and Silverman, Arnold. *The Case Against Having Children*. New York: David McKay Co., Inc., 1971.

Veevers, J. E. "Voluntary Childlessness: A Neglected Area of Family Study." *The Family Coordinator* 22: 199-206, 1973.

Suggested Films

How To Make A Woman (1973, 58 min.) Polymorph Films, Inc., 331 Newbury Street, Boston, Mass. 02115.

Human Physiology: Male and Female Reproductive Systems (1972, 41 min.) Schloat Productions, 150 White Plains Road, Tarrytown, N.Y. 10591.

Population and the American Future (1972, 59 min.). Modern Talking Picture Service, Inc., 10 Rockefeller Plaza, New York, N.Y. 10020.

Three Lives (1971, 70 min.). Impact Films, 144 Bleeker Street, New York, N.Y. 10012.

To Be A Man (1970, 13½ min.) and *To Be A Woman* (1969, 13½ min.). Billy Budd Films, 235 E. 57th Street, New York, N.Y. 10022.

Wait Until Your Father Gets Home! (1970, 11 min.). Churchill Films, 662 N. Robertson Blvd., Los Angeles, CA 90069.

Chapter 14

Work, Money, And Relationships

A family's social status is usually determined by the man's job even if the woman works, too. A married woman's job rarely takes precedence over her husband's job as the determiner of status. When her job is recognized, it is usually recognized for itself rather than for family status. Even when the wife works, the husband usually makes the most money, determines where the family will live, and is considered the head of the household. These generalizations about work and money affect the relationships in a family.

Occupational Roles: His and Hers

The goals a man has for his family may be hinged on his job aspirations more than on his aspirations as a husband and father. If he sees his role as being the top businessman as well as the best provider for his family even if it means overtime work, his family may suffer more than it gains. To be the best in his job and the best in his family is an almost insolvable dilemma. Some men, however, assume that their jobs as family men are satisfied if they are good providers and want little part in the household or family.

Women have almost always been thought of as homemakers even though they worked alongside men in establishing this country. The feminist movement could not have moved forward, however, had it not been for an avenue for women to work outside the home. Still, less than half of all women in the United States today are in the public work force. Although law and culturally accepted sex roles are sometimes blamed for so few women working, women's lack of socialization to be aggressive in the business world is also a culprit. The educated woman who cannot gain fulfillment from being only a parent and homemaker is still seen as deviant. It may be that women would not be led to believe they must be fulfilled by homemaking if more opportunity to work at good pay with relief from housework and childcare were available.

Women who do stay home with their children today probably get too involved with them. Both mother and child may feel abused, and the husbands may feel left out. In fact, it seems that the mother who stays home and resents it has as bad an effect on her children's development as does the mother who works and resents working. The factor of whether the mother works is not as crucial to her children's development as her attitude toward what she is doing (Hoffman 1961).

To alleviate some of the problem of too little time for family life, the husband could live closer to his work; to alleviate some of the problem of too much time with the children, the wife could use group care for the children at any hour of the day or night. To alleviate the differentiation of roles at home, the husband and wife could become versatile in all household tasks and repairs so that their roles were interchangeable. At a time in marriage when the husband and wife need to continue their own pair relationship—the years when the children are small—they seem to be the most separated.

The disillusionment from job monotony (Kristol 1973) is spilling over into the family. People have internalized such a need for higher and higher consumption levels that they must continue to work. Even so, fear of becoming a robot is ever present. The need to interact with people seems not to be met adequately on the job or in the family.

The cultural lag problem is again at work. Those families who have aspired to and achieved a way of life that is interesting, fulfilling, but different are well apart from or beyond the cultural description of "happy" but very bored families. Eventually the life styles of families that were once thought of as deviant may become the norm.

Teaching Techniques

1. *To gain knowledge about the work hours and attitudes of students' parents, the desire of work hours and compensations of the students, and the plans the students have for coping with the dilemma of all work and no family life.*
   a. Survey the class, anonymously, with the following questionnaire. Take the questionnaires up, redistribute them, and tally them in class by a raising of hands. Each student will be raising his hand for an anonymous paper, and no one need feel hampered.

(Circle one – Male, Female)

	Father	*Mother*	*What student would like*
(1) No. of hours a day works	______	______	______________
(2) No. of hours a day commutes	______	______	______________

	Father	*Mother*	*What student would like*
(3) Type of work			
construction	______	______	________________
industry	______	______	________________
delivery	______	______	________________
service	______	______	________________
manager	______	______	________________
office	______	______	________________
executive	______	______	________________
(4) Type of household task			
clean	______	______	________________
cook	______	______	________________
care for children	______	______	________________
laundry	______	______	________________
(5) No. of children	______	______	________________

How has the number of children added to work load? ________________________________

(6) Likes work (yes)	______	______	________________
(7) Likes pay (yes)	______	______	________________

b. To make some preparation for not getting caught in the work bind of most families, what do you propose in the following areas? Make a thorough study of self and plans. Interview and observe families and employers.
   (1) Preparation for type of employment
   (2) Dual knowledge about housework and childcare
   (3) Family planning
   (4) Variety in leisure activities
c. Study the civil rights legislation to know what the laws provide for both men and women. Report on various steps that have been taken. Divide the reports into these areas:
   (1) Original Civil Rights Law of 1964
   (2) National Organization of Women

(3) Affirmative Action plans for employers
(4) Equal Rights Amendment
(5) Differences in work laws for men and women in your state
(6) Day Care availability
(7) Tax deduction for child care payments
(8) Employment figures for men and women
(9) Lending and credit regulations which differ between women and men

2. *To understand that the conflict when the wife goes to work is based on former expectations of both partners.*
   a. Debate: When the wife goes to work and/or makes more money than the husband, there is a threat to a husband's self-concept because of a possible balance in power and difference in cultural expectations. Debate: When the wife has to work because of financial necessity, the husband helps with the housework less gracefully.
   b. Discuss the following research finding:
   The husband's share of the housework is 15 percent when the wife is not working and 25 percent when the wife is working (Blood 1973).
   Questions for Discussion
   (1) Why isn't the sharing 50 percent?
   (2) Does she share in his former household tasks?
   (3) Does she not want him to share because of notions of cultural role? Or does she actually want to do certain jobs?
   (4) How does she approach him to share?
   (5) If she does not make the money he makes, does he consider this fact to mean she should do more of the housework?
   (6) What if he does not do the quality of work to her satisfaction?
   (7) Is he treated like a child?
   (8) Would she do the jobs he assigns if he decided the sharing?
   (9) Why is there not usually the sharing of the husband's traditional work but a sharing of the wife's traditional work?

3. *To evaluate male success in terms of occupational roles using the culturally accepted criteria below.*
   a. Speculate on how widely accepted are the following criteria for success of fathers and husbands (these criteria are not given as absolutes). The man should:
   (1) Make enough money to provide an adequate living for his family
   (2) Make more than his wife
   (3) Have a culturally acceptable method of making money
   (4) Work for his money
   (5) Work in a "masculine" job
   b. Evaluate these "negative" actions of men who cannot meet the

above criteria by applying behavior generalizations given after the actions list.

Actions

(1) Desert their families bodily or through intoxicants or drugs
(2) Criticize their wives and children
(3) Refuse to help with housework
(4) Quit work entirely
(5) Overemphasize maleness as sufficient for their position

Behavior Generalizations

(1) When a person's self-image is threatened, he tends to protect it by striking back, overemphasizing his own importance, or by withdrawing.
(2) When demands are higher than can be met, a person tends to quit trying.
(3) Punishment causes behavior to cease but does not necessarily stop the desire to carry out the behavior.

c. Evaluate the effect of overemphasis of men to attain the role of successful breadwinner.

Examples

(1) Less time with family allowing it to be female-socialized
(2) Increased tension resulting in mental and physical breakdown of self and disruption of family.
(3) Model for socializing children to expect the same if father is successful in both work and family or to reject if father has disrupted harmony of household because of it.

Read *A Letter to My Wife* (Koffend 1972) for a man's interpretation of the effect of the "masculine mystique."

d. Apply the criteria set for men in their *occupational* role to wives and mothers who work outside the home, and discuss why women are not put under as much stress at work even though they may have a job that requires more effort than men.

e. Discuss some situations when fathers and/or husbands are not held to the criteria for being the breadwinner.

(1) Disabled
(2) Student
(3) Retired

f. Create a set of criteria for husbands and fathers that would be more in keeping with equalitarian and/or democratic ideals.

Examples

(1) The husband and wife are both responsible for earning enough to support themselves and their families adequately. The division is entirely their decision.
(2) The method of earning should be in keeping within the dictates

of their own consciences, their own reference group, and the law.

g. Discuss the type of personal traits a man would have in order to meet the responsibility of providing for himself and his children without meeting the specific cultural dictates.
   Examples
   (1) Comfortable with his own sexual identity, whatever it is
   (2) A wife who is comfortable with her own sexual identity
   (3) Creative and individualistic without ulterior motives to "prove something."
h. There has been a long-standing belief that public assistance to parents will undermine their desire to work and will encourage larger families. Debate the issue using some of the following sources:
   Guaranteed Income (Theobald 1964)
   The Politics of a Guaranteed Income (Moynihan 1973)
   "The Agency Game" (Berne 1964), a psychological strategy used in reality by people working in agencies that administer public assistance.
i. Compare the socialization of male children now in comparison to several years ago with respect to male superiority, male breadwinner role, and masculinity.
   (1) If your four-year-old son asked for a toy sewing machine, would you buy it?
   (2) If your twelve-year-old son asked for a real sewing machine, would you buy it?
j. Bring new children's books to class to show how the stories and pictures are depicting varying roles and occupations for men and women. The 1973 and later editions are beginning to make changes.

4. ***To evaluate those criteria that place female success in terms of the homemaker role.***
   a. Speculate on how widely accepted are the following criteria for success of wives and mothers (these criteria are not given as absolutes):
      (1) Be supportive of her husband so he can be successful in his occupation.
      (2) Manage the home so that there is adequate food, clothing, sanitation, etc.
      (3) Manage the household spending not to exceed the income, yet be adequate.
      (4) Be knowledgeable and capable of rearing children to be successful.
      (5) Add to the family income if needed

b. Analyze the "negative" actions of women who cannot meet the above criteria by applying behavior generalizations:

Actions

(1) Criticizes husband and children
(2) Overcomplains about burdens of housework
(3) Neglects housework with abandonment
(4) Deserts home and family bodily or through intoxicants or drugs
(5) Covertly or overtly begs for personal attention

Behavior Generalizations

(1) When demands are greater than ability to perform, a person tends to withdraw.
(2) When too little reinforcement (either intrinsic or extrinsic) is given, a person stops performing.
(3) When a person's self-concept is demeaned, she strives to protect it by striking out, withdrawing, or making excuses.

c. Discuss why wives who are not employed outside the home can get by with not meeting the rigors of cultural expectations.

Examples

(1) Products of performance are not open to public scrutiny.
(2) Family members tend to hide behaviors at home that are believed to be unacceptable to others.
(3) Some behaviors that would not be acceptable in employment are described as "feminine" and therefore are made acceptable if they are done by homemakers.

d. Write a case study of a woman who takes the role of major breadwinner and with it the role of expecting to be fed, clothed, and cared for as many husbands now do.
(1) What are your problems in writing the case?
(2) What are your feelings in writing the case?
(3) Empathize with the woman in the case fully.

e. Discuss some of the statements of the opponents of the Equal Rights Amendment.
(1) Women would in fact have unequal rights because of the burden of pregnancy.
(2) Women would have unequal rights because of the average smaller muscular build. Read *The Natural Superiority of Women* (Montagu 1953).

5. *To understand how some industries might change to meet the needs of families without there being a threat to the success of the industry.*

a. Start the discussion by these statements:
(1) Ten-hour shifts, four days each week, three days off
(2) Half-day employment five to six days each week

(3) Alternating shifts from one week to the next
(4) Variety in assembly-line jobs; some products are finished by a crew, who do more than one-item assembly-line job.

b. Read "Is the American Worker 'Alienated'?" (Kristol 1973) to understand why assembly-line work and non-creativeness alienates the worker.

c. Discuss the following method of assigning work in one commune, Twin Oaks (Kinkade 1973).
(1) Jobs are described by the work hours per day necessary for that job.
(2) Each person lists his preference in jobs.
(3) Each person's responsibilities are then scheduled so that he gets some jobs he likes and some he does not.
(4) If he dislikes a job he earns more credits per hour for that job; if he likes a job, he earns fewer credits.
(5) Each person must earn a certain number of credits per week.

6. *To understand the reconciliations involved when the husband and wife exchange traditional work roles.*

a. Show a picture of a man doing work usually classified as feminine.

Discussion Questions
(1) Why is this activity acceptable?
(2) Why is it funny?
(3) Speculate on why he does it.
(4) Why not?
(5) What would men like to do but will not because of fear of ridicule?
(6) What ways do men use to meet creative, esthetic needs? Covert? Overt?
(7) What is the cultural lag in this area? (Cultural lag is when behavior changes but culture has not.)

b. Some men, disabled or not, do all the housework and care for the children.
Read the following:
"Mother Went to Work and Father Stayed Home" (Lueloff 1973)

Discussion Questions
(1) When a man is disabled, how can he keep house and care for the children?
(2) What changes in men's and women's concepts about roles have to occur to make the change successful?
(3) What is the difference in the approach a man uses to keep house and the approach a woman uses?
(4) What is the difference in the approach a single woman uses to

manage money and the home and the way a married man or single man would?
(5) How do other cultures allow a man not to go to war or work without condemnation?
(6) Does our culture ever allow a man to *choose* to keep house whereas his wife or other women provide the income? Under what circumstances?
(7) Would you consider a role reversal? For a year?

7. ***To analyze conflicts in families which stem from the work ethic.***
Review and report on the following articles:
"Is the Work Ethic Going Out of Style?" (Time 1972, pp. 72-73)
"Is the American Worker 'Alienated'?" (Kristol 1973, p. 12)
"Business Technology and the American Family: An Impressionistic Analysis." (Koprowski 1973, pp. 229-234)
The Greening of America (Reich 1970)

Money, Personality, and Behavior

What people do about money is one manifestation of their culturally conditioned needs, desires, and expectations. Whether or not a person can live by a plan for spending probably has as much to do with whether he wants to as whether he has the computational ability. What a person spends his money for probably has as much to do with what he thinks he needs as what is adequate. How much a person will work for money probably has as much to do with how he sees the work or how he sees the use of money as maintaining an existence. How well two or more people spend the family income probably has as much to do with beliefs about what people "ought" to do as with sound business management principles.

Since money is necessary for purchasing both necessities for survival and some things that make life more worth living, it is a source of concern in families. Some basic management practices must take place, but the particular manner is probably less important than whether the needs and desires of the family are met. Whether or not one concept of spending is better than another is probably more a matter of a person's values than it is a matter of better business management. Who manages the money is probably as much a cultural expectation or possibly a personality trait of dominance as it is who is more capable. Controlling the spending may be as much a matter of manipulating the other as it is either a dominance trait or capability.

Money is blamed for conflicts in families when a lack of it, too much of it, or mismanagement of it are only the overt culprits. Too little and mismanagement of money can be real problems, however. What happens is that conflicts bring out stresses and strains, belittling of self-concepts, thwarted desires, overload of pressures, and unmet needs which make living very uncomfortable. Too much money has its drawbacks in a false notion that everything can be bought, that more than enough for necessities is enough for everything, that if one has the money, then one has the right to spend it at will.

Easy credit–not just credit–has given some people a false feeling of having money when they have none. They then live as if they did have money, with the double problems of indebtedness or bankruptcy and the notions that money can buy anything.

Teaching Techniques

1. *To gain a picture of student beliefs about money.*
   a. Survey the class with an anonymous questionnaire to find out their beliefs about money.

Questionnaire on Your Beliefs About Money

1. What is an adequate income for a married couple in their early twenties?____________________

   Why?____________________

2. How much of this income should be earned by the husband?____

   Why?____________________

3. When should a husband or wife work overtime or at two jobs (one of which is fulltime)?____________________

   Why?____________________

4. What working hours should the husband have?____________________

   Why?____________________

5. What working hours should the wife have?____________________

   Why?____________________

6. What types of products should be purchased on credit?__________

   ____

   Why?____________________

7. What types of products should be purchased in cash?__________

   ____

   Why?____________________

8. Who should keep the bills ____________________

   Why?____________________

9. What household appliances should you have in your first home?

   ____

   Why? ____

b. Write your attitudes and training in the area of money. Compare your list with another student's list. Could you two live together harmoniously?

2. *To analyze a person's **belief about money** as a way to **study** his **personality**, to predict his behavior, and to understand his interpersonal **relations**.*

   a. First, ask the students as a class to answer on paper the questions below to set the stage. After the whole class has answered the questions, ask a student to volunteer to be the one to be questioned, and have the class members begin to determine his personality and attempt to predict his behavior and interpersonal relations. Only questions concerning money may be asked. The student is instructed not to answer anything that does not pertain to money and not to answer any question he does not want to answer in front of the class. Some examples of questions are these:

      (1) Have you ever earned money? If not, where does your money to spend come from?
      (2) What does money buy for you?
      (3) If you were cut off from your present income source, what would you do? Why?
      (4) If you had to ask someone else to manage all your money, whom would you ask? Why?
      (5) Which has more importance to you–a $5.00 shirt or a $25.00 shirt? Why?

      After the questions have been asked and the student has given several answers, ask the class members to use the answers in describing and understanding the student being questioned.

   b. Ask the class to make comments about the following statements:

      (1) Seventy-four-year-old man:
          "If I could draw as much money as I wanted from the family (grown sons) business on the condition that my wife could draw the same amount, then I wouldn't draw any!"
      (2) Twenty-eight-year-old wife:
          "I think I should draw a salary for the work I do around home."
      (3) Twenty-two-year-old man:
          "I don't care how much my wife makes–the more, the better!"
          "I don't think people should have to account for all their money."

"You should borrow some money early in life to establish a credit rating."

"A well-dressed man is a woman's greatest asset."

(4) Nineteen-year-old girl to father:

"I want this car even though it doesn't have air conditioning. At least it has a furry rug and a checked top panel. I don't care if it does cost more than one with air conditioning."

3. *To understand how* ***childhood conditioning*** *(or parental and cultural values) about money* ***affects the adult spending*** *patterns.*

a. Read the following paragraph and have the class speculate on why two sons from the same family are totally different in adult spending patterns.

Tom's father never made much money, but he always kept account of every penny he made or spent. He made his boys do the same. Tom continues to do so to this very day, but not his older brother who has been in and out of bankruptcy several times.

After students speculate on the reasons, give them the following generalizations to help substantiate some of their conclusions or to spark further discussion.

(1) Sons tend to pattern after their fathers when their fathers are nurturant and permissive (Levin 1958).

(2) Sons tend to be the opposite of their fathers when they see their fathers as different from their own expectation of a father (Levin 1958).

(3) First-born children tend to be more rigidly disciplined and to be expected to achieve more than children born later (Schachter 1963).

(4) People are born with a different tolerance threshold for either rigidity or freedom (Kagan and Moss 1962).

(5) People can be conditioned to bolster their confidence with material possessions (Skinner 1953).

4. *To understand that* ***beliefs about money*** *as much as having too little money* ***can result in bankruptcy.***

a. Give this questionnaire to your students.

How Likely Are You to Get Head Over Heels in Debt?

(If you answer "yes" to most of the questions, you are a likely candidate for bankruptcy.)

1. Do you have as many as five credit cards?
2. Do you use these credit cards without keeping a running tally on purchases?
3. Do you like credit cards because they allow you to buy what you want on the spur of the moment?

4. Do you believe that you are entitled to the following items immediately upon marriage: automobile, TV, washing machine, dryer, dishwasher, air conditioner, and stereo equipment?
5. Is your family income almost entirely from wages or salaries?
6. Is your family income near the national average?
7. Are you in your late twenties or early thirties?
8. Do you have children?

b. Study the National Bankruptcy Act (see the Family Service Association representative).

Under this act debtors have the protection of counsel without ever going into bankruptcy. The counselor will advise you how to work your way out of your dilemma. An estimate of what percentage a person can pay on indebtedness is about 3 percent each month for three years. For example, it is recommended that a couple with an indebtedness of $1000 pay $30.00 each month; with an indebtedness of $6000 pay $200.00 each month. This schedule, of course, must fit their ability to have enough money to pay for food, rent, etc. No new debts are allowed to be accumulated.

6. *To analyze* ***money problems*** *by* ***applying generalizations of human relationships.***

a. Read the following story to the class and discuss the human relationships problems.

Amy and Sam had both worked prior to marriage and had both managed their own money. After marriage Sam said, "I'll handle the money since I am the man of the house. My father always handled the money." Amy responded, "But, Sam, you know very well you can't take care of the checkbook. It would be a wreck in no time. Keeping books is my job." Sam replied, "I thought you'd want me to be the head of the house. Don't you love me?" Amy cooled off and said, "Of course I love you. Let's don't talk about it anymore." Two years after this Amy was having to dodge bill collectors and was trying to keep the home together. Finally she said, "I'm tired of living like this. From now on I'll take charge of the money. You almost had us in bankruptcy." Sam yelled back, "I don't give a damn! Take it over if you think you can do any better!"

Discussion

How do role expectations and desire to keep peace in the family affect one's knowledge that the person to do a particular job is the person most qualified?

7. *To understand that although* ***social class*** *is heavily measured by family income,* ***the way the money is spent*** *and the life styles are also important measures.*

a. Review some of the described levels of social class to ascertain the facets which imply attitude and behavior along with income and education as criteria. Discuss how people from differing classes may have conflict.

(1) The upper class–Aside from being rich, educated, and living in an environment with every material necessity and quality furnishings, the upper class thinks differently. They were born in security. They know they set the rules. They learned social graces from modeling after their families.

(2) The upper middle class–Their work or profession is synonymous with their identity and it governs every move. Although they can provide for all material necessities, they know they have to work for them. They are very rule conscious but have a feeling they can influence change. Their social graces were consciously taught.

(3) The lower middle class–Their job is their livelihood, but their identity is more attached to their families' and friends' concepts of them. They believe in the virtue of honesty as the important characteristic. They are followers but only when they want to be. Their social graces are based on treating people like "home folks."

(4) The lower class–They have no job skill and see work as necessary if they need the money. By not having the pressure to succeed in a job, they are free to act as they please so long as they don't get clobbered by the law or by their neighbors.

(This is a composite of descriptions based on many studies from Feldman and Theibur (1972), Hollingshead (1949), Parker (1972), Reissman (1959), Warner (1949), and many others.)

b. Read *Goodby Columbus* (Roth 1959) or see the movie (1970) to get a picture of a family who moved up two social classes in one generation on the income and housing facets, but not on the behaviors facet. One particular example is that meals were being served in an expensively furnished and appointed dining room but were being eaten as it they were a picnic. Many other examples are exposed.

c. Discuss the following observation.
Many parents spend a great deal of money on piano lessons for their children so that the children will have an aesthetic appreciation for music; then the child speaks and his diction "kills it all." Would it not have done more to have given him diction lessons than piano lessons?

d. Discuss the problems of the married pair when:

(1) The husband's family had more money but less education than the wife's.

(2) The husband's and wife's families had equal amounts of money but differing levels of education (his higher) (hers higher).
(3) Both families had little money, but his family was cultured and hers was not.
(4) Both families had little money, but hers had higher aspirations and mental abilities.
(5) The wife's family saw money as something to spend both to make more and live better, and the husband's family saw money as something to save, almost with fear of investment.

e. Empathize with the parents and young couple when the couple aspires to move one to two social levels above their parents but realize they must give up some of the parental contact to do it. Points to consider:
(1) If family and friends want to keep in touch with a couple who is moving upward, they must move with them behaviorally, if not financially.
(2) An upwardly mobile couple literally cannot *afford* to keep family and friends as companions if the family and friends cannot pay their own way or will not change their attitudes and behaviors.

f. Analyze the college campus as an insular setting where people tend to reinforce each other's behavior giving a false notion of social equality.
Read the following case of Jack and Nancy.

THE CASE OF JACK AND NANCY*

"I met Jack when we were in college," Nancy told the counselor. "He was the captain of the football team. Every girl on the campus wanted him. On Saturday nights when our team had won, it was thrilling to be the one he chose. I got excited—yes, even sexually—when I got close to the 'hero.' I felt like the Roman women must have felt when they saw their victorious soldiers coming home from battle.

"In those days, I had never had any doubt that I wanted to marry him, even though I knew that he was from a background very different from mine. His mother and father were as poor as church mice. His father had been an alcoholic, and his mother never was able to earn very much. They lived in a slum, but I always used to think it was to Jack's credit that he pulled himself up enough to stay in high school and to get a football scholarship to college. It made me love him even more, because I felt sorry for him, I guess.

"My father is the vice-president of a large corporation in San Francisco. I know now that he was very much opposed to my marrying Jack, although he said very little about it before we were married. We

*From pp. 100-101 in *Marriage and Family Relationships* by Richard H. Klemer. Copyright © 1970 by Richard H. Klemer. Used by permission of Harper & Row, Publishers, Inc.

had a big wedding, and then we went to live in a little town near our college, where he had a job as an assistant football coach. For two or three years we had a good marriage. Our first child was born there, and at first we were happy. But the friends he brought home were kind of rough, and we had almost nothing in common to talk about. I had majored in fine arts, and Jack knew almost nothing about painting or music. Moreover, we had a hard time of it financially. My folks tried to help out, but he resented the things they gave us. I think he was unhappy in that little town, or perhaps because he knew I was missing the kind of life I had lived before I went to college, and this made him feel more guilty than he had to be. Actually, I don't think he was any great shakes as a coach anyway. So our marriage got to be a little unhappy, and he took to either staying away or bringing his friends in to drink beer. I got pretty disillusioned. He was a nice dresser before we were married, but afterward he used to sit around the living room in his underwear and watch television. He never wanted to do the things that my father used to do (before Daddy got rich), like cutting the grass and painting the house. He just didn't seem to care what the yard looked like. I had to go out myself and cut the grass.

"Shortly after our first child was born, my father saw to it that Jack got an offer from the same industrial firm in San Francisco that employs Daddy. It was a good job as an expediter. I was delighted, of course. We moved away from the little town and back to San Francisco, where I had grown up and where my parents lived.

"But instead of making Jack happy, this only seemed to make him worse. He didn't like my friends there, and he didn't seem to want to make any new ones. He said that my friends had grown up having everything and that they were snobbish and didn't like him. This wasn't so at all. They tried hard to make him a part of the group. They wanted him to try going sailing and skiing, which he had never done, but he said they just wanted to show him up.

"Before long, he got very depressed and sat around the house in his undershirt watching television even when there weren't any sports events on. By this time I didn't seem to love him anymore. I couldn't get the least bit excited about the despondent man who didn't seem to know where he was going. Sex relations became an unwelcome tolerance, and pretty soon I began to resent him altogether.

"He never wants to go anywhere with my friends or do anything culturally interesting. What am I going to do?"

When Jack came in to see the counselor, he started right out with the issue of her friends. "She and her snooty friends," he exploded. "When we were back in that small town where we started our marriage, she wouldn't have anything to do with my friends. Now she expects me to like hers. They're the country-club set, and all they can think about is sailing or golf. They're so smug I can't stand them.

"When we were in college, I thought Nancy and I had a lot in common. She used to want to come and watch me play football, and she knew a lot about the game. She liked the people I knew then, or at least she pretended to. They were all in college just like us. She didn't make any fuss about my wearing a T-shirt then. Now she hits the sky if

I sit in the living room without my coat on. What's a man's home supposed to be, anyhow?

"She's scared to death of what the neighbors are going to think about us. The grass never gets a half-inch high before she's out there cutting it. She says that I never do it, but the truth of the matter is that she never gives me a chance. Her old man is the rigid type, too. He's so bad that he has to have the points of the pencils on his desk all pointing in the same direction or he throws a tantrum. She says that she wants to be happy, but she's never going to be happy until she relaxes a little and stops worrying about what other people think.

"The most important problem in our marriage right now is sex. She's completely frigid now. When we were first married, I thought she was one of the best sex partners I ever had. But now she doesn't want sex anymore.

"I can't understand what's come over her. She hit the ceiling when I told her about some of the girls down at the office, and yet she won't extend herself a bit to be sexy with me. Actually, I think she was all tied up about sex as a kid: You know, she was a goody-goody girl. Her parents made her that way. You would almost think that sex wasn't natural the way they didn't talk about it.

"Anyway, if she doesn't start coming around soon, I'm going to step out on her. I've told her that before, but this time I mean it."

Points for Discussion

(1) Different behaviors are reinforced off campus from those on campus.

(2) Childhood-conditioned needs are difficult to change.

(3) Wives adjust more easily to upward mobility of husbands than to downward mobility.

(4) Culturally-conditioned male dominance makes it easier for males to be of the higher social class if the couple is of different social classes.

(5) People tend to become more like their parents as they reach maturity.

(6) If children admired their opposite sex parent, they are more likely to expect their spouses to be like that parent.

g. Empathize with the couple in the case of Susan and Rudolph whose objectives were the same, but their means for reaching these objectives differed because of their conditioning.

THE CASE OF SUSAN AND RUDOLPH*

"I've been married to Susan for seven years," Rudolph said to the marriage counselor, "and in all that time she's never been able to hold on to a nickel for more than a few hours at a time. Money goes through

*From p. 38 in *Marriage and Family Relationships* by Richard H. Klemer. Copyright © 1970 by Richard H. Klemer. Used by permission of Harper & Row, Publishers, Inc.

her hands like water, and she can't save either. She won't even mend a rip in a torn sheet!"

When the counselor talked to Susan, she said, "Rudolph is the cheapest, the tightest, the most miserly man there ever was. Why, he even expects me to mend torn sheets! Can you imagine that?"

While it was clear to the counselor that this wasn't the only problem in this marriage, it was also evident that the torn sheet symbolized the deep division in the couple's emotional attitudes toward spending family income. After airing some other overlying resentments, Rudolph volunteered the following information: He was the son of a widowed mother from New England. He grew up with his four brothers in a small, semirural community whose values were "use it up, wear it out, make it do." His mother constantly impressed upon the developing consciousness of her five boys that a good husband–not a wastrel and a profligate like their late father had been–should save his money for the inevitable rainy day. These attitudes acquired in childhood had intense emotional significance for Rudolph.

In due course, Rudolph grew up, went into the army, was sent to California, and there met and very quickly married the happy-go-lucky daughter of a happy-go-lucky Glendale family. In Susan's neighborhood "gracious living" was an important value. The popular attitude was "spend your money, that's what it's for." It was important to keep up with the Joneses. Moreover, those people who did spend (sometimes beyond their means) for houses often made a substantial profit in the California real-estate market and therefore had even more money to spend.

Each of these partners thought his mate was trying to punish him with silly notions that were contrary to the best interests of the family. "But I'm only trying to save it for my family's future," Rudolph said emphatically. Susan pleaded, "We are entitled to some kind of adequate living now when we are young enough to enjoy it." Susan and Rudolph had been to see divorce lawyers, who recommended that they consult a marriage counselor.

Points for Discussion

(1) People can agree on the ends and disagree violently on the means because belief about the means has moved into the moral realm.

(2) Telling a person he is wrong does not change his behavior until his perception changes.

(3) A person's "script" (childhood set of expectations as described by Berne 1964 and English 1973) may never really be changed.

(4) Proving equal costs in the long run does not change a person's belief that his means is not as good as another.

(5) To condemn a person's method of spending is to condemn him as a person, so close are spending and beliefs.

(6) What one sees as overspending, the other may perceive as selected spending.

8. ***To understand the difficulty in teaching children about money management and that parents can rarely teach their children how to manage money by revealing their own incomes and methods.***

   A person's income is so personal and so private that he guards the secret as he would his most prized possession. To tell a child is to run the risk of its being told. To let a child know the bad financial moves a parent has made is to risk losing the child's confidence. To let a child know how difficult it is to meet the financial burdens is to put too much on a young shoulder.

   What are your suggestions for ways parents can teach children to handle money by seeing how parents manage?

Summary

The cultural roles for men and women in the areas of work and money are changing very slowly even though more women are working outside the home. Many of the relationships problems blamed on money may be caused by the cultural expectations which almost force a person to take a role in which he may be neither capable nor interested. Yet the conditioning to fulfill the roles is very compelling.

Money and work are so much a part of people's lives that this whole chapter has been devoted to teaching techniques involving how a person believes and behaves in these areas. Information in preceding chapters was applied in this chapter. The next chapter is about handling crises which are really extensions of all the problem areas and understanding of human behavior discussed thus far.

References

Berne, Eric. *Games People Play*. New York: Grove Press, Inc., 1964.

Blood, Robert O. "Division of Labor in Two-Income Families." In *Marriage Means Encounter*, edited by George Roleder. Dubuque, Iowa: Wm. C. Brown Company, Publishers, 1973.

English, Fanita. "TA's Disneyworld." *Psychology Today* 6: 45-50, 1973.

Feldman, Saul D., and Theibur, Gerald W. *Life Styles: Diversity in American Society*. Boston: Little, Brown, and Co., 1972.

Hoffman, Lois W. "Effects of Maternal Employment on the Child." *Child Development* 32: 187-197, 1961.

Hollingshead, August B. *Elmtown's Youth*. New York: Wiley, 1949.

"Is the Work Ethic Going Out of Style?" *Time*, 30 October, 1972, pp. 72-73.

Kagan, Jerome and Moss, H. A. *Birth to Maturity*. New York: Wiley, 1962.

Kinkade, Kathleen. "Commune: A Walden-Two Experiment." *Psychology Today* 6: 35-42, 1973.

Klemer, Richard H. *Marriage and Family Relationships*. New York: Harper & Row, 1970.

Koffend, John B. *A Letter to My Wife*. New York: Dell Pub. Co., 1972.

Koprowski, Eugene. "Business Technology and the American Family: An Impressionistic Analysis." *The Family Coordinator* 22: 229-234, 1973.
Kristol, Irving. "Is the American Worker 'Alienated'?" *The Wall Street Journal,* January 18, 1973.
Levin, H. "Permissive Childrearing and Adult Role Behavior." In *Contributions to Modern Psychology*. Edited by D. E. Dulany, R. L. DeValois, D. C. Beardsley, and M. R. Winterbottom. New York: Oxford University Press, 1958, pp. 307-312.
Lueloff, Jorie. "Mother Went to Work and Father Stayed Home." In *Marriage Means Encounter*, edited by George Roleder. Dubuque, Iowa: Wm. C. Brown Co., Publishers, 1973.
Montagu, Ashley. *The Natural Superiority of Women.* New York: Macmillan, 1953.
Moynihan, Daniel P. *The Politics of a Guaranteed Income.* New York: Random House, 1973.
Parker, Richard. *The Myth of the Middle Class.* New York: Liveright, 1972.
Reich, Charles. *The Greening of America.* New York: Random House, 1970.
Reissman, Leonard. *Class in American Society.* New York: The Free Press, 1959.
Roth, Philip. *Goodbye Columbus.* New York: Bantam Books, 1959.
Schachter, S. "Birth Order, Eminence and Higher Education." *American Sociological Review* 28: 757-767, 1963.
Skinner, B. F. *Science and Human Behavior.* New York: The Free Press, 1953.
Theobald, Robert, ed. *Guaranteed Income.* Garden City, New York: Anchor Books, Doubleday & Co. Inc., 1964.
Warner, W. Lloyd; Meeher, Marchia; and Eels, Kenneth. *Social Class in America.* Chicago: Science Research Associates, Inc., 1949.

Chapter 15

Crises

A crisis is any event which causes changes in a person's or family's normal behavior. What is defined as a crisis by one person may not be defined as a crisis by another; therefore, a crisis has a perceptual factor as well as an objective factor. What is labeled as a crisis also tends to have an era factor since events defined as a crisis in one era may not have the same impact in another, purely because of the change that must take place rather than the precipitating event. Some precipitating events which cause crisis situations are discussed after the beliefs about how different people handle crises. The events discussed are (1) divorce, (2) the disabled family member, and (3), death.

Handling Crises

It has been postulated that the reasons for defining situations as crises and for handling crises differently by different people, different families, different societies, and even these three in different eras, may be (1) the extenuating circumstances of the situation, (2) the resources available including past experience in solving problems, and (3) whether or not the event is a threat to the status of the people concerned (Hansen and Hill 1964). The range of outcomes of crisis situations is from complete disintegration to a stronger position.

The following teaching ideas will be presented as if the overall goal is for greater understanding of why people vary in their abilities to handle crises. Obviously the ultimate goal is for the students to be better able to handle crises because of this knowledge and understanding. The specific objectives will cover a variety of crises faced by families.

The presentation of teaching techniques includes these behavioral objectives: (1) to be aware of the reasons families meet crises differentially, (2) to be empathetic with those people in perceived crisis situations, (3) to understand social-psychological aspects of crises, (4) to analyze crises, and (5) to evaluate proposed solutions to crises (Glasser and Glasser 1970; Irwin 1971).

Teaching Techniques

1. *To become aware of the reasons that cause families to meet crises differently.*
   Put the following list of possible crises on the board and ask the students to select one person in the family to which each situation might occur and then to state on paper whether or not it would be a crisis and how the person would handle it. The notion of how people define and handle crises could precede this assignment or could be an outcome of this assignment.

   Pregnancy
   Irreparable bodily damage
   Death
   Loss of a job
   Will not graduate
   Reduced income
   Broken leg
   Relative coming to live with family
   Divorce

   Others could be added. The discussion will center around the facts that pregnancy, for example, would be welcomed and not a crisis for one's married sister who had been hoping to get pregnant for three years, whereas it would be a crisis for an unmarried girl whose boyfriend had just left the country, and who had conservative, distant parents who had little money. On the other hand, pregnancy for a particular married woman could very well be a crisis, whereas pregnancy for a particular unmarried woman might be just as welcome as any other event. The students are then given an opportunity to present some of their notes about handling crises in their own families to the class. (The rule of "telling only what you want to tell about your family so long as you understand why you do not want to tell" still holds here. See Chapter 1 on The Empathetic Approach.) This personal application of the generalizations about crises will help the students gain insight and will also cause them to remember the generalizations longer.
2. *To show empathy with differing definitions of crises and to empathize with other people who may see events as crises even if the events are not seen as crises by others.*
   Read one of the following articles (or similar ones) to the class (or assign some students to report a crisis in a personal way) and discuss whether or not the event would be a crisis to the students. All three of the articles

are reprinted in *Families in Crisis* (Glasser and Glasser 1970). Use the questions given to guide them to see how the event was a crisis to the family involved. (See Chapter 2 on the Literature Approach. One paperback can be disassembled to distribute articles for the reading assignments.)

"Living Poor: Providing the Basic Necessities; Priorities and Problems" (Jeffers 1970)

"The Old Love and the New: Divorce and Readjustment" (Waller 1970)

"A Family as Seen in the Hospital" (Richardson 1970)

Questions

a. What were your immediate feelings about the situation–disgust, pity, scorn?
b. How did the persons get into this situation?
c. How are the persons facing the crisis?
d. Assuming you had these same circumstances, would you have faced the crisis in the same way?

3. *To gain knowledge about the **social-psychological** aspects of a crisis situation.*

a. Have students list and discuss some specific events under each of the following categories of crises (adapted from Hansen and Hill 1964).

Addition or deletion of a family member	*Change in family socioeconomic station*	*Conflict in family roles*	*Demoralization of one or more family members*
Examples:	Examples:	Examples:	Examples:
Birth	Loss of job	Woman makes more money	Birth of a handicapped child
Death	Promotion	Man is incapacitated	Alcoholism
Relative is coming to live	Money inherited	Child is belligerent	Infidelity
Divorce	Loss of property	Man is embarrassed at being a father	
Child is leaving home			

Note that a combination of these events is often more likely than only one occurrence.

b. Sometimes life itself is characterized as a crisis. In effect, the efforts in meeting of the developmental tasks in each stage of the family life cycle may or may not be crisis producing. The notion that inadequate meeting of tasks in former stages of the family life cycle and the lack of knowledge about the developmental tasks of future stages in the family life cycle lends evidence that there is a great probability that there will be crises in families.

Give out one set of Duvall's (1971) developmental tasks for one stage in the family life cycle (such as the one given below) and discuss how attempts at meeting these tasks could become a crisis:

*Launching Stage**

(1) Rearranging physical facilities and resources
(2) Meeting the costs as launching-center families* (college, weddings, etc.)
(3) Reallocating responsibilities among grown and growing children
(4) Coming to terms with themselves as husband and wife
(5) Maintaining open systems of communication within the family and between the family and others
(6) Widening the family circle through release of young adult children and recruitment of new members by marriage
(7) Reconciling conflicting loyalties and philosophies of life

Questions to Stimulate Discussion

(1) If these developmental tasks were yours, but not your parents', to meet at this particular moment, how would you meet them?
(2) How have some crises seemed to take families by surprise when they are almost inevitable?
(3) What preparation can a family make for being ready for this stage?
(4) What types of things could cause this period to be crisis producing?

4. *To analyze **crisis situations***

a. Have someone (a student or an outsider) report a crisis situation, and instruct the class members to question the person in an attempt to analyze the situation as to:
(1) Why it is defined as a crisis to the teller.
(2) What resources he has for facing the crisis.
(3) What changes it will make in the family.
(4) What experience the family has had in problem-solving or crisis-meeting.
(5) What help relatives and friends can be.
(6) The philosophy of the individual as causes or reasons for crisis situations (bad luck, brought on as punishment, just happened, lack of planning, etc.)

*That stage in the family life cycle in which the children become adults and are "launched" into the adult world.

b. Compare sudden crisis situations with insidious situations (slowly building crises) in order to analyze the processes and apply the strengths for handling them.
Insidious problems include such things as aging, disenchantment, alcoholism, and poverty. Although one would think that since these problems slowly build they could be taken care of, there is a wearing effect that is not a factor in sudden crises.

c. Analyze a crisis situation from the theory that role conflict exists when there are two opposing expectations for an individual at one given time. The crisis occurs when the person "blows his stack."

Examples of Crisis Situations Involving Conflicting Values

(1) The wife who earns as much money as her husband yet is made to feel that her job is unimportant except for her income.

(2) The mother-in-law who sees her son as the breadwinner and tells her daughter-in-law she is just "helping out" when both son and daughter-in-law make the same income.

(3) The son who is told he is too old to be doing "such childish things," and in the same breath he is told he must quit trying to give his "opinions."

(4) A fifteen-year-old boy becomes a father.

d. Sudden unemployment affected some of the middle- and upper-middle-class families in the early 1970s. Discuss these areas which hit the families hardest: blow to self-concept, disbelief, inability to switch male-female roles, attempt to continue to live in same style, etc. (Gallese 1972).

5. *To evaluate solutions to crisis situations*

a. Apply the following postulate to some of the proposed solutions to crises listed below.
To the extent that lack of (education) is the cause of a problem, increased (education) will be the answer. (The word that is placed in the parentheses may vary from "cohesiveness" to "money" to "kin network" to "experience.")

(1) Solution: The cycle of poverty will be broken when the children of poverty-stricken, uneducated parents are given the education to get good paying jobs. (Lack of education is admittedly *one* of the reasons for chronic poverty levels, but other factors such as mental ability, social expectations, and temperament may also weigh heavily.)

(2) Solution: A man who regularly beat up his wife was being talked to by a court counselor after one rather severe beating of

his wife. The usual in-depth searches for why he needed to hit his wife were made to no avail. The counselor finally realized that in that man's social setting beating one's wife is expected. When the counselor told him that beating one's wife is just not acceptable by most of society, the man looked astonished and said, "They don't?" He quit beating his wife. Could this be the reason? To the extent that lack of knowledge of social sanction was the cause of the wife-beating, knowledge that wife-beating isn't socially sanctioned by most of the people was the reason for stopping.

(3) Apply the postulate to this case: Mrs. X's children (eleven) range in age from one to twenty. The first five were born while she was married to a man whom she later divorced. The sixth child was born illegitimate, and the last five were born while she was married to a man who rarely added to the support of any of her children. Mrs. X has applied to AFDC for the maximum allowance. She perceives lack of money as her problem.

Divorce

Divorce is steadily increasing in the United States, but the regional differences are so great that the probable reasons for divorce specific to those regions is perhaps more important than knowing the average increase in divorce across the United States. The divorce rate* for the United States as a whole is 2.6 per 1000 population; 4.2 per 1000 population on the West Coast; and 1.1 per 1000 population in the Northeast (Vital and Health Statistics 1970).

The concommitant changes with the increase in the divorce rate are the "no-fault" divorce laws of some states, do-it-yourself divorce, a proposal for national divorce legislation, and an increase in divorce counseling. The "no-fault" divorce law is being implemented to eliminate an alleged guilty party and a defendant in order to allow people who are incompatible to separate with as little psychological damage as possible. Legal fees for divorce are expensive even when the divorce is uncontested. There are more written directions for handling your own divorce without costly legal fees. One of the problems in divorce is, and always has been, that divorce laws differ from state to state, which probably causes as great a problem as the conflict in the

*Rate is different from ratio. Rate means number per thousand population, whereas ratio means number of divorces in one year compared to number of marriages in that year.

marriage or the frustrations during the divorce proceedings. Therefore, national divorce legislation is being considered. Divorce counseling, both for helping those people concerned understand the emotional problems and for managing the divorce, has increased along with the increase in divorce rate.

Although divorce laws were made for the benefit of the persons involved, the laws were also an attempt to stabilize society. The increase in divorces and the ensuing tragic hardships in money, time, and emotions have encouraged the no-fault divorce and divorce counseling so that the divorce does not devastate the partners and the children. All of this change is evidence of more humane treatment of people rather than a breakdown of society. An increase in marriage enrichment and alternate marriage forms are two ways of attempting to curtail the need for a marriage to reach divorce.

Teaching Techniques

1. *To understand the cultural reasons for legislation about divorce.*
   a. Compare societies with and without legislation about divorce.
      (1) Divorce laws were rescinded between 1917 and 1936 in Russia with the result of a near breakdown of the family with a lack of security and socialization of all family members (Mace and Mace 1963).
      (2) Moslem countries have recently made their divorce laws more strict. Prior to this, a man could divorce his wife merely by saying three times, "I divorce you." Men and women now have to show just cause.
   b. Read the entire divorce laws in your state (from the *General Statutes*) and compare with Litwak's (1956) "Three Ways in Which Law Acts as a Means of Social Control: Punishment, Therapy, and Education: Divorce Law a Case in Point."
2. *To analyze why divorce laws are changing.*
   a. Are the following major changes in divorce laws in some states more humane? From adultery as the only grounds to other reasons? From two years' separation to six months? From having to have an aggrieved partner and a faulted partner to "no fault"?
   b. Apply the cultural lag concept (that behavior changes before culture changes) to the changing divorce laws and previously changed behavior of the people.
   c. Compare the new "no-fault" divorce laws (in fourteen states by 1973) with the former separation by mutual consent laws which had been in effect for decades.

"No-fault" divorce laws, even though they eliminate the need for an accused partner, require proof that the marriage has had an irretrievable breakdown with no reconciliation likely.

d. Compare the "no-fault" divorce laws with the former divorce law which required that one of the partners had committed an act detrimental to the other spouse (Gough 1972; Monahan 1973; and Robbins 1973).

e. The movement toward equal rights has been instrumental in changing divorce laws so that they are more humane.
Read about humanistic philosophy to understand one of the philosophies behind the divorce law changes (Cantor 1972; Foster 1972; and Rogers 1972).

3. *To become aware of* ***divorce procedures****.*
   a. Check with the local Social Services Department (Welfare Department in some states) to get information about free legal advice for welfare recipients.
   b. Check with a local lawyer to learn local legal procedures in your state.
   c. Have someone recently divorced or a lawyer tell about procedures.

4. *To assess* ***divorce counseling*** *as a means for alleviating anxieties and legal and financial problems in a divorce.*
   a. Read "How to Make a Good Divorce" (Rogers 1973).
   b. Check the local Family Services Association for divorce counseling in your community.

5. *To understand the process of* ***adjusting to a divorce****.*
   a. Apply the process of adjusting to the alcoholic who has been institutionalized to the adjusting to a divorce. People tend to meet crises in a patterned progression. At first there is a numbness and a denial that the event has occurred. As the numbness wears off, the persons involved become disorganized and begin to show their resentments. Conflicts soon develop and there is a strain on relationships. The degree to which all this happens is influenced by the personal and financial resources available as well as the problem-solving ability the people have. Eventually a lowest level occurs, and life begins to be worth living again (Jackson 1961).
   b. Apply the ways people meet crises to divorce.
   c. Read the following stories and book for greater insight into the problems of divorce.

      "Moses Supposes" (Currie 1958)
      "Love and Like" (Gold 1959)

"Ixion" (Swarthout 1958)
Of the Farm (Updike 1966)

A more complete list may be found in *Family Insights Through the Short Story* (Somerville 1964).

The Disabled Family Member

Family members may be born with a disability or may become disabled. The disability may be physical, mental, emotional, or a combination of these and may be manifested in such ways as mental retardation, long-term illness, cerebral palsy, alcoholism, dementia, blindness, and leukemia, to mention only a few.

No matter what the disability is there are four factors which will affect that person and his family. One is the development of a good self-concept by the disabled person and members of his family; a second is non-exploitation of the disabled person or his family; a third is adequate financial resources; and a fourth is the social acceptance of that disability. Lack of one or a combination can disable the entire family.

Teaching Techniques

1. *To understand the **importance of a good self-concept** when one is disabled or has a disabled family member.*
   a. Discuss the comments as they relate to self-concept:
      "Why does this have to happen to me?"
      "I can't stand to look at a disabled person."
      "I'm glad I'm not that person."
      "I wish I could play football."
   b. Parents seem to be able to accept a child's disability which was caused by the environment better than one which was inherited (Farber 1959).
      (1) Discuss the "bad seed" psychology.
      (2) See the movie "Bad Seed" (a feature film) or read the book.
   c. Discuss the family dynamics when it is announced that one of the family members will be disabled.
      (1) Who might take the lead in constructive effort? Why?
      (2) Who might be most upset? Why?
      (3) Who might overreact or become overly kind? Why?
      (4) Would anyone insist on a concerted effort?
      (5) Would all family members including the disabled be allowed to be individuals?

d. What do you say when your son says he is sorry he was born with so many handicaps–astigmatism in one eye, flat feet, muscular legs, slight overweight–when in reality he is very bright, very handsome, beautifully formed? He does happen to wear glasses for reading and wears insteps in his shoes. Do we all feel we're different?

2. *To understand the circumstances under which* ***exploitation*** *occurs.*

a. The disabled person can use the family members by playing on their sympathies, but the family members have reinforced this or it would not continue.

Role play this scene:

Eight-year-old with cerebral palsy: Carry my books.
Twelve-year-old sister: OK.
Eight-year-old: Turn on Channel 2 and bring me a glass of milk.
Twelve-year-old: I want Channel 8.
Eight-year-old: You don't like me. I'm going to tell Mama.
Twelve-year-old: . . . .

b. Families with disabled members can use the disabled persons as scapegoats for their own shortcomings or as a release from their feelings of guilt (Vogel and Bell 1968).
Discuss these statements:
"If it weren't for Alice, we could go to the beach."
"I can't go tonight; I have to stay with Charles."
"We'd have a larger house, but you know the expenses we have."

c. How can a disabled parent exploit his spouse and children?

d. Have a counselor for disabled persons talk to the class about family members' roles.

e. Discuss the postulate that "every person is both an actor and a reactor" (Stryker 1959).

f. Discuss jealousy of siblings when a handicapped child is pampered.

3. *To gain knowledge of the* ***expenses*** *involved and the* ***agencies*** *that can assist with a disabled person.*

a. Assign students to visit agencies such as Vocational Rehabilitation, Lions Club International, Cerebral Palsy Association, Society for the Mentally Retarded, etc., that give assistance to disabled persons.

b. Compare the costs of various disabilities.

c. Study the occupations for which the various disabilities will not be a hindrance.

4. *To understand the* ***medical nature of the disability*** *and the attitude of the public toward it.*

a. Ask a medical doctor to explain the medical nature of several disabilities which may be represented in the class or community.

Include what behaviors are to be expected as normal and what treatment is necessary.

b. Assign each student or group of students to study one type of disability and to report on it. Combine this study with the reading of a story or book on families with disabled members (listed under #5) to enrich the meaning of this assignment.
   (1) What is the nature of the disability?
   (2) What is the medical treatment?
   (3) How have societal attitudes changed?
   (4) What is the difference in attitude and effect on family if the disability is temporary, permanent, or will terminate in death in a few years?

5. *To gain insight through reading literature into the total family relationships when there is a disabled member.*

   "We're All Guests" (alcoholism) (Clay 1955)
   "Morning Sun" (emotional disturbance) (Deasey 1953)
   A Child Called Noah (autism) Greenfeld 1973)
   "Thoughts in the Dark" (physical impairment) (Ishikawa 1953)
   "Holiday" (permanently disabled) (Porter 1962)

   A more complete list may be found in *Family Insights Through the Short Story* (Somerville 1964).

Death Education

One of the topics which is best studied by the literature approach is death. Much of the great literature handles death and crises in some way; yet textbooks on the family give little space to it.

Death itself is the only inevitable occurrence of everyone's life. It happens in everyone's family and circle of acquaintances. But because it is both irreversible and inevitable, even the thought of it is whisked away. The less preparation for it and the less perspective we have about it, the greater the shock when it occurs.

There are many factors which may accompany a particular death: accidental nature, prematurity, suicide and homicide, aging, long illness, euthanasia, legal death, guilt, bereavement, funerals, financial and psychological preparation, and the concerns for what happens to the deceased after death. Several of these factors may accompany each death.

Teaching Techniques

1. *To explore one's own feelings about assumed causes of death. (Care must be taken when discussing these causes in class. Students may have recently experienced some of them.)*

a. Compare reactions to accidental death, suicide, homicide, aging, illness, and euthanasia.
   What would you say if you read in the paper that a man known to you all, but not a close friend or relative, died in one (take each one separately) of the above ways?
   What would be your reaction if he were a close friend or relative?
b. Read the following stories about suicide and discuss.
   "The Apple Tree" (Galsworthy 1942)
   The Death of a Salesman (Miller 1949)
   "I'm Really Dead" (Schor 1973)
c. Read *Love Story* (Seigal 1970) and discuss the difference in the outcome or feelings about the story if the couple had been older, if the type of illness had been different, if the financial circumstances had been different, and if there had been a child.
   (*Love Story* is about the love and death of a twenty-five-year-old girl who was married to a young lawyer. She died of an incurable disease. They had no children.)

2. *To understand the* ***behavior of*** *the* ***dying aging person*** *as well as the one alive.*
   a. Read Updike's *Of the Farm* (1966) to study the ways the author reacts to the probable, but not imminent death, of an aging mother and the ways an aging mother may manipulate people as she prepares for death.
      Compare this story with Kubler-Ross's psychological death (1969), a period of behavior which seems to be a necessary part of accepting death and breaking away from the rest of life.
   b. Discuss possible reasons for deathbed promises to the aging:
      To alleviate guilt for not having been more comforting.
      To ease the aged person's mind.
      To assure the inheritance.
   c. Discuss the possible feeling of freedom with associated guilt upon the death of an older person:
      If the person has been controlling.
      If the person has had long suffering.
      If the person has had great medical expense.

3. *To evaluate the* ***decisions*** *surrounding a person's* ***imminent death*** *because of an illness.*
   a. Euthanasia is advocated by many who believe it is no mercy to the dying one or the family for a person to live and never again be aware. Discuss the pros and cons.
      (1) Contact the Euthanasia Society of America, New York City, for more information.
      (2) Read "Death with Dignity" (Alverez 1971).

b. Legal time of death is presently described to be when the doctor proclaims a person dead.
   Discuss the proposals to change criteria for death to include an evaluation of brain wave patterns.
c. Whether to tell the patient about his imminent death may be more debatable in this culture than euthanasia and legal time of death. A debate would be appropriate in class by well-prepared students. Or have the whole class read fiction about telling a patient about his imminent death (Glaser and Strauss 1965; Gorer 1965).
d. Donation of sound organs, the entire body, or having an autopsy is a decision which may be legally made by the person even before he becomes a patient or by the family members after death. Discuss the feelings and myths involved in these decisions.

4. *To understand the background of* ***euphemisms surrounding death.***
   a. How do various people express that someone has died? He passed away. She had a coronary arrest. He went away. She's gone. He's dead. He didn't make it. She's not with us any longer. He was called to Heaven.
      These expressions are illustrations of the conditioning of the people. How do you categorize these expressions with these types of people:
         Practical, rational
         Superstitious
         Philosophical
   b. Read parts of "Neglect of Dying Patients' Emotional Needs Linked to Cultural Inability to Face Death" (Hicks 1970) to get class discussion on need for euphemisms.

5. *To explore one's own* ***beliefs about death.***
   a. Give students a revised form of the questionnaire published in *Psychology Today* (Shneidman 1970). Compare the students' answers with those of the readers' in *Psychology Today* (Shneidman 1971). From the questionnaire it was found that the readers' attitudes seemed to be ambivalent toward death–awe and attraction; risking death, yet loving life; wanting happiness, yet acting in self-destructive ways; taboo on death, yet an insistence on being more permissive; an obsession with war, yet a concern for spiritual rebirth.
   b. To understand the superstitions surrounding death.
      (1) How do the following behaviors belie the superstition that if something is planned it will happen?
          Reluctance to make a will, buy cemetery lots, plan a funeral, or put a death clause in a contract.
      (2) There are few jokes and cartoons about deaths because of the fear that laughing about so serious a matter will make it happen.

Read the following joké to get at the students' feelings about death as its theme.

Patient: Doctor, will I die?

Doctor: That's the last thing you will do!

6. *To become aware of the many factors about conducting funerals and disposing of the body. (If there has been a recent death of any students' friends or family members, you may not want to choose this exercise.)*
   a. Conduct an in-class survey of the types of funerals students have attended.
   b. Compare the varieties of ways of disposing of the body and discuss the beliefs surrounding each one:

      Burial
      Cremation
      Mausoleum
      Freezing the body
      Medical science use of the body (include here autopsies prior to burial or cremation)

      (Bowman 1964; Haberstein and Lamers 1963; Mitford 1963; and Jackson 1963).
   c. The sociopsychological function of funerals is sometimes ignored as people try to get the "ordeal over with."

      "The Covenant" (Casill 1966)
      "We Know Your Hearts Are Heavy" (Gerber 1965)
      "I Knock at the Door" (O'Casey 1960)

      Many other references may be found in "Death Education as Part of Family Life Education" (Somerville 1971).
7. *To understand how guilt, grief, and bereavement are handled.*
   a. Expression of grief is necessary to the continuing growth of the people who are alive.
   b. That life goes on even after death is a truth which must be faced but is easier when the person is not pushed. Read "A Gentleman from San Francisco" (Bunin 1962) and "The Magic Mountain" (Mann 1929) for insights.
   c. Become alert to overly great displays of emotion surrounding funerals. Guilt has been associated with large funerals, bedside promises, pressuring people to cry, premature deaths (premature deaths are sometimes associated with the dead person's lack of adequate self-concept and therefore there is no need to take care of one's self).
   d. Vulnerability during grief is noted in the following observations.

      More secrets are told between the time of death and the funeral than any other time.

Larger funerals than one can afford are usually contracted for after a death rather than before a death.

The widow or widower is visited *immediately* by salesmen with ways to spend the money.

Read *The American Way of Death* (Mitford 1963).

8. ***To create new ways of applying generalizations about meeting peoples' needs at a time of death and after.***
   a. Read about and discuss the recent movement that encourages people to discuss death (*Washington Post*, December 30, 1972).
   b. Suggest to students that they might want to listen to people whose friends or relatives have died. Often a person manages the crisis better when he talks about the person who has died. Caution will need to be taken lest that person believe that one who is dead should not be talked about. Also, caution is given not to push a person to talk, but be willing to listen and talk when the person needs to talk. People who have had a friend or relative die need to talk about that person and reminisce in order to work through the fact of death, to remember the person who died, and to move on with their own life (Satir 1972).

Summary

Crises are periods in life when changes from the usual pattern of living must be made. The result of the handling of a crisis may or may not be devastating. It could be productive. The events that trigger crises vary because of differences in the way the event affects people. Some events do not precipitate a crisis purely because the ensuing change is not defined as a crisis. The ability to handle a crisis depends on the resources available. Some crises require more money, some require nurturing friends, and some require problem-solving ability.

Some events discussed as crisis producing in this chapter were divorce, the disabled family member, and death. The postulates of how people handle crises were applied in many of the techniques suggested.

This chapter on crises was purposely not placed at the end of this book because the implication might be that a crisis is the end of marriage and the family. Even though divorce or becoming a widow may be a crisis event, the resulting single state may or may not be crisis producing. The next chapter is on the single state.

References

Alverez, Walter C. "Death with Dignity." *The Humanist* 31: 12-14, 1971.

Bowman, Lercy. *The American Funeral: A Way of Death*. New York: Paperback Library, 1964.

Bunin, Ivan. "A Gentleman from San Francisco." In *A Gentleman from San Francisco and Other Stories*. New York: Vintage, 1962.

Cantor, Donald J. "A Matter of Right." In *Marriage and Family in a Decade of Change*, edited by Gwen B. Carr. Reading, Massachusetts: Addison-Wesley Publishing Co., 1972.

Casill, R. V. "The Covenant." In *The Happy Marriage and Other Stories*. Purdue University Studies, 1966.

Clay, George R. "We're All Guests." In *New World Writing*. Eighth Mentor Selection. New York: New American Library, 1955.

Currie, Ellen. "Moses Supposes." In *New World Writing*, Fourteenth Mentor Selection. New York: New American Library, 1958.

Deasey, Mary. "Morning Sun." In *The Best American Short Stories 1953*, edited by Martha Foley. New York: Ballantine, 1953.

Duvall, Evelyn. *Family Development*, 4th edition. Philadelphia: J. B. Lippincott Co., 1971.

Farber, Bernard. "Effects of a Severely Mentally Retarded Child on Family Integration." *Monographs of the Society for Research in Child Development* 24: 13, 1959.

Foster, Henry, Jr. "Reforming a Divorce Law." In *Marriage and Family in a Decade of Change*, edited by Gwen B. Carr. Reading, Massachusetts: Addison-Wesley Publishing Company, 1972.

Gallese, Liz Roman. "The Breaking Point." *The Wall Street Journal*. Spring 1972, p. 1.

Galsworthy, John. "The Apple Tree." In *Great Modern Short Stories*. New York: Random House Modern Library, 1942.

Gerber, Joan Merrill. "We Know Your Hearts Are Heavy." In *Stop Here, My Friend*. Boston: Houghton Mifflin, 1965.

Glaser, Barney G., and Strauss, Anselm L. *Awareness of Dying*. Chicago: Aldine Publishing Co., 1965.

Glasser, Paul H., and Glasser, Lois N., eds. *Families in Crisis*. New York: Harper and Row, 1970.

Gold, Herbert. "Love and Like." In *The Best American Short Stories 1959*, edited by Martha Foley and David Burnett. New York: Ballantine, 1959.

Gorer, Geoffrey. *Death, Grief, and Mourning*. Garden City, New York: Doubleday, 1965.

Gough, Aidon R. "Divorce Without Squalor: California Shows How." In *Marriage and Family in a Decade of Change*, edited by Gwen B. Carr. Reading, Massachusetts: Addison-Wesley Publishing Co., 1972.

Greenfeld, Josh. *A Child Called Noah*. New York: Warner Paperback Library, 1973.

Haberstein, Robert, and Lamers, William. *Funeral Customs the World Over*. Milwaukee: Bulfin, 1963.

Hansen, Donald A., and Hill, Reuben. "Families Under Stress."In *Handbook of Marriage and the Family*, edited by Harold T. Christensen. Chicago: Rand McNally & Co., 1964.

Hicks, Nancy. "Neglect of Dying Patients' Emotional Needs Linked to Cultural Inability to Face Death." *The New York Times*. 26 August, 1970: 13.

Irwin, Theodore. *How to Cope with Crises* (No. 464). New York: Public Affairs Committee, 1971.

Ishikawa, Tatsuzo. "Thoughts in the Dark." In *New World Writing*, Fourth Mentor Selection. New York: New American Library, 1953.

Jackson, Edgar. *For the Living.* Des Moines: Channel, 1963.

Jackson, Joan. "Adjustment of the Family to Alcoholism." *Marriage and Family Living* 23: 3, 11, 1961.

Jeffers, Camille. "Living Poor: Providing the Basic Necessities; Priorities and Problems." In *Families in Crisis*, edited by Paul H. Glasser and Lois N. Glasser. New York: Harper Row, 1970.

Kubler-Ross, Elizabeth. *On Death and Dying.* New York: Macmillan, 1969.

Litwak, Eugene. "Three Ways in which Law Acts as a Means of Social Control: Punishment, Therapy, and Education: Divorce Law a Case in Point." *Social Forces* 34: 214-223, 1956.

Mace, David, and Mace, Vera. *The Soviet Family*. New York: Dolphin Books, Doubleday & Company, Inc., 1963.

Mann, Thomas. *The Magic Mountain.* New York: Knopf, 1929.

Miller, Arthur. *Death of a Salesman.* New York: Viking, 1949.

Mitford, Jessica. *The American Way of Death.* New York: Simon and Schuster, 1963.

Monahan, Thomas P. "National Divorce Legislation: The Problem and Some Suggestions." *The Family Coordinator* 22: 353-358, 1973.

O'Casey, Sean. *I Knock at the Door.* New York: Macmillan, 1960.

Porter, Katherine Anne. "Holiday." In *Prize Stories 1962: The O'Henry Awards.* Greenwich, Conn.: Fawcett, 1962.

Richardson, Henry B. "A Family as Seen in the Hospital." In *Families in Crisis,* edited by Paul H. Glasser and Lois N. Glasser. New York: Harper Row, 1970.

Robbins, Norman. "Have We Found Fault in No Fault Divorce?" The Family Coordinator 22: 359-362, 1973.

Rogers, Carl. "A Humanistic Conception of Man." In *Marriage and Family in a Decade of Change,* edited by Gwen B. Carr. Reading, Massachusetts: Addison-Wesley Publishing Company, 1972.

Rogers, John G. "How to Make a Good Divorce." *Parade Magazine.* July, 1973, p. 18.

Satir, Virginia. *Peoplemaking.* Palo Alto, California: Science and Behavior Books, Inc., 1972.

Shneidman, Edwin S. "Death Questionnaire." *Psychology Today* 4: 67-72, 1970.

———. "You and Death." *Psychology Today* 5: 43-45ff, 1971.

Schor, Lynda. "I'm Really Dead." *Redbook*, August, 1973, pp. 79-80.

Seigal, Erich. *Love Story*. New York: New American Library, 1970.

Somerville, Rose. "Death Education as Part of Family Life Education: Using Imaginative Literature for Insights into Family Crises." *The Family Coordinator* 20: 209-224, 1971.

———. *Family Insights Through the Short Story*. New York: Teachers College Press, Columbia University, 1964.

Stryker, Sheldon. "Symbolic Interaction as an Approach to Family Research." *Marriage and Family Living* 21: 111-19, 1959.

Swarthout, Glendon. "Ixion." In *New World Writing*, Thirteenth Mentor Selection. New York: New American Library, 1958.

Updike, John. *Of the Farm*. New York: Alfred A. Knopf, 1966.

Vital and Health Statistics, NCHS, U.S. Department of Health, Education and Welfare. *Increases in Divorces, U.S., 1967,* PHS Publication No. 1000, Series 21, No. 20. Rockville, Maryland, December, 1970.

Vogel, Ezra F., and Bell, Norman W. "The Emotionally Disturbed Child as the Family Scapegoat." *A Modern Introduction to the Family*, 2nd ed., edited by Norman W. Bell and Ezra F. Vogel. New York: Free Press, 1968.

Waller, Willard. "The Old Love and the New: Divorce and Readjustment." In *Families in Crisis*, edited by Paul A. Glasser and Lois N. Glasser.New York: Harper & Row, 1970.

Washington Post, December 30, 1972.

Suggested Films

Cathy Come Home (economic stress) (1970, 78 min.). Time-Life Films, 43 W. 16th St., New York, N.Y. 10011.

Changing (crisis in a blue-collar family) (1971, 26 min.). National Audio-Visual Center, Washington, D.C. 20409.

Divorce (1972, 15 min.) National Instructional Television Center, Box A, Bloomington, Ind. 47401.

He Lived with Us, He Ate with Us, What Else Dear? (LSD) (1970, 26 min.). Paulist Prod., 17575 Pacific Coast Highway, Pacific Palisades, CA 90272.

Like Other People (sexual life of the handicapped) (1972, 30 min.). Perennial Education, Inc., 1825 Willow Road, Northfield, Ill. 60093.

Though I walk Through the Valley (terminal case) (1973, 30 min.). Pyramid Films, P.O. Box 1048, Santa Monica, Ca. 90406.

The War of Eggs (child as scapegoat) (1971, 26½ min.). Paulist Prod.

The Worlds of Abraham Kaplan: Death (1971, 29 min.). University of Michigan Television Center, 310 Maynard St., Ann Arbor, MI 48108.

Chapter 16

The Singles

Many of the more recent personal information forms list only two categories of marital status: married and single. A divorced or widowed person is considered to be single on these forms. The status of divorced, widowed, single, or married all still have legal rights and responsibilities as well as cultural expectations; nevertheless, divorced and widowed persons are also legally single!

A particular status in any culture in any one era usually has certain sanctions and is encouraged for stability and continuance of that culture. The married state or some other legal state in which the children could be socialized and the adults have security has always been encouraged. The single state has nearly always been discouraged unless that culture has found it to be productive. Although marriage is by far the largest state, the single state (never married, divorced, and widowed) is increasing because it can be and is productive. Moreover, it is being recognized that even the two-parent family and the marriage without children can be devastating if there is an atmosphere of degradation.

Staying Single in Pro-marriage World

Because of the emphasis on marriage, the single person must swim against the tide to stay single. He may even lead himself to believe that he wants marriage even if he does not. With the greater realization that the single state can be productive, the pressure is somewhat less.

Teaching Techniques

1. *To understand the greater acceptance of the single state.*
   a. Study the numbers of single men and women in the married, never-married, divorced, and widowed states below. Note that in every age category, there are more never-married men than never-

Number of Never-Married, Widowed, Divorced, and Married Men and Women by Age in 1970

	Never-Married	*Widowed*	*Divorced*	*Married*
Male				
14 years old and over	20,426,937	2,130,932	1,926,597	44,597,574
14 to 17 years old	8,098,673	7,508	6,614	71,528
18 to 24 years old	7,636,138	16,350	118,893	3,248,080
25 to 34 years old	1,890,462	38,770	378,778	9,369,909
35 to 44 years old	884,372	75,546	405,882	9,464,269
45 to 64 years old	1,285,524	550,809	760,143	16,686,539
65 and older	631,768	1,441,949	256,287	5,757,249
Female				
14 years old and over	17,624,105	9,615,280	3,004,278	44,481,843
14 to 17 years old	7,573,262	17,803	10,585	206,608
18 to 24 years old	5,835,542	67,164	234,960	5,226,687
25 to 34 years old	1,263,803	158,024	585,129	9,973,286
35 to 44 years old	672,255	353,760	646,547	9,578,573
45 to 64 years old	1,331,557	2,930,892	1,155,157	15,550,221
65 and older	947,686	6,105,637	371,900	3,946,468

Source: U.S. Department of Commerce, *Marital Status and Living Arrangements of the Population in the United States: 1970,* May, 1973.

married women; however, women usually marry men older than they are. Therefore when two-to-four-year discrepancies are compared, there are more never-married women than men.

b. Survey the students about their marital status and expectations. (Keep a record similar to this one, but choose the ages for your own research information over the years.)

	Male					*Female*				
Age of student	Married	Single	Expect to marry by 22	Expect to marry by 30	Expect to stay single	Married	Single	Expect to marry by 22	Expect to marry by 30	Expect to stay single
16										
18										
20										
25+										

c. Compare the reasons given and not given (maybe not known) for wanting to marry, for wanting to stay single, and for wanting a divorce. Discuss the more recent change in willingness to state certain desires.

Possible Reasons for Wanting:

To Marry	*To Stay Single*	*To Get a Divorce*
(1) Want to live with that person	(1) Want freedom	(1) Cannot stand to live with that person
(2) Want to have continued partnership	(2) Want variety	(2) Feel hurt
(3) Want to rear children	(3) Want to be alone a great deal	(3) Cannot take the disagreement over children
(4) Both partners see things alike		(4) See life differently

Reasons That Are Not Usually Known For Wanting:

To Marry	*To Stay Single*	*To Get a Divorce*
(1) Fear of being left out	(1) Fear of a close relationship	(1) Want to be rid of responsibility
(2) For revenge	(2) Fear of control	(2) Want to be alone
(3) To be accepted as adult	(3) Fear of the unknown	(3) Want freedom
		(4) Want variety

2. *To analyze* ***cultural pressures on single never-married people.***
   a. Explain the reasons behind the cultural pressures as illustrated in these comments. What is implied?
      (1) "Are you married yet?"
      (2) "When do you plan to marry?"
      (3) "Do you live alone? Do you like it?"
      (4) "Don't ever get married."
      (5) "Wait a while before you marry."
      (6) "Have you decided marriage is for the birds?"
      (7) "Do you hate women (men)?"
      (8) "You're not married?"
      (9) "I'm having only couples over. I knew you'd understand."
      (10) "Bring your date and come."
      (11) "We're having a stag party."
      (12) "Live a little before you marry."
   b. Discuss the singles in a paired society.
      (1) More than 90 percent of the population marry by the age of 45. Why? Could the following factors have an effect?
         (a) Cultural pressure
         (b) Desire to have security
         (c) Desire for children
         (d) Need to be like others
         (e) Need to have sexual relations in a legal relationship
         (f) Desire to build future family investment

(g) Need for a permanent boy- or girlfriend
(h) Cultural lag
(i) Self-fulfilling prophecy

(2) Consider these possible differences in the married and never married person.
(a) Personality
–Singles are more likely to be on the extreme ends of personality trait continuum (Klemer 1970).
–Some singles are not suited to close confining relationships with a peer.
(b) Reasons for not marrying other than personality
–Goal of education or career
–Need to care for aged parents or other family member
–Opposite sex not available
–Desire to live alone
–Marriage gradient (tendency for men to marry same or lower social class women leaving some women out)

(3) How and why society is geared to a paired relationship
(a) Pairs were believed to be better able to care for each other.
(b) Those not paired were treated as "deviants" with all its connotations because someone *had to care* for them when they did not want to.
(c) Married couple or person is assumed to be more capable and non-threatening–Examples: Married person has adult status for borrowing money. Another married woman is not as envied as unmarried woman is by wives.
(d) Couple parties.
(e) Companies tend to hire married people because it is assumed they will be more settled, have a calming influence on others, and are eager to get ahead (therefore more production for department).

(4) What changes are occurring? (Discuss cultural lag concept–some of the following are not yet accepted even though they occur.)
(a) Women can earn a living.
(b) Women can prevent conception.
(c) Singles can adopt children.
(d) Aged and ill family members can be cared for by society.
(e) Men can hire people to do housework or do it themselves.
(f) Age of youth or young adult has increased to thirty-five years old and is increasing.
(g) People are getting better educated and can see the pitfalls of marriage and children.

(h) Single-person apartments are acceptable.
(i) Single women are being taught physical self-protection.
(j) Single men are expected to be home managers.
(k) New group and singles bars and gatherings.

(5) People need to have some independence

(a) To share when one person is not dependent on the other person takes a great deal of altruism and planning. (When the wife was dependent, she was conditioned to *want* to wait on her husband. When the husband could not buy services, he was conditioned to *want* to care for the wife.)

(b) Men and women can take just so much pressure.
–A man or woman works all day and needs a little time not to be pressured by family matters.
–Just after the children get put to bed, the husband or wife approaches the other for some personal attention.

(6) Can these basic needs be met in the single state?

Maslow (1954)	*Erickson (1964)*	*Thomas (1925)*
Physical needs	Identity	Recognition
Companionship	Intimacy	Response
Self-esteem	Generativity	New Experience
Self-actualization		Security

3. ***To gain insight into discrepancies in one's own values about the single state (Rokeach 1971).***

Have students rank the following list of values (give them the values in this paragraph form).

A comfortable life, an exciting life, a sense of accomplishment, a world at peace, a world of beauty, equality, family security, freedom, happiness, inner harmony, mature love, national security, pleasure, salvation, social recognition, self-respect, true friendship, and wisdom.

Ask the students to indicate their attitudes toward a single (never married) person as being head of their school by checking one of the four categories below.

I: Yes, I think a single never-married person is capable, but I would not choose a single over a married person or a married person over a single person.

II: Yes, I think a single never-married person is capable and would choose a single person over a married person.

III: Yes, I think a single never-married person is capable, but I would prefer a married person.

IV: No, I do not think a single never-married person should be head of this institution.

Then have each student put their rank numbers of the values "wisdom" and "equality" under the category they checked. Find the difference between the rank numbers.

The person who checked category IV will probably have a greater discrepancy between the rank numbers of "wisdom" and "equality" than do those people who checked category I. Those students who are for *either* a single or a married person probably ranked wisdom high and equality high.

5. *To evaluate the single state in light of personal rewards.*
   a. Discuss the types of personalities that are better off single.
      (1) I've never been the kind of person who liked to be with other people very long at a time. I tire of people quickly unless there is a true respect for the other's privacy. You can tell a child to go away or that you are tired and he goes out, but you cannot tell an adult that, especially if he happens to be your husband. Closeness is oppressive to me.
      (2) Divorce is ugly no matter how easy it is legally. It is much better to let a love die in freedom than to have to tear at each other after the love is gone.

Single Again: Divorced and Widowed

To be single again is different from being single never-married because of the attitudes of other people and one's own attitudes about being single again. The single-again person may be divorced or widowed. In either case the previous marital state may or may not have been satisfactory. The fact that divorced men and women are far more likely to remarry than widowed men and women indicates that being married itself was probably not the problem. Some of the feelings, attitudes, and problems of the single-again person are similar to yet different from those of the never-married person.

Teaching Techniques

1. *To understand the difference in being single again as opposed to never having been married.*

   Compare possible feelings of single-never-married person with the person who is a single-againer after being married (Lyman 1971).
   a. Possible feelings of the single-never-marrieds (men and women)
      (1) They wonder what is wrong if they do not marry when pressured by society.
      (2) Some are taunted by envious married people.
      (3) Some would rather be alone but are pressured to date.
      (4) When they do not date or do not have a date, they feel cultural indignation and have to explain.

(5) Some are not sure their single life is as wonderful as some people would lead them to believe.

b. Possible feelings of the *single-againers*—either divorced or widowed (or even singles who have broken up) (Lyman 1971).

(1) When they understand that, even though each situation is unique, the single-again situations are all very similar; then they can begin to rebuild their lives.

(2) Self-pity is to be expected and should be expressed in moderation but then should be cut out.

(3) All of them feel as if the world is coming to an end and most of them hope it will.

(4) The absence of a person for companionship, conversation, and consultation is greatly felt.

(5) Widows, divorced people, and those who have recently broken up feel as if they have been left holding the bag.

(6) All feel rejected by other couples.

(7) All have guilt feelings about what they should have done.

(8) All need to withdraw some because they cannot handle the inputs at the time.

(9) Some are actively angry at the one who left (even widowed).

(10) Some are *free* at last!!

2. *To understand the **difference between men and women who are single again** (Lyman 1971).*

a. Compare possible feelings of women single-againers and men single-againers.

(1) Possible feelings of women single-againers

(a) They feel and are treated like a fifth wheel more than men are.

(b) They are sometimes purposely not appointed to committees or invited to take important posts.

(c) They are perhaps considered a threat to a marriage because of other wives' insecurity.

(d) Women single-againers are *believed* to be in need of sex, and men are ready and willing.

(e) They may never have learned to manage and work for a living.

(f) They begin to feel unwanted; their self-concept lowers.

(2) Possible feelings of men single-againers

(a) If they are divorced, probably they had to leave home and children and live in one room or apartment.

(b) They are lonely.

(c) Spending money is cut if they are having to pay alimony or child support.

(d) They are relieved from nagging wife and children.
(e) They have the children and do not know what to do.
(f) They can initiate dates.
(g) They may have to refuse dates initiated by women.
(h) They have to accept help from well-wishers who feel sorry.
(i) If they are Catholic widowers, divorced women are off limits.
(j) They will probably marry sooner than single-again women.

3. *To empathize with the feelings and behavior of single-again people.*
   a. Read the following case.

   A thirty-five-year-old woman without children almost immediately after becoming a widow was pursued by men to go out with them and without exception to have sexual intercourse with them. Although she was not averse to having male company, she found that the men did not fit her image of a companion. She said they were either much older, married, or unacceptable personally.

Questions

(1) Why is a widowed woman pursued?
(2) Why do men think women need them sexually more than any other way?
(3) Why is she disappointed in the pursuers?

   b. Read the following case.

   A man of twenty-nine years without children almost immediately after becoming a widower was pursued by women of all ages. They invited him to dinner and eventually to bed. He accepted as many as time would allow. Rejection was almost always because of time allowance and not because of personal attributes of any woman.

Questions

(1) Why might widowed men and women see pursuers differently?
(2) Why might a man not see age and personal attributes as a deterrent as women do?
(3) How might the culture compare the freedom of divorced or widowed men and women?

   c. Read the two cases above substituting "never married" and "divorced" for "widowed" and discuss whether or not the rest of the case would remain the same.

   Question

   Where do the differences lie–in the individuals or in the culture?

Single Males and Females with Children

Single parents–female, male, unwed, divorced, widowed, adoptive–are all different, yet very much alike. They each have to rear a child or children without a spouse. Sometimes this is a better situation than having a spouse; sometimes it is worse. Some people choose single parenthood, some do not; but those who choose single parenthood are unique. Society is only barely beginning to accept choosing to be a single parent. Society has at times accepted the widowed single parent, tolerated the divorced single parent, and rejected the unwed single parent. Although a woman can choose to have her own child with or without marriage and even with or without male contact, a man can never make this choice. To have his own child, he would have to have a woman to bear him a child, with or without marriage. Both, of course, may choose to adopt a child without any other person's consent (except legal authorities).

The big change is that parenthood and marriage are not totally culturally tied together. In the past single parenthood was frowned on for fear that the child would be in jeopardy. It seems now that a child can be reared by a single parent as well as by two parents. The similarity is in the environment provided. Stories are legend as to the devastation of children in some two-parent families. Some individuals are simply refusing to put up with the old problems involved in some marriages just to have the legal and cultural right to have children.

The decision to be a single parent is not a rebellion but a decision to live the way one sees as best.

Teaching Techniques

1. *To evaluate the* ***single-parent experience*** *in relation to the* ***two-parent experience.***
   a. Collect evidence that some children from fatherless homes are as well developed as those from two-parent homes. Present the evidence under the generalization that it is the adequacy of the single parent in financial means, self-concept, knowledge of child development, decision-making ability, and outlook on life and the opposite sex which determines how well the children develop. (See Chapter 3 on The Research Approach for justification for studying the minority findings.) (Bigner 1970; Biller 1971; Herzog and Sudia 1968; Hetherington 1973; and Klein 1973).
   b. In the *Mirages of Marriage* (Lederer and Jackson, 1968) the myths of the idyllic situation of marriage are exploded. Compare some of these myths with the myths of the idyllic situation of the single parent.
2. *To understand role-specific situations of the single parents that perpetrated their* ***problems*** *in this culture.*
   a. Compare the possible problems that are peculiar to each of the different types of single parents and discuss why. Challenge or support the cultural attitude.

(1) Divorced woman with custody of children (Lyman 1971):
  (a) Usually works and keeps house
  (b) Feels compelled to provide male-oriented activities and role models.
  (c) Rarely is helped by anyone because other people see her as a threat to other marriages.
(2) Divorced man with custody of children (Lyman 1971):
  (a) Usually works and hires a housekeeper
  (b) Feels inadequate for the expressive relationship
  (c) Is pitied for his assumed helplessness
(3) Divorced woman without custody of children (Lyman 1971):
  (a) Traditionally seen as worst of her sex
  (b) Is seen as a threat to all marriages
(4) Divorced man without custody of children (Lyman 1971):
  (a) Usually has had to leave home and live in one room or apartment.
  (b) Has to pay child support and sometimes alimony
(5) Widowed woman (Lyman 1971):
  Similar to (1) except not as rejected
(6) Widowed man (Lyman 1971):
  Similar to (2) but helped more
(7) Unmarried natural mother (some are choosing this state over marriage or adoption) (Parker 1972):
  (a) Faces a hostile rejecting culture
  (b) Is treated as very low socially and help is begrudgingly given
  (c) Child or children are similarly rejected
  (d) Very often is young and has little way to make money
(8) Unmarried natural father (Pannor et al 1971):
  (a) Ignored by society and even encouraged to feel free of responsibility.
  (b) May have deep regrets but cannot own them in light of cultural attitudes.
  (c) If vocal and bragging about his progeny yet irresponsible, he is rejected more.
(9) Unmarried adoptive mother (Klein 1973):
  (a) Is seen as a charitable person
  (b) Has to force people to believe she is a normal heterosexual
  (c) Has to face people who ask why
  (d) Feels compelled to be the perfect mother and father
(10) Unmarried adoptive father (Klein 1973):
  (a) Is seen as a curiosity
  (b) Has to prove heterosexual beliefs, attitudes, and behavior
  (c) Feels compelled to be perfect father

3. *To analyze* ***why single-parent families*** *are many times* ***excluded***—*even rejected*—*from two-parent family activities in this society.*
   a. Challenge and/or support some reasons given for exclusion of the one-parent family from two-parent family activities:
      (1) One parent cannot rear children properly, and *therefore* his children would be harmful to children in two-parent families.
      (2) Children from a one-parent family would become a nuisance by looking for attention.
      (3) The single mother would be a threat to the wife in the two-parent family.
      (4) The divorced single parent might encourage others to divorce to join the free life.
      (5) The single parent would expect too much attention.
      (6) The single parent, especially if divorced, is inadequate as a spouse, a parent, and as a person.
   b. Apply generalizations about behavior which explain or refute the above attitudes toward the single parent family.
      (1) People of similar values and behaviors tend to socialize together because their very similarity reinforces their belief that they are right.
      (2) Long-standing cultural beliefs which have deep emotional overtones are very difficult to rationalize because the belief is internalized (becomes a part of the person).
      (3) There is *no* great evidence that the single parent cannot adequately rear children, produce in his job, develop his own personality, be an asset to the community (Herzog and Sudia, 1968).
      (4) Children from unhappy unbroken homes are more likely to experience adverse effects on development than those from happy broken homes.
      (5) Children reared in a single parent home are adequately socialized when the parent still has respect for the opposite sex, has a good self-concept, and has a good perspective on life (just as a married parent should have these same qualities in order to be a good parent).
      (6) The child's own inherent constitution and body image may have as much to do with developmental adversities as environmental influences.
   c. Have an individual who is unknown to the class be introduced as and *play the part* of a child from a single parent home or *play the part* of a single parent by telling some sad episode in his life but not mention his parents or position. (If you have two sections or can divide the class so that only half hears the story at a time, have this

same person *play the part* of the child from a two-parent home or *play the part* of a married person by telling the same sad episode in his life.)

(This can be in person or on tape.)

After the person leaves or after the tape is over, give the class the semantic differential shown below (see Chapter 9 on Understanding Human Behavior). Compare the responses of the two sections to see if their views were swayed by a pre-set attitude against the single parent. (This same idea can be used to compare pre-set attitudes toward people from different social classes, from different races, from different ethnic groups, or of different genders. (See Chapter 3 on The Research Approach.)

SAD EPISODE

When I was in high school, I usually made average grades and had some friends. Well, one time I didn't have as much time to study for a test as I should have, but I needed to make a better than average grade. I had set aside the night before to study and a friend whom I had not seen in a long time came through town and called me. He wanted to come over. I was eager to see him, and we talked and talked. My study time was shot. The next morning one of the other students who had seen the test questions told me some of them and I looked up the answers. I made a very good grade, but I was accused of cheating. I was not sure in my own mind where I stood. I still don't know.

Give students this scale to mark.

Directions: Place an (X) mark on the line which would best describe the person.

	7	6	5	4	3	2	1	
Honest								Dishonest
Trustworthy								Not trustworthy
Pleasant								Unpleasant
Clean								Dirty
Appealing								Repulsive
High Masculinity (f a male)								Weak Masculinity
High Femininity (if a female)								Weak Femininity
Effective								Ineffective
Happy								Sad

Directions to the Teacher (see Chapter 3 on Research)

Take up the papers and redistribute. Tally the responses of the class members by a raise of hands. (Students will not mind revealing the responses when they are not their own.)

Because of high student interest at this time, discuss the results even though the comparison with the second section is not yet available. When the second section's results are tallied, then compare the responses of the two sections revealing the experiment to discover similarities and differences, and discuss these in reference to the cultural beliefs and human behavior generalizations.

(If you are very strictly research-oriented, you may want to subject these responses to a statistical analysis, but for class purposes inspection of the data is sufficient for engendering class discussion.)

4. ***To understand why people choose to become a single parent.***

   a. Read the following situations:

ATTITUDES OF OTHERS*

"I was doing some shopping one afternoon last week on my way back here from my mother's, and I had Timmy in the pram. In the street I bumped into a woman I haven't seen since I was in the sixth form with her daughter at the County High, five or six years ago. 'Why, it's Penny!' she said, 'I'd recognize you anywhere! How simply marvelous to see you again, how *are* you?' Fine I said, fine, I was at teacher-training college now. Well, good Lord, she said, I still looked as though I was eighteen. Then she looked at Timmy sitting up in his pram. 'Oh, isn't he beautiful!' she said. 'But gracious, don't tell me he's yours, is he?' He most certainly is, I said; why, didn't she think he looked like me? 'Oh, yes, of course he does!' she said. 'Absolutely the spitting image! How wonderful though, oh, aren't you lucky to have such a gorgeous baby! But doesn't time fly, I mean it seems only last week you and Helen were in Miss Martin's class at school together. I've often thought about you, Penny, because you were one of Helen's very best friends, she'll be so thrilled when I tell her I've seen you. But honestly, I just can't get over it; you know, I mean, well we didn't even know you were married!'

'I'm not,' I said."

DECISION TO KEEP CHILD**

"So I came back to London without having said anything. It was only about eight or nine weeks later that Simon was born. Odd, isn't it? Up till then I'd thought after he was born I'd have him adopted; but after actually having him, and looking after him in the hospital, there was no question of it. If anyone had asked me before, or I'd ever thought about it, I'd have said without hesitation I was going to give him for adoption.

"That was another way the Wel-Care social worker was so good.

*From p. 88 in *In No Man's Land* by Tony Parker. Copyright © 1972 by Tony Parker. Used by permission of Harper & Row, Publishers, Inc.

**From pp. 31-32 in *In No Man's Land* by Tony Parker. Copyright © 1972 by Tony Parker. Used by permission of Harper & Row, Publishers, Inc.

She never tried to influence me, simply told me what alternatives there were and left it to me to make up my own mind. When I decided afterwards I would try and get a job, and did in fact get a small temporary one more or less to keep myself occupied, she helped me find a foster-mother I could leave Simon with, and then another one again when that didn't work out. She was really marvelous.

"I had rather a difficult time for a few months: Elizabeth had had to give up the flat because she got a new job in the Midlands. I couldn't afford to keep it on by myself, let alone with Simon. I still wasn't quite twenty-one by a few months, so I'd no money to play with, which meant there'd have to be a few gap-bridging arrangements.

"There seemed no sense in going on not telling my parents, particularly as they were beginning to mention our next summer holidays in their letters, asking me where I'd like to go. So I plucked up courage and went home for the week-end. I didn't take Simon with me; as soon as I got them alone after the friends who'd been there had departed, I told them quite straightly and simply. They were surprised, and I think a bit hurt that I hadn't told them that I was pregnant at Christmas. But it was a *fait accompli*, there was nothing much they could say. They kept the news absolutely to themselves, presuming I was going to have it adopted when I went back to London I suppose. They didn't ask me questions at all; who the father was, or anything. I came back to London for a few more weeks, then I rang them up and said I was coming home for another week-end. That time I took Simon with me; I told them I'd made up my mind to keep him, if I could find somewhere decent in London to live, and work out a way of financing myself.

"My father said very little, but only made a practical suggestion: that he'd make me a loan which would carry me through in reasonably comfortable furnished accommodation until my next birthday which would be the one when I came into the money from the trusts. Which in fact is what he did, and when the time came I got the money and bought this place, and here I am. Which brings us up to the present day, doesn't it?"

DECISION TO HAVE A BABY*

"When the divorce was through I was in a bit of a state then. I was thirty years old, going on thirty-one, and I thought for Christ's sake what in hell have I got to show for my life, absolutely nothing of my own at all. So I 'phoned up Michael where he was working, I asked him could we meet for a coffee because there was something I wanted to ask him. When we met I said now that the divorce was all final and everything, would he give me a baby so I could at least have something, but he said no.

"So then I asked Roy, I told him I wouldn't make any demands on him for it, which was a pretty damn fool thing for me to say I guess, because of the financial aspect I mean. In the end he said well if I promised then O.K. he would, and he did: we had to try only a

*From p. 51 in *In No Man's Land* by Tony Parker. Copyright © 1972 by Tony Parker. Used by permission of Harper & Row, Publishers, Inc.

couple of times and I got pregnant. And that's how it happened that things are this way now. I thought having a baby might change me, help me get back some kind of identity of my own. Only so far it hasn't worked out."

DECISION TO HAVE SEVERAL CHILDREN*

"–I suppose I can't really put it into words at all," she said softly; "only that once I had so little, and now I have so much. . . ."

"My name is Sally Morrison. I'm twenty-two and I have two children, a three-year-old boy called Peter and a baby daughter of seven months whose name is Jemma. I'm not married. I never have been married, and I don't think I ever shall be, and certainly can't ever see myself wanting to be. I live on my own with the children in two rooms which have a connecting kitchen in between, on the ground floor of an old-fashioned semi-detached house in what can't be described as anything more than a small and totally characterless town on the outskirts of London. It's like dozens of others: the sort of place which isn't quite near enough to London to be part of it, and not far enough away to have developed any sort of individuality of its own.

"I don't work for my living, not unless you call bringing up two small children working. I certainly often feel it is; but I mean other than that I don't have a job. I live on Social Security Benefit, and have done so for the past three years; it's enough to get by on, but only just. . . .

"As I said earlier on, by the time Peter was a year old I was very conscious of the inherent dangers to him in the situation of being an only child and having only one parent. I was in exactly the same position myself in childhood, but at least I did have some kind of substitutes in my grandparents. With Peter too there was the additional complication that he was a boy, and I didn't want him to grow up in an atmosphere of close single relationship to and with his mother, without anyone else in the picture at all.

"So from that time on, I always intended to have one other child at least, if not possibly three altogether. Though that's something I haven't made up my mind about one way or the other yet. As it is now, with Jemma still very much an infant, and both of them very demanding and tiring, the mere idea seems too awful to contemplate; but as she gets older no doubt I shall feel up to giving it a bit more rational thought.

"When I'd settled in here and become confident about my ability actually to make a go of things with Peter, I decided the time had come to start looking for someone to have another child by. I suppose this can't very well sound anything else but cold and calculating; and I suppose by only looking at it one way there's no escaping the truth that it is. I wouldn't want to try to pretend, either, that I had Jemma purely and simply for Peter's benefit, because I didn't; I enjoy her very much myself; I like babies, I like being a mother.

"What I don't like, and wouldn't like, is to be somebody's wife,

*From pp. 109, 110, 130-132 in *In No Man's Land* by Tony Parker. Copyright © 1972 by Tony Parker. Used by permission of Harper & Row, Publishers, Inc.

or at least not yet. Possibly I might change my mind when I'm older, and if I ever met somebody I fell in love with and who'd take me with two children of my own already, I might consider it. But as I am at the moment, and I can only talk as I am and as I feel now, I really don't want to have to share my life with anybody else except my children. I simply don't think I could.

"Which means that I don't want to share them, my children, with anybody else either. And that I regard them as my children and in no way part of, or belonging to, anyone else at all. Perhaps this is due to the kick in the teeth I got from Steve when it was made so clear to me Peter was mine. But I think that's not entirely true, because I'd already fallen out of love with Steve before Peter was born; even if he had wanted to come back with me and share him, I'm certain I wouldn't have agreed.

"However, to get back to Jemma and Malcolm. Having made up my mind I wanted to have another child for both my own benefit and Peter's, I began to keep my eyes open for someone suitable to father it. I drew up a kind of list of qualifications in my mind. In the first place, it couldn't be a man who was already married, because I'd no desire to seduce somebody else's husband, with all the complications that might lead to. Secondly I felt it would have to be somebody reasonably near my own age; also it had to be someone I liked and felt a bit physically attracted to, because I didn't want it just to be a casual pick-up or a one night stand affair purely and simply to get myself pregnant.

"I think I felt also it would have to be somebody I was reasonably friendly with and knew quite well, because it would involve more than just a sexual relationship. I hoped for the child's sake I could remain on fairly good terms with its father in the future, and not end in the same sort of situation I'd had to face with Peter. So whereas it's true to say to a certain extent I did sort out someone I thought would be right, on the other hand I didn't go as far as being predatory and actually going out hunting. I just waited for a suitable person to turn up.

"Malcolm, I realize now, wasn't at all right. Perhaps I'm deceiving myself, and always was, in thinking there ever could be any such person. I think the main fault was and still is that he's too young to cope with it emotionally. At the moment, even though he does come round two or three times a week we don't get on at all well, and sometimes we hardly even speak. In all these calculations you see, I'd overlooked one factor; which was that he might fall, as indeed he did fall and still is, in love with me. This is something I feel rather guilty and unhappy about; it's what I meant when I said he was not emotionally old enough for the situation. And I know this is fundamentally my fault for involving him in it, not his own."

b. Challenge other reasons for wanting to get pregnant which have been delineated such as:
   (1) Desire to punish parents
   (2) Desire to push a social issue as interracial birth, liberation of women

(3) Desire to be accepted as an adult
(4) Curiosity to know what pregnancy is like
(5) Personality characteristic of being a good mother (or father), but not a good wife (or husband)
(6) To give and get the love missed as a child
(7) To give the child to someone else who needs one (in this case, the person would only be the parent who gave birth)
(8) Desire to prove femininity, but no desire to marry

c. Discuss these questions:
(1) Does single parenthood attract many of those people who do not have the strength to fulfill the responsibility? (Not anymore than parenthood in marriage does.)
(2) When the children grow up, do they continue to fulfill the needs that the parents had when they fantasized their role as baby parents? (Some people are best at being baby parents, some are little boy parents, some are young girl parents, some are teen-age children parents; rarely are they all.)

5. *To evaluate the **probabilities of success** of the person who wants to become **a single parent** when the culture and the childhood conditioning are for the married two-parent life (see Parker 1972 and Klein 1973 for case studies and situations or write some).*

a. Apply the following generalizations to anyone who chooses to be a single parent. (These generalizations also apply to mixed marriages, divorce, exchange of male-female roles, etc.)
(1) When an action is taken because it is desired as good instead of a move to "get back at" someone, the behaviors of the person are constructive.
(2) When a person lives in a neighborhood of people who reinforce that particular action, the action becomes self-reinforcing.
(3) When a person has the financial means so that the action does not depend on others, the action is less fraught with interference.
(4) When a person has knowledge of the disapproval of the culture and the reasons for the disapproval, steps can be taken to buttress one's own position without uncertainty.
(5) When a person has a good self-concept and confidence that he is making the right choice, he can make decisions and act with stability.

b. Apply the following generalizations that will probably affect the "best laid plans of mice and men"—that is, affect even the apparently strong personalities.
(1) When a person is under stress, he tends to regress to such childlike behavior as belligerence, crying, and refusal to move.

(2) Recently changed attitudes or desires (or performances) are likely to leave a person when the reinforcements leave.
(3) Strong and powerful aversive stimuli as rejection, taunts, and accusations can change a person's behavior.
(4) When a decision is made that also involves another person, the control of the situation is not as easy as doing something alone.
(5) Childhood conditioning is very strong and lasting.
(6) A person tends to become more like the culturally expected norm as he gets older.
(7) Peer enthusiasm for a person's project wanes as they get other interests, leaving the person to handle all the problems and enjoy the fruits alone.

6. *To understand the concerns about* ***adoption by a single person*** *(Klein 1973).*

a. Read the law in your state as it applies to adoption by a single person.
In the North Carolina General Statutes of 1973 the law essentially states:

> Any person over twenty-one years of age may adopt a child; *if* that person has a spouse, then both of them must agree to the adoption.

b. Consult an adoption agency to find the interpretation and execution of the law for adoption by single parents.
The interpretation is usually in this manner:
(1) The adoptive parent(s) must have enough income to provide basic necessities.
(2) The adoptive parent(s) must be a normal heterosexual.
(3) The adoptive parent(s) must be emotionally stable.

c. Invite a single adoptive parent to talk to the class.

d. Discuss the single male as opposed to the single female adopting a child.

Questions for Discussion

(1) Would the problems of a single male adopting a child be like those of a widowed or divorced father?
(2) Would you suggest a boy or girl for adoption? Would the agency make any differentiation?
(3) What concerns about housekeeping and child care would you have?
(4) What principles of human development would be particularly applicable to this situation?

e. If a single person wanted to adopt two children rather than one, what would be your suggestions based on knowledge of human development and relationships?

f. Discuss the background of these attitudes toward the single father that might or might not be attributed to the single mother.
   (1) Is he a normal heterosexual?
   (2) Why does he want to nurture a child?
   (3) Why does he want to keep house?
   (4) Why does he not want to get married?
   (5) What does he know about rearing a female child?
   (6) Could he face the opposition from the culture?

7. *To become aware of possibilities of single parenthood through various methods of conception now under experimentation (Francoeur 1972 and Rosenfeld 1969).*
   a. Discuss the following possibilities and compare with present problems of a single parent:
      (1) Artificial insemination (for women themselves or for women and men separately who choose the woman to incubate their child) with a choice of genetic backgrounds.
      (2) Transfer of fertilized egg from another female's uterus to one's own uterus.
   b. Discuss the following probabilities and compare with present problems of a single parent.
      (1) Selection of sperm and egg from a bank to develop a child in a laboratory.
      (2) Asexual pregnancy without use of a sperm.
      (3) Cloning (taking part of one's body and causing it to develop a replica of that person).

8. *To understand the purposes and results of efforts to support single-parent families in light of the problems they face. (These efforts are not geared to saving a marriage; rather, they are geared to supporting a family.)*
   a. Review these three efforts.
      (1) Parents without Partners, Inc. (Burgess 1970; Gould 1968; and Weiss 1973).

      Goals are to share common experiences, to learn from each other, to gain companionship, and to help parents rear healthy children. Some of the activities include programs on child development, group discussion of personal and parental problems, family activities, substitute Mom or Dad Day when the children meet with the Dads if they do not have one or the Moms if they do not have one. Special projects are aimed at helping the parents and children with crises.

(2) United Methodist Church Study Guide, *The One Parent Family* (Douglas 1971).
(3) How to Make a Good Divorce Counseling Service (Rogers 1973).

Summary

The single state has been discouraged throughout the centuries because of the belief that it was non-productive in that no legal children were born and that many of the adult singles had to be cared for by others. Now the single state is gaining some favor because it can be productive.

This chapter presented ways to study the problems and the desires of single people whether they are never-married, divorced, or widowed. The one-parent family was discussed from both the perspective of problems in child and adult socialization and the perspective of its strength.

Although the one-parent family probably makes up the greatest bulk of variation from the two-parent nuclear family, the next chapter presents other forms of families now in existence and those proposed for the future.

References

Bigner, Jerry. "Fathering: Research and Practice Implication." *The Family Coordinator* 19: 357-362, 1970.

Biller, Henry B. *Father, Child, and Sex Role: Paternal Determinants of Personality Development.* Lexington, Massachusetts: Heath Lexington Books, 1971.

Burgess, Jane K. "The Single-Parent Family: A Social and Sociological Problem." *The Family Coordinator* 19: 137-144, 1970.

"Coping with Change" (entire issue). *Forum.* New York: The J. C. Penny Company, Inc., Fall/Winter, 1971.

Douglas, William. *The One Parent Family.* Nashville, Tennessee: The Methodist Publishing House, 1971.

Erikson, Erik. *Childhood and Society.* New York: W. W. Norton & Co., 1964.

Francoeur, Robert T. *Eve's New Rib: Twenty Faces of Sex, Marriage and the Family.* New York: Harcourt Brace Jovanovich, 1972.

Gould, Ethel P. "Special Report: The Single-Parent Family Benefits in Parents Without Partners, Inc." Journal of Marriage and the Family 30: 666-671, 1968.

Herzog, Elizabeth, and Sudia, Cecelia. "Research of Fatherless Homes." *Children* pp. 177-182, 1968.

Hetherington, E. Mavis. "Girls Without Fathers." *Psychology Today* 6: 47-52, 1973.

Klein, Carole. *The Single Parent Experience.* New York: Walker and Co., 1973.

Klemer, Richard H. *Marriage and Family Relationships.* New York: Harper & Row, 1970.

Lederer, William J., and Jackson, Don D. *The Mirages of Marriage.* New York: W. W. Norton, 1968.

Lyman, Howard W., *Single Again.* New York: David McKay Co. 1971.
Maslow, Abraham. *Motivation and Personality.* New York: Harper & Row, 1954.
Pannor, Fred Massarik, and Evans, Byron. *The Unmarried Father.* New York: Springer Publishing Co. Inc., 1971.
Parker, Tony. *In No Man's Land.* New York: Harper & Row, 1972.
Rogers, John G. "How to Make a Good Divorce." *Parade Magazine,* 1 July 1973, p. 18.
Rokeach, Milton. "Persuasion that Persists." *Psychology Today* 5: 68-71, 1971.
Rosenfeld, Albert. "Science, Sex and Tomorrow's Morality." *Life Magazine,* 13 June 1969, pp. 37-50.
Thomas, William I. *The Unadjusted Girl.* Boston: Little, Brown & Co., 1925.
U.S. Department of Commerce. Bureau of the Census. *Marital Status and Living Arrangements of the Population in the United States: 1970.* PC(S1)-40, May, 1973.
Weiss, Robert S. "The Contributions of an Organization of Single Parents to the Well-Being of Its Members." *The Family Coordinator* 22: 321-326, 1973.

Chapter 17
Differing Family Patterns Now And In The Future

There always have been different family patterns and there always will be. Of major concern to students in a family relationships class is the need to understand and to know the generalizations about relationships in the varieties of families extant in this culture. This chapter will be presented in three sections: the various aspects of family patterns, remarriage, and predicting the future of the family.

Family Patterns

Although only marriages of one woman to one man at a time (monogamous) are legal in the United States and the nuclear family is the normative type, some other living patterns are found whether they are legal or illegal, normative or not. There are many proponents of the belief that monogamy has failed and that the nuclear family can no longer meet the needs of individuals (Gordon 1972; Otto 1970b; and Sennett 1972).

Teaching Techniques

1. To gain perspective about differing family patterns.

a. Describe families that would fit the following legal components of a family:

(1) *Marriage and Divorce*. To live together legally as husband and wife, two people of the opposite sex, usually above eighteen years of age in most states, must have obtained a marriage license and must have had the ceremony performed by a specified person such as a clergyman or a legal official. (In some states, common law marriage is legal.) To become single again after having been married, one must follow a legal procedure.

(2) *Children*. Children are legitimate when they are born to married people or are adopted.

b. Describe families that fit the 1970 census definition: A family consists of a household head and one or more other persons living in the same household who are related to the head by blood, marriage, or adoption (U.S. Department of Commerce 1973).

Examples

(1) A husband and wife who live in the same household with one or the other of the parents or brothers or sisters.
(2) An unmarried woman and her child living with her mother and father.
(3) Brothers and sisters (or cousins) living together.
(4) Grandparents and grandchildren living together.

c. Describe some culturally accepted families which have no legal ties of inheritance or responsibility.
Example: Two or more unrelated people of the same sex who live as a family without sexual relationships. (Two or more unrelated people of the opposite sex even without a sexual relationship are still not generally accepted.)

d. Describe families that may lack general cultural acceptance but may take responsibility for family members.

Examples

(1) Two or more unmarried people of the opposite sex living together and having a sexual relationship.
(2) Two or more people of the same sex living together and having a sexual relationship.
(3) Two married people living together with one or more people of either sex and having sexual relationships among all of them.
(4) Parents and children and other close kin, such as siblings, or uncles and aunts, and nieces and nephews living together and having sexual relationships.
(5) Married couples in which one or both are participating in extra-marital sex.

e. If a sexual relationship is the one and only thing which is unacceptable in a family (other than between husband and wife) which is ostensibly operating for the common good of all in the areas of food, shelter, clothing, and personal development, what is it about the sexual relationship in each of the above five families that would not be for the common good of all?

The usual answers are these:

(1) Non-related people having a non-culturally sanctioned sexual relationship who do not have their reference group's positive reinforcement for their behavior will not be as comfortable or productive.

(2) People of the same sex are not able to add to the continuation of the population.

(3) Close blood kin having sexual relations increase incidents of jealousy and break down the power structure or organization.

f. Describe families in which there are no illegal sexual relationships, but in which there are too few or no responsibilities taken for the welfare of the family members.

Examples

(1) Families in which there is physical abuse of any family member.

(2) Families in which severely inadequate sanitation, food, shelter, clothing, and personal development are provided.

(3) Families in which little or no effort is made for providing money (from income, welfare payments, or social security) to provide for basic necessities.

(4) Families in which degradation is inadvertently or purposely carried out.

2. *To understand that there are* ***variations*** *in the usual* ***legal*** *and accepted* ***families patterns*** *which might increase the general good of all in the areas of food, shelter, clothing, and personal development.*

a. Determine which of these arrangements would be most likely to be a variation(s) you would choose.

(1) Androgyny–No sex-role differentiation in responsibilities (Osofsky 1972).

(2) Communal living without sexual relationships except between members of a married pair–Joint ownership of property; organized sharing of responsibilities including child care, feeding, and care of the home; joint use of all income; and a goal to work toward (Berger 1972).

(3) Network of families–Living in separate houses or apartments, several families who have made some joint decisions about certain responsibilities as child care, emergency care, etc. (Stoller 1970).

(4) Serial monogamy–The remarriage of persons after one or more divorces or stages of widowhood (Alpenfels 1970).

(5) Adoption of children by single people–The adoption by either male or female (Klein 1973).

(6) Human-actualizing contract–A contract along with the marriage license to learn and use knowledge for greater growth of all members (Satir 1970).

b. How do the variations from the current legal normative family become problems? (Which of the following answers seems to be most logical?)

(1) Since androgyny, communal living, network of families, and human-actualizing contract all require knowledge of human development and human learning processes, the problem would come in re-educating the individuals.

(2) Since these living conditions are choices, and the re-education would not be a common education for all children in all families, then the future marriage of the progenies might suffer.

3. *To understand that some **variations in family patterns** might be better for the common good of all even though they are at the moment **not** yet legally or culturally **acceptable** for the ususal family.*

   a. Select the one you would be most comfortable with and tell why.

      (1) Two-step marriage–The first step would be a marriage for couples alone, but to have children a second license or contract would have to be obtained (Mead 1970).

      (2) Living together unmarried but with no children–Wide acceptance of and encouragement of contraception is necessary.

      (3) Open marriage–The agreement to any activity which would enhance the growth of each marriage partner from separate domiciles to reversal of traditional roles to extramarital sexual relationships (O'Neill and O'Neill, 1972b).

      (4) Polygyny after sixty–The marriage of more than one woman to one man without the loss of economic or social status.
      The uneven ratio of women to men after sixty could be justification (Kassel 1970).

      (5) Homosexual marriage–Two or more members of the same sex who want to make their responsibility to each other legal as well as to live in a sexual and social relationship (Kelly 1972).

      (6) Group marriage–The marriage of two or more women to two or more men (or all the same sex) to make responsibilities for each other and the children both legal and easier economically (Ellis 1972).

   b. How do the legal variations from the usual legal family become problems other than from the lack of the positive reinforcement from social sanctions?

      The expectation of acceptance of responsibility for others is not as apt to be carried out if there is no law which allows punitive action when the responsibility is not taken as in the expectation of unmarried persons to use contraception.

4. *To understand how **variations in family patterns became** more culturally **acceptable** and maybe eventually legal or at least not illegal.*

   What process of evolvement did each group go through to get the limited cultural acceptance each has now?

a. Serial monogamy–One or more remarriages has legal sanction and is beginning to have cultural sanction.
b. Adoption of children by single people, male or female. (One-parent families because of divorce or widowhood have proven they can be successful in many cases and this arrangement has given credence to the families with single adoptive parents.)
c. Communities in the past were a network of families with an unwritten rule of helping the neighbors. The newer idea stems from a revitalizing of the old principle because in a mobile society families find themselves without traditional and long-time friendships.
d. Polygyny after sixty–Because of the excess of females to males after sixty and because of a legal loss of certain incomes, men and women have already begun to live together without the legal sanction of marriage.
e. Living together unmarried–Since most of the restraint about premarital sex was because of the likelihood of pregnancy, effective contraceptives have taken away the greatest reason against it.

5. *To become aware of* ***current trends in family living*** *through the articles in current magazines.*

   Ask the class members to make a survey of the current articles about the family in magazines and newspapers currently on the newsstands to assess the topics, the information given, the approach used, the research backing the article, and the appeal made. (Divide the class into thirds with only one third checking the current popular magazines, one third checking the quasi-professional, and one third checking the professional research journals.)

   Discuss these current issues as to why these family patterns are "popular" at this time and how they will affect the family and how valid (even in the research journals) the information is. Find the supporting research for the current popular article and compare the two reportings.

Remarriage

Remarriage is not for everyone, just as first marriage is not for everyone. For some people, remarriage is not probable because they did not like being married or they think that remarriage is an act of unfaithfulness. Remarriage circumstances are different from first marriages in these ways: feelings of vulnerability, the specter of the former partner, and/or children involved. Other circumstances that might seem different are older age, fewer available partners, or a sour outlook on life, but these factors could apply to never-married people also. Even so, divorced and widowed people are more likely to marry than never-marrieds of their own age group.

The following table shows the differences in rates of first marriage and remarriage rates* for men and women at various ages for 1969.

	Women		Men	
Age	*First Marriage*	*Remarriage*	*First Marriage*	*Remarriage*
14-24	100.8	432.9	73.0	521.1
25-29	146.9	291.6	188.5	523.8
30-34	76.3	206.3	102.6	359.6
35-44	35.8	100.6	47.1	245.9
45-64	9.9	24.9	13.8	102.0
65 years and over	0.9	2.5	2.7	19.0

Source: Health Resource Administration. *Remarriage, United States*. Rockville, Md.: National Center for Health Statistics, December, 1973.

Remarriage rates* for divorced and widowed men and women increased from 1960 to 1969. Remarriage rates for men are more than three times those for women, mainly because there are more widowed and divorced women in the population. Divorced men and women have a higher marriage rate than widowed men and women. The remarriage rates in 1969 for all divorced men was 221; for all divorced women, 135; for all widowed men, thirty-nine; and for all widowed women, ten. First marriage rate for women in 1969 was approximately eighty for all ages, and remarriage rates for all divorced and widowed women were approximately thirty-seven. However, the remarriage rate for both men and women is far higher than the first marriage rate in the younger ages (Health Resources Administration 1973).

Teaching Techniques

1. *To apply the following **generalizations about** divorced and widowed men and women that would increase their chances for **remarriage**:*
   Continued respect for the opposite sex
   Ability to meet the other's emotional needs
   Ability to put former marriage in perspective
   Ability to deal with children of either marriage
   Ability to meet financial and work responsibilities
   a. Apply the above generalizations to a greater probability of divorced than widowed people remarrying.
   b. Apply the above generalizations to a greater probability of divorced or widowed men remarrying than women.
2. *To understand that the **effect of remarriage on children** is based on many of the same generalizations that operate in the biological parent-child relationship in a marriage (Duberman 1973).*

*Rates are based on number per 1000 population in the designated category.

a. Compare the similarities and differences in the biological parent-child relationship and the step-parent-child relationship. Children in a step-parent situation:
   (1) May feel rejected by both the natural parent and the step-parent because the natural parent may feel the need for another person's love besides the child's.
   (2) Adjustment is likely to be better to stepfathers than to step-mothers. Even natural fathers have been separated more from their children by virtue of their work and by less expressiveness, and therefore the new stepfather is not expected to interact as much.

   Apply the above characteristics to the natural parent-child relationship, and discuss the similarities as well as the differences. Examples of natural parent-child relationships for the above characteristics:
   (1) Children will attempt to get one parent's attention and openly say, "See Mama likes me better than she does you, Daddy."
   (2) Children who have had some serious blows to their self-concepts will say to both parents, "You don't like me. You wish I'd never been born." Or they may withdraw completely.
   (3) The closeness of a mother-child relationship is evidenced in the greater inability of people to call their mothers-in-law by the same name they called their own mothers.

b. Review children's classics to understand the negative feelings toward step-parents (Cinderella, etc.).

3. *To understand that the attitude of children toward remarriage can be both overzealous or resentful, affecting the possibilities of remarriage.*
   a. Discuss these points about single parents who do not want to remarry:
      (1) Some parents want to be single and alone.
      (2) Some parents want to date and enjoy social life.
      (3) Some parents resent their children's guardianlike or match-making behaviors.
      (4) Fathers can keep their more intimate friendships out of scrutiny of children better than mothers can because mothers still greet their men friends at home.
      (5) Dating-age children may resent the competition of dating parents.
   b. Debate this point: Children should not become involved in helping the parent *decide* whether or not to marry.
   c. Role play the point in the debate above.

      Parent to child: You know how nice Mr. Smith is and how much he likes you? Well, I might consider marrying him, but I want you to help me think it over.

Child: (You set the age or allow the students to set the age or replay this with various ages.)

4. ***To analyze the behavior of the divorced partner when the other partner remarries.***

Read the following case:

Bette had been divorced three years when her former husband remarried. She immediately went into a depressed state and also demanded more support money for the children.

If the former husband complies, what are his probable reasons?

Generalizations Operating

a. When two people who are in possible competitive roles appear to be in the same circumstances, then there is less resentment toward the other.
b. When one person is successful in something the other also wants, the unsuccessful person usually reacts in a regressive manner.
c. When a person feels he is in the wrong and at the same time is enjoying his behavior, he tends to overcompensate by giving others more than is necessary.

Rewrite the case so that the woman is the one who remarries. Discuss the former husband's feelings.

Predicting the Future of the Family

Predictors of the future usually have one of three philosophies (Flechtheim 1971). The three roads along which the future may theoretically move are (1) complete breakdown and doom, (2) greater equality and peaceful coexistence, or (3) accommodation through rational compromise. The three may be adapted to the family: (1) families are doomed; (2) families will become altruistic; (3) families will continue to have problems and happiness, but a rational view will be taken. As the future of the family is taught, note the students' philosophies.

Teaching Techniques

1. *To evaluate predictions of the family of the future.*
   a. Have students read at least one prediction about the future of the family from three different eras of time (or have groups of students read from a different era). Discuss the differences in the bases on which the predictions were made and the outcomes of the predictions. Using the self-fulfilling prophecy (see p. 308). How have some of the predictions come true and how have some of them changed?

      Suggested Readings

      Several decades ago: (Huxley 1932; Terman 1938; and Westermarck 1936) One to three decades ago: (Goode 1963; Hill 1964; and Mace and Mace 1960) Present prediction: (Farson 1969; Francoeur 1972; Otto 1970a; and Toffler 1970)

b. Select a thirteen- or fourteen-year-old boy or girl whom you know very well and predict his or her family life for the next fifty years. Use reasonable justifications for your predictions in light of technological changes and other predictions from experts.

c. Assume that the following are prevalent.
Discuss or write a paper on what should or could be done to alleviate some of these possible disappointments in life.
(1) Unbalanced sex ratio—too many women
(2) Mentally retarded persons marrying and procreating
(3) Parents inadequate for the task of nurturing, even though excellent progenitors
(4) Disenchantment in marriage
(5) Too many children born in inadequate circumstances
(6) Unsatisfactory sexual relationships
(7) Inadequacy of adults (not married to each other) to express affection
(8) The position of women as less than equal
(9) The great differences among men and women with all men put in one mold and all women put in one mold

2. *To evaluate various* ***methods of predicting*** *the future of the family.*

a. *Extrapolation* from present trends (Francoeur 1972; Hill 1964; Nye 1967; O'Neill and O'Neill 1972a; Parke and Glick 1967; and Toffler 1970):
Advantages: Figures available from census
Disadvantages: Data did not take into account possible social and technological changes

b. *Inferences* from three-generational studies (Hill and Foote 1970):
Advantages: Data from similar settings
Disadvantages: Data gathered at one time did not take into account the unrecognized changes in people's perceptions about themselves as they recount their younger years.

c. *Inferences* from an assessment of technology (Francoeur 1972):
Advantages: Knowledge of what is possible makes it easier for people to make changes.
Disadvantages: Data did not take into account the human use of technology which can vary markedly.

d. *Assessment* of the effects of family specialists (Pollock 1967 and Nye 1967):
Advantages: People still tend to want to hear others' opinions. They even want to know what is "right" and do tend to follow what they think the expert has said as Otto Pollock predicted in 1967.

Disadvantages:They may be contradictory and change in a short time span.

e. *Predictions* from science fiction (Kenkel 1969 and Huxley 1932): Advantages: Science fiction allows one to be creative and philosophical without any binders.
Disadvantages: It is usually too far out for people to glean the implications.

3. *To predict the future of the family by the use of the two prongs of the **self-fulfilling prophecy**: what will be because it is prophesized; what will be because the prophecy is not acceptable and major effort is made to alleviate it.*
   a. Debate the two sides of the self-fulfilling prophecy:
      (1) The family of the future will follow lines of what is predicted such as more divorce, fewer children, fewer marriage contracts, more intentional one-parent families, etc. (Or write a paper on these predictions.)
      (2) These trends must be averted (using the plan of the marriage enrichment and human potential advocates). (Or write a paper on the movements to avert the more "doom" type prophecies.)
   b. Draw silhouettes from Kristin Lai (1972), "Who will we be by 1990?" Ask students to explain the motivational level of each silhouette. Discuss. Will we as self-actualizers be too selfish for marriage?

Survival Man

Little room for moral and aesthetic niceties

Security Man

Seeks order, strong rulers, punishment for deviants, highly structured religious belief

Adapted from "Who Will We Be by 1990?" by Kristin Lai, *Los Angeles Free Press*, May 20, 1970, by permission of the publisher.

c. Role play an alternate family form such as group marriage. Have students react and then discuss problems and advantages in such an arrangement.

Summary

Present family patterns already vary to some extent, but there are many other variations being tried or being described. Present or future family forms will be judged on their adequacy in promoting self-actualization and good interpersonal relationships.

Although there are many alternatives to marriage being tried, monogamy is still the only legal marriage. The major family form different from the two-parent family is the single person with or without children discussed in the previous chapter. Along with the increase in single parent families, there is an increase in remarriages which seems paradoxical. However, the increase in divorce is more rapid than the increase in remarriage.

The future of the family has been predicted for years in various ways. Although some predict a wave of brotherly love, the greatest probability is that the big changes that do occur in the family will be made rationally and for the purpose of better human relationships.

Because family relationships are so very personal to every person, evaluation of learning appears to be difficult. However, in the next chapter the thesis about evaluation is that family relationships are based on generalizations about human behavior from sound research and that evaluation of progress toward learning and applying these generalizations can be done.

References

Alpenfels, Ethel. "Progressive Monogamy: An Alternate Pattern." In *The Family in Search of a Future*, edited by Herbert Otto. New York: Appleton-Century-Croft, 1970.

Berger, Bennett; Hackett, Bruce; and Millar, R. Mervyn. "The Communal Family." *The Family Coordinator* 21: 419-328, 1972.

Duberman, Lucille. "Step-Kin Relations." *Journal of Marriage and the Family* 35: 283-292, 1973.

Ellis, Albert. "Group Marriage: A Possible Alternative." In *The Family in Search of a Future*, edited by Herbert Otto. New York: Appleton-Century Crofts, 1970.

Farson, Richard, ed. *The Future of the Family*. New York: Family Service Association of America, 1969.

Flechtheim, Ossip K. "Teaching the Future." In *The Future of Time*, edited by Henri Yaker, Humphrey Osmond, and Frances Cheek. New York: Doubleday & Co., Inc., 1971.

Francoeur, Robert T. *Eve's New Rib: Twenty Faces of Sex, Marriage and the Family*. New York: Harcourt, Brace, Jovanovich, 1972.

Goode, William J. *World Revolution and Family Patterns*. New York: Free Press, 1963.

Gordon, Michael. *The Nuclear Family in Crisis*: The Search for an Alternative. New York: Harper & Row, 1972.

Health Resources Administration. *Remarriages, United States* (74-1903). Rockville, Md.: National Center for Health Statistics, December, 1973.

Hill, Reuben. "The American Family of the Future." *Journal of Marriage and the Family* 26: 20-28, 1964.

Hill, Reuben, and Foote, Nelson. *Family Development in Three Generations.* Cambridge, Massachusetts: Schenkman Pub. Co., 1970.

Huxley, Aldous. *Brave New World.* New York: Bantam Books, 1932.

Kassel, Victor. "Polygyny After Sixty." In *The Family in Search of a Future,* edited by Herbert Otto. New York: Appleton-Century-Croft, 1970.

Kelly, Janis. "Sister-Love: An Exploration of the Need for Homosexual Experience." *The Family Coordinator* 21: 473-476, 1972.

Kenkel, William. "Marriage and the Family in Modern Science Fiction." *Journal of Marriage and the Family* 31:6, 1969.

Klein, Carole. *The Single Parent Experience*. New York: Walker and Co., 1973.

Lai, Kristin. "Who Will We Be by 1990?" In *Marriage and Family in a Decade of Change*, edited by Gwen B. Carr, Reading, Massachusetts: Addison-Wesley Publishing Co., 1972.

Mace, David, and Mace, Vera. *Marriage East and West.* Garden City, New York: Dolphin Books, 1960.

Mead, Margaret. "Marriage in Two Steps." In *The Family in Search of a Future*, edited by Herbert Otto. New York: Appleton-Century-Croft, 1970.

Nye, Ivan. "Values, Family and a Changing Society." *Journal of Marriage and the Family* 29: 241-248, 1967.

O'Neill, Nena, and O'Neill, George. *Open Marriage.* New York: M. Evans, 1972a.

———. "Open Marriage: A Synergic Model." *The Family Coordinator* 21: 403-410, 1972b.

Osofsky, Joy D., and Osofsky, Howard J. "Androgyny as a Life Style." *The Family Coordinator* 21: 411-418, 1972.

Otto, Herbert, ed. *The Family in Search of a Future: Alternate Models for Moderns.* New York: Appleton-Century-Crofts, 1970a.

Otto, Herbert. "Has Monogamy Failed?" In *Marriage and Family in a Decade of Change,* edited by Gwen B. Carr. Reading, Massachusetts: Addison-Wesley Publishing Company, 1970b.

Parke, Robert J., and Glick, Paul C. "Prospective Changes in Marriage and The Family." *Journal of Marriage and the Family* 29: 249-256, 1967.

Pollock, Otto. "The Outlook for the American Family." *Journal of Marriage and the Family* 29: 193-205, 1967.

Satir, Virginia. "Marriage as a Human Actualizing Contract." In *The Family in Search of a Future,* edited by Herbert Otto. New York: Appleton-Century-Crofts, 1970.

Sennett, Richard. "The Brutality of Modern Families." In *Marriage and Family in a Decade of Change*, edited by Gwen B. Carr. Reading, Massachusetts: Addison-Wesley Publishing Company, 1972.

Stoller, Frederick H. "The Intimate Network of Families as a New Structure." In *The Family in Search of a Future*, edited by Herbert Otto. New York: Appleton-Century-Crofts, 1970.

Terman, Louis. *Psychological Factors in Marital Happiness.* New York: McGraw-Hill, 1938.

Toffler, Alvin. *Future Shock.* New York: Bantam Books, 1970.

U.S. Department of Commerce. Bureau of the Census. *Marital Status and Living Arrangements of the Population in the United States: 1970.* PC(Sl)-40, May, 1973.

Westermarck, Edward. *The Future of Marriage in Western Civilization.* New York: The Macmillan Co., 1936.

Suggested Films

The Family: Life Styles of the Future (1971, 22 min.). Hobel-Leiterman Productions, 21 Woodlawn Avenue E., Toronto 7, Ontario, Canada.

Lucy (unwed pregnant girl) (1970, 13 min.). Pictura Films Dist. Corp., 43 West 16th St., New York, N.Y. 10011.

Marriage (1971, 17 min.). E. C. Brown Trust Foundation, Box 25130, Portland, Ore., 97225.

The Year of the Communes (1972, 53 min.). R. C. Productions, Box 24642, Los Angeles, CA 90024.

Young Children of the Kibbutz (1972, 28 min.). Education Development Center, 39 Chapel Street, Newton, Mass. 02165.

Part Three

Evaluation in Family Relationships

Measuring progress and placing a value on that measure continues to be a concern for teachers of family relationships. The dilemma usually comes when teachers, students, families, and administrators are not clear about their goals. Chapter 18 shows how students' progress may be evaluated and Chapter 19 poses the question of how family relationships education may be evaluated in the future. The philosophy that evaluation is an integral part of the total process of any venture is used in presenting the discussion in both chapters.

Evaluation must be related to both the objectives and the activities carried out whether they be a part of the classroom teaching or a part of the overall planning in the whole field of family relationships. Just as teachers must not plan goals that students cannot reach, teachers must not plan, or allow others to plan, goals for themselves that are unobtainable. A goal for students to interact beautifully with their families and others for the good of mankind is commendable but not possible for just one course in family relationships. Equally as impossible is a goal for family relationships courses (and the field itself) to settle all social ills. This situation being so, teachers must plan attainable goals for both the classroom and for their own professional future.

The outlook for family relationships education is exceptionally bright because of the greater amount of substantive theory in the field of the family and in human behavior and the greater acceptance of the value of education in the formerly personal domain of the family.

Chapter 18

Evaluation in the Classroom

Evaluation in family relationships has been claimed to be difficult because of the personal nature of the subject matter. However, the subject matter itself is based on generalizations about human behavior derived from sound research and, therefore, it can be taught and evaluated as other subject matter can be. A person's own family relationships may be personal, but the generalizations explaining the relationships are objective.

In order for evaluation to be valid, there must be a relationship between the (1) objectives, (2) the teaching-learning experiences, and (3) the evaluation items. The relationship is that all three must be stated on the same cognitive level and must be based on the same generalizations. When the objectives are stated in the behaviors expected of the students, then the learning experiences and evaluation items must include these behaviors. In fact, objectives, teaching-learning experiences, and evaluation items should have such a common relationship that many of the teaching-learning experiences suggested in this book can also be used as evaluation items. The following five statements are our beliefs about evaluation:

1. Objectives, teaching-learning experiences, and evaluation must be related if the evaluation is valid.
2. Objectives stated in behavioral terms must indicate the behaviors expected in the teaching-learning experiences and the evaluation items.
3. Teaching-learning experiences and evaluation items can be interchangeable.
4. Evaluation items must be on the same cognitive level as the teaching-learning experiences and the objectives if the evaluation is valid.
5. Cognitive objectives in family relationships are based on concepts and generalizations about human behavior.

Examples of evaluation items will be given for each of the five beliefs listed. The evaluation devices will be taken from some of the chapters in Part Two: General Areas of Family Relationships and Techniques for Teaching.

Relationship Among Objectives, Teaching-Learning Experiences, and Evaluation

Examples

1. Chapter 9, Understanding Human Behavior

Objective

To understand that needs change from time to time, that the order of precedence of needs changes, and that the intensity of needs changes from time to time (p. 124).

Teaching-Learning Experience

Predict what your family life would be like if your parents still had the same needs as they had when you were born. State what their needs and desires were then and see if satisfying those needs and desires would be beneficial to you or to them now (p. 124).

Evaluation Item

Explain why a marriage may be dull for a couple who attempts to keep their marriage interesting and growing by doing the same things after ten years of marriage that they were doing after one year of marriage.

2. Chapter 10, Communication

Objective

To *evaluate* the communication resulting from a lack of selectivity (p. 154).

Teaching-Learning Experience

Evaluate this communication: A child rushes in from school on a hot day and the mother says, "What did you do at school today?" His answer is, "Nothing" (p. 154).

Evaluation item

Evaluate the following two communications based on the criterion of selectivity.

a. A man who has a terminal illness said, "What will you do when I'm gone?" His wife said, "Don't worry. I won't need you."

b. A student said, "Ah, movies again! We're not working today!" The teacher answered, "Isn't it good that you learn and don't even know you're working."

3. Chapter 12, Interpersonal Relationships in any Family

Objective

To understand that conflict is more likely the greater the number of people in a family (p. 196).

Teaching-Learning Experience

Show the class the algebraic formula for finding how the number of relationships increases as each family member is added (p. 196).

$$x = \frac{y^2 - y}{2}$$

x = number of relationships
y = number of people

Evaluation Item

Discuss the various conflict possibilities in a family with five children and a grandmother, even if all the family members desire good relationships.

Expected Behaviors Stated in Objectives Teaching-Learning Experiences, and Evaluation

Examples

1. Chapter 9, Understanding Human Behavior

Objective

To *apply* the belief that everyone has certain basic needs (p. 123).

Teaching-Learning Experience

Apply the belief that people have certain basic needs to show how advertisements succeed (pp. 123-124).

Evaluation Item

Apply generalizations about basic needs to explain why people tend to want the "latest thing," tend to like the song "I Want to Be Me," and tend to succeed even more when they have recently succeeded.

2. Chapter 10, Communication

Objective

To *analyze* communication difficulties by using the transactional analysis framework (p. 162).

Teaching-Learning Experience

Play a tape-recorded conversation about some issue between a couple who have relationships difficulties and *analyze* the conversation.

Evaluation Item

Play a different tape-recorded conversation showing communication difficulties and *analyze* the difficulties based on the transactional analysis framework.

Interchangeability of Objectives, Teaching-Learning Experiences, and Evaluation

Examples

1. Chapter 9, Understanding Human Behavior

Objective

To understand that first perceptions about others are difficult to change because that which is first learned has less interference. (p. 128).

Teaching-Learning Experience (not in the chapter)

Discuss what happens to a jury when a piece of evidence is revealed, but the judge says, "Strike that evidence from the books." He also means strike it from the minds of the jurors.

Evaluation Item (listed in the chapter as a learning experience)

Read the story of "The Piece of String" by Guy de Maupassant and explain why the major character was never able to clear up the accusation (p. 129).

2. Chapter 11, Intergenerational Relationships

Objective

To make some judgments about actions toward people in the older generation who feel alienated when they are no longer needed (p. 176).

Teaching-Learning Experience

Based on the generalization that relationships are better when people have a good self-concept, what are some valuable decisions to make about aging, but not old, parents?

Evaluation Items

Apply the generalization to:

A couple with no children are living with the husband's parents while their new house is being built next door. Just prior to the completion of the house, his father dies. The husband is an only child. Should the couple move to the new house and the mother stay in her house? (p. 177).

3. Chapter 13, Human Sexual Identity

Objective

To analyze conditioned role behavior of men (p. 230).

Teaching-Learning Experience

Apply the cultural lag theory in analyzing the dilemma of men in today's equalitarian society (p. 230).

Evaluation Item

Analyze the conditioned role behavior of men as it affects the taking of the father role in today's society.

Cognitive Level of Objectives, Teaching-Learning Experiences, and Evaluation

Examples

1. Chapter 9, Understanding Human Behavior

Objective

To *understand* that perception is truth to the individual and that perception, not just facts, must change for any change in behavior to occur (p. 126).

Teaching-Learning Experience

Note how your first perception and course of action about the whole situation changed as your perception changed in the case of Mike (p. 127).

Evaluation Item

Show a contradictory picture and direct students to give two possible perceptions and two courses of action according to the perception.

2. Chapter 10, Communication

Objective

To *become* a more responsible listener (p. 156).

Teaching-Learning Experience

Read Craik's quotation on p. 157. Divide the class into groups of three. Have one of the group tell some foolish situation he has found himself in to one of the others. The listener must use the points in the quotation for empathetic listening. The third person observes. Rotate until all have listened.

Evaluation Item

Keep a record of the number of times and the number of ways you *were* a responsible listener for one week. Describe briefly the situations.

3. Chapter 14, Work, Money, and Relationships

Objective

To *evaluate* success of husbands and fathers in terms of occupational roles using the culturally accepted criteria below (p. 242).

Teaching-Learning Experience

Evaluate these "negative" actions of men who cannot meet the criteria of the successful husband and father (p. 243) by applying generalizations about human behavior (p. 243).

a. When a person's self-image is threatened, he tends to protect it by striking back or overemphasizing his own importance.
b. When demands are higher than can be met, a person tends to quit trying.
c. Punishment causes behavior to cease but does not necessarily stop the desire to carry out the behavior.

Evaluation Item

Evaluate the effect of overemphasis of men to attain the role of successful breadwinner.

Objectives, Teaching-Learning Experiences, and Evaluation Based on Generalizations

1. Chapter 9, Understanding Human Relationships

Objective

To understand how values gain or lose status (based on the generalization that values gain or lose status when there is no longer a need for holding that value) (p. 162).

Teaching-Learning Experience

By induction, arrive at a generalization about the status of values by seeing the similarities and differences in the statements on p.142 about how these values are losing status.

Evaluation Item

Use the same teaching-learning experience, but use a list of statements about losses of different values.

2. Chapter 12, Interpersonal Relationships in Any Family

Objective

To understand that power in a family changes as the bargaining position changes (p. 198).

Teaching-Learning Experience

Make a chart of attributes of a husband and wife and discuss the strength of these attributes as to the power they carry (p. 198).

Evaluation Item

Read the case of Marian and Alex (p. 200) and discuss it in light of the generalization that power changes as bargaining position changes.

3. Chapter 11, Intergenerational Relationships

Objective

To apply the theory that how one reacts to life in each stage predicts what he will be like in each succeeding stage (Developmental Task Theory) (p. 170).

Teaching-Learning Experience

Interview persons twenty-to-thirty years older than you are; find their satisfactions in each of their stages of the family life cycle, including the present, and use the Developmental Task Theory to explain their degree of satisfaction (p. 171).

Evaluation Item

Compare Erikson's Eight Stages of Man with Duvall's Family Development Theory to further support the Developmental Task Theory. (pp. 168-169).

Summary

This chapter was written to show a belief that objectives, teaching-learning experiences, and evaluation items must be related in cognitive level and in the generalization being taught. To show this relationship, the specific behaviors of the students should be stated in the objective and either stated or implied in the teaching-learning experience, and in the evaluation item. If they are truly related, it is quite possible to use the same types of situations for teaching-learning experiences as evaluation items and vice-versa.

A list of separate evaluation items was not written for this chapter because they may not be related to the objectives or to what was taught. Therefore, presenting such a list would be in opposition to the philosophy in this chapter.

The final chapter is about the future of teaching about family relationships which is essentially an evaluation of where we are now and a prediction about the importance of family relationships education.

Chapter 19
The Future in Teaching About Family Relationships

Families of many types will continue to be the primary source of socialization for children in this society. Although varieties of changes in family forms are occurring, basic principles of human relationships will continue to operate. With more substantive theory about family relationships coming from recent research, the base of knowledge from which to teach is strengthened. Because of (1) a basic belief that better human relationships happen when people know more about themselves and others and know about how certain types of interaction takes place, (2) a belief that people can be taught how to relate better, and (3) a movement toward more humanizing relationships, the prediction is made that teaching about family relationships has a bright and enduring future.

The era of the sixties affected teaching about the family in two ways. The zeal of many teachers to teach human sexuality; the eagerness of students to learn about relating; the movement toward individualism, humanism, and freedom; the wide dissemination of information through the mass media; and the low degree of cultural integration of family relationships subject matter both *helped* and *hurt* the teaching of family relationships. It *hurt* the future of teaching about family relationships in that it caused some people to become reactionary in their effort to keep control over society. It also *helped* the future of teaching about family relationships, however, because there were those people who believed that a change in family relationships was beneficial, and they used all the research findings they could to bolster their view.

Many of the proponents of family relationships education now advocate the problem-solving and productive-thinking approach of scholars. For example, good family relationships teaching now emphasizes the application of theories, principles, generalizations, and postulates to the explanation of behavior. Too often, in the past, family relationships teaching has been limited to simple facts that were rarely applicable in more than a few situations or limited to teaching specific value stances as if they were absolutes.

Advances in educational theory as well as in psychological and sociological theories have improved the teaching of family relationships. More and more teachers are planning courses with sound goals that can be achieved.

Family relationships teachers, however, will have to continue to be very careful when people talk about "accountability." At no time should family relationships teachers allow themselves to be held accountable for such so-called social ills as divorce, premarital pregnancy, and alienation of affection. Each of these problems is influenced by complex factors, and each of them could be a social good according to the circumstance. One way to keep those people who claim to hold others accountable from expecting the impossible is to be certain about goals. The goals of family relationships courses must be stated very clearly, and teachers must be willing to be held accountable for doing their part of the teacher-student contract: present the subject matter in the best teaching-learning manner of which they are capable. Teachers must also be willing to be held accountable for knowing their subject matter and knowing the educational theory. However, at no time should the teacher be willing to be held accountable for the students' and parents' not holding up their part of the contract of the teaching-student situation. The students' part is to make the effort necessary to learn the subject to the degree they are capable. Parents have the responsibility and must also be held accountable for providing the home atmosphere and the support of which they are capable. Teachers must be held accountable, but so must students and parents. Teachers can teach students to comprehend and apply in the classroom, but teachers cannot be held accountable for value judgments students make outside the classroom.

It is hoped that it is clear that this book is concerned with teaching theories, principles, and generalizations of family relationships so that they are meaningful to the students. The methods were presented in two different ways—from the description of general methods with examples from family relationships and from the subject matter outline with examples of methods most suitable for teaching for those objectives—so that teachers could become experts in their own field.

Family relationships teaching will be enriched and students will relate better when realistic goals are made and when viable methods are used for attaining the goals. Better teaching about family relationships is destined to make better family relationships.

Index of Concepts in the Objectives

Index